Praise for
Acting for the Camera

DEIDRE HALL, People's  **ner**

"Tony Barr's *Acting for the Camera* is ~~~~ practical acting book I've ever ~~~~"

JERRY LONDON, D ~~~~

"Tony is a top notch director ~~~~ and *Acting For the
Camera* is realistic and easy to understand for the pro or the
novice."

JEFFREY HAYDEN, Director

"*Acting for the Camera* is a godsend, and I've re-read it from
cover to cover. It's still the best book written on the subject,
and I owe you a great debt for it."

ELLIOT SILVERSTEIN, Director

"A helluva book for the newcomer, especially the section on
'The Machinery of Film.'"

**ERNEST FRANKEL, Frankel Films,
Director/Producer/Writer**

"I believe actors will find it invaluable. Congratulations on a
superb job."

HENRY WINKLER

"It's always fabulous when someone can finally write a coher-
ent, helpful guide to what acting on film is all about without
losing the understandig of the craft. TONY BARR HAS
DONE IT, FOLKS!"

THEATER-TRAINED ACTORS:

If you're a theater-trained actor, you need this book in order to learn how to work in front of the camera. Although the foundation of good acting is the same in both media—listening—as an actor, you need to understand what the screen requires from you and what creative adjustments you need to make to achieve your best performance.

These pages explain it all in detail.

ACTING FOR THE CAMERA

•••••••••••••••••••

Tony Barr

with exercises by
Eric Stephan Kline

HarperPerennial
A Division of HarperCollinsPublishers

To my wife, Barbara, whose help has been invaluable;
to my beautiful children, Suza, John, and David;
my wonderful granddaughters, Danielle Nicole and Jessica Rose;
and to all my students, my best teachers.

HarperCollins books may be purchased for educational, business, or sales promotional use. For information please write: Special Markets Department, HarperCollins Publishers, Inc., 10 East 53rd Street, New York, NY 10022.

FIRST EDITION

Designed by Nancy Singer

Library of Congress Cataloging-in-Publication Data

Barr, Tony.
    Acting for the camera / Tony Barr ; exercises by Eric Stephan Kline. — Rev. ed.
        p.   cm.
    Originally published: New York : Perennial Library, 1986.
    Includes index.
    ISBN 0-06-092819-0
    1. Motion picture acting.   I. Kline, Eric Stephan. II. Title.
PN1995.9.A26B37   1997
791.43'028—dc21   97-993

    00 01 ❖/RRD 10

Contents

Foreword

●●●●●●●●●●●●●●●●●●●●●●●●●●●●●●●●●●●●

Actors are always looking for that teacher or that book which will supply the magic that transforms them from aspiring young talents to geniuses. When I was starting out, I was one of those actors, and I did my share of reading. I'm still reading, and one book I just read is Tony Barr's *Acting for the Camera*.

There is no teacher like performing. Whether the performance is on Broadway, in a little theater in a small town, in summer stock, or in dinner theater; whether it is in a major feature for MGM, in a little non-union film, or in a student film; whether it is in a commercial or industrial film or documentary or religious film—whatever and wherever, there is nothing better for the actor than to do it.

The questions actors must ask themselves are, "How do I do it better? And sooner?" And that's where the teachers and books come in.

I've read a lot of material about acting and actors. I've certainly talked enough about them during my lifetime to fill volumes, because the subject of acting never fails to get me excited. What it all must boil down to eventually is, "What have I learned that I truly understand, and that I can actually put to use?"

When doing *Ages of Man*, Sir John Gielgud was asked what was the most difficult thing for him in acting, and he replied, "Making it simple." Tony Barr has made it eloquently simple with *Acting for the Camera*. It is fast reading, easily understood, and beautifully laid out. Now I understand what I do.

Ed Asner

Preface

In 1960, a talented director friend of mine, David Alexander, approached me to find out if I would form an acting school with him. I agreed.

One of the principal reasons behind the decision was that Hollywood was full of charlatans and con men passing themselves off as teachers, publicists, agents, etc., and unwary neophytes had no way of knowing when they were being bilked by these exploiters who prey on the unsuspecting and innocent. A reputable school would certainly be a plus.

We started the Workshop (David left it soon after to direct full time), devoting ourselves to teaching acting as we had been taught it and as we had applied it in our years in the theater. Our teachers had used Stanislavsky literally; we used Michael Chekhov, Lee Strasberg, Robert Lewis, and a number of other lesser and greater exponents of what had become known as "the Method." And David had his own technique.

I soon became aware that every teacher had his or her own pet tools and, consciously or otherwise, eliminated those teaching and acting tools that did not fit into a particular mold. I was as guilty as everyone else, focusing primarily on intention and emotion-recall exercises. It took about five years for me to realize that something was missing, and that what we were teaching, however effective it might be from time to time, was too limited.

As the years passed, I also realized that there was virtually no professional acting work to be found on the stage if one was based in Hollywood; careers and livelihood depended on television and feature films. It became painfully clear that my teaching focus was wrong. I bought videotape equipment and began to study the specifics of working in the film media and to teach my students what I learned about the difference between stage and camera. The inner drives (that is, the emotions, the sensory responses) are the same for the actor whichever medium he is working in, since under given circumstances the same stimulus will cause the same reaction in a person no matter what the medium. For example, if I kill your mother, your feelings would be the same for television as for the Hollywood Bowl.

On the stage, the actor must work through the other actor so as to project to the back row of the theater, wherever it might be. On camera, in a close-up, the back row of the theater is, in effect, on the shoulder of the off-camera actor. In a master shot, the back row is only a few feet away, where the lens is. In other words, the only major technical difference lies in the *distance of communication*. On the stage, it is across theatrical, or unreal, space. On camera, if the scene is between two people at a table, they need only project as far as the other actor. If at opposite ends of a room, across that distance; in a love scene, the audience is practically in bed with the actors. *For the camera, you need only to communicate across real space.*

The film medium also has specific techniques, specific technical needs, specific mechanical needs and abilities, and the actor's work is affected by those mechanics. Therefore, he must be so completely familiar with them that he is able to take them into account automatically as he gives his real attention to his performance.

This book is written primarily from the point of view of my own experiences in Hollywood, because I have lived and worked here since 1947. The approach works just as well, however, for the people making films in New York, San Francisco, Germany, France, or any other place where the actor's work is viewed by a camera. And very importantly, *if I were teaching for the stage, I would start in the same place: stop acting, start listening; keep it simple, without loss of passion!*

There are already a number of good acting books that discuss philosophies of acting, the relationship of the actor to the community, and so forth. Therefore, I have confined myself to the pragmatic aspects of acting for the camera. In addition there is some basic information about Hollywood and the studios that will be helpful to those actors who come here to seek a career. I hope it will also be informative and interesting for those readers who build their careers elsewhere.

The term *actor* as used in this book is generic, meaning both actors and actresses. The same is true of the words *director, producer,* and *author,* since the doors have finally been opened to talented women in all areas of the entertainment world. In the interest of simplicity, I will use *actor* when I am speaking generally and *actor* or *actress* when speaking specifically. Similarly, I will use the pronoun *he* when speaking generally.

What follows is a collection of critiques, discussions, and thoughts selected from work done since my focus shifted to the camera media. I've been learning a lot, and I hope you will, too.

Acknowledgments

This book would not be complete without an acknowledgment of the help and encouragement I received in its original preparation from the following people:

Loreen Arbus
Ed Asner
Robert Cohen
Karl Malden
Quinn Martin
Ted Post
Elliot Silverstein
David Swift
Henry Winkler

My special thanks to the actors Joanne Kasch and Heath Kizzier for allowing me to use their photographs in the book. And thanks to my very talented former associate, Sal Acquisto, and my friend and former secretary, Jennifer Meynard.

For this revised edition, I must also add my thanks to my very inventive and dedicated friend and associate Eric Kline, who started teaching for us at the Film Actors Workshop in 1980 and is one of the finest acting teachers and coaches I know. Eric designed the exercises that appear at the end of this book, and which are now a very important part of it.

A very special thank you to my wife, Barbara, who was the administrator of the Film Actors Workshop for fifteen years, who made sure the place was kept to the highest standard, and who made the Workshop a happy and creative home for all of our students.

ACTING FOR THE CAMERA

Tony Barr

with exercises by
Eric Stephan Kline

HarperPerennial
A Division of HarperCollins Publishers

To my wife, Barbara, whose help has been invaluable;
to my beautiful children, Suza, John, and David;
my wonderful granddaughters, Danielle Nicole and Jessica Rose;
and to all my students, my best teachers.

HarperCollins books may be purchased for educational, business, or sales promotional use. For information please write: Special Markets Department, HarperCollins Publishers, Inc., 10 East 53rd Street, New York, NY 10022.

FIRST EDITION

Designed by Nancy Singer

Library of Congress Cataloging-in-Publication Data

Barr, Tony.
    Acting for the camera / Tony Barr ; exercises by Eric Stephan
Kline. — Rev. ed.
        p.   cm.
    Originally published: New York : Perennial Library, 1986.
    Includes index.
    ISBN 0-06-092819-0
    1. Motion picture acting.   I. Kline, Eric Stephan. II. Title.
PN1995.9.A26B37   1997
791.43'028—dc21   97-993

        00 01 ❖/RRD 10

Contents

● ●

Foreword

●●

Actors are always looking for that teacher or that book which will supply the magic that transforms them from aspiring young talents to geniuses. When I was starting out, I was one of those actors, and I did my share of reading. I'm still reading, and one book I just read is Tony Barr's *Acting for the Camera*.

There is no teacher like performing. Whether the performance is on Broadway, in a little theater in a small town, in summer stock, or in dinner theater; whether it is in a major feature for MGM, in a little non-union film, or in a student film; whether it is in a commercial or industrial film or documentary or religious film—whatever and wherever, there is nothing better for the actor than to do it.

The questions actors must ask themselves are, "How do I do it better? And sooner?" And that's where the teachers and books come in.

I've read a lot of material about acting and actors. I've certainly talked enough about them during my lifetime to fill volumes, because the subject of acting never fails to get me excited. What it all must boil down to eventually is, "What have I learned that I truly understand, and that I can actually put to use?"

When doing *Ages of Man*, Sir John Gielgud was asked what was the most difficult thing for him in acting, and he replied, "Making it simple." Tony Barr has made it eloquently simple with *Acting for the Camera*. It is fast reading, easily understood, and beautifully laid out. Now I understand what I do.

Ed Asner

Preface

In 1960, a talented director friend of mine, David Alexander, approached me to find out if I would form an acting school with him. I agreed.

One of the principal reasons behind the decision was that Hollywood was full of charlatans and con men passing themselves off as teachers, publicists, agents, etc., and unwary neophytes had no way of knowing when they were being bilked by these exploiters who prey on the unsuspecting and innocent. A reputable school would certainly be a plus.

We started the Workshop (David left it soon after to direct full time), devoting ourselves to teaching acting as we had been taught it and as we had applied it in our years in the theater. Our teachers had used Stanislavsky literally; we used Michael Chekhov, Lee Strasberg, Robert Lewis, and a number of other lesser and greater exponents of what had become known as "the Method." And David had his own technique.

I soon became aware that every teacher had his or her own pet tools and, consciously or otherwise, eliminated those teaching and acting tools that did not fit into a particular mold. I was as guilty as everyone else, focusing primarily on intention and emotion-recall exercises. It took about five years for me to realize that something was missing, and that what we were teaching, however effective it might be from time to time, was too limited.

As the years passed, I also realized that there was virtually no professional acting work to be found on the stage if one was based in Hollywood; careers and livelihood depended on television and feature films. It became painfully clear that my teaching focus was wrong. I bought videotape equipment and began to study the specifics of working in the film media and to teach my students what I learned about the difference between stage and camera. The inner drives (that is, the emotions, the sensory responses) are the same for the actor whichever medium he is working in, since under given circumstances the same stimulus will cause the same reaction in a person no matter what the medium. For example, if I kill your mother, your feelings would be the same for television as for the Hollywood Bowl.

On the stage, the actor must work through the other actor so as to project to the back row of the theater, wherever it might be. On camera, in a close-up, the back row of the theater is, in effect, on the shoulder of the off-camera actor. In a master shot, the back row is only a few feet away, where the lens is. In other words, the only major technical difference lies in the *distance of communication*. On the stage, it is across theatrical, or unreal, space. On camera, if the scene is between two people at a table, they need only project as far as the other actor. If at opposite ends of a room, across that distance; in a love scene, the audience is practically in bed with the actors. *For the camera, you need only to communicate across real space.*

The film medium also has specific techniques, specific technical needs, specific mechanical needs and abilities, and the actor's work is affected by those mechanics. Therefore, he must be so completely familiar with them that he is able to take them into account automatically as he gives his real attention to his performance.

This book is written primarily from the point of view of my own experiences in Hollywood, because I have lived and worked here since 1947. The approach works just as well, however, for the people making films in New York, San Francisco, Germany, France, or any other place where the actor's work is viewed by a camera. And very importantly, *if I were teaching for the stage, I would start in the same place: stop acting, start listening; keep it simple, without loss of passion!*

There are already a number of good acting books that discuss philosophies of acting, the relationship of the actor to the community, and so forth. Therefore, I have confined myself to the pragmatic aspects of acting for the camera. In addition there is some basic information about Hollywood and the studios that will be helpful to those actors who come here to seek a career. I hope it will also be informative and interesting for those readers who build their careers elsewhere.

The term *actor* as used in this book is generic, meaning both actors and actresses. The same is true of the words *director, producer,* and *author,* since the doors have finally been opened to talented women in all areas of the entertainment world. In the interest of simplicity, I will use *actor* when I am speaking generally and *actor* or *actress* when speaking specifically. Similarly, I will use the pronoun *he* when speaking generally.

What follows is a collection of critiques, discussions, and thoughts selected from work done since my focus shifted to the camera media. I've been learning a lot, and I hope you will, too.

Acknowledgments

This book would not be complete without an acknowledgment of the help and encouragement I received in its original preparation from the following people:

Loreen Arbus
Ed Asner
Robert Cohen
Karl Malden
Quinn Martin
Ted Post
Elliot Silverstein
David Swift
Henry Winkler

My special thanks to the actors Joanne Kasch and Heath Kizzier for allowing me to use their photographs in the book. And thanks to my very talented former associate, Sal Acquisto, and my friend and former secretary, Jennifer Meynard.

For this revised edition, I must also add my thanks to my very inventive and dedicated friend and associate Eric Kline, who started teaching for us at the Film Actors Workshop in 1980 and is one of the finest acting teachers and coaches I know. Eric designed the exercises that appear at the end of this book, and which are now a very important part of it.

A very special thank you to my wife, Barbara, who was the administrator of the Film Actors Workshop for fifteen years, who made sure the place was kept to the highest standard, and who made the Workshop a happy and creative home for all of our students.

• • • • • • • • • • • • • • • • • •

ONE

Acting

1

Film and Stage— Two Sides of the Same Coin

The actor's primary function is to communicate ideas and emotions to an audience. If you remember that, it will be easier for you to understand what the prime and very simple difference is between acting for the stage and acting for the camera.

In the theater, the audience may be anywhere from a few feet away from you to two balconies away from you, and it is your obligation to communicate everything to the people in the furthermost parts of the auditorium. Therefore, energy must be greater, speaking volume must be louder, physicalizations must be bigger, and tiny subtleties may well get lost. Yet, you can get away with a lot on the stage, because the audience, unable to see the subtleties, will assume that they are there even if they are not. A performance that is "indicated," or merely made up of superficial gestures, looks, and movements that have no real impulse behind them, may seem to be real to all members of the audience except those sitting in the very first rows.

When you're working in film, the audience is generally only a few feet away from you (the position of the lens), so communicating ideas and emotions to the audience is no more difficult than communicating with someone sitting across the table from you. The camera is practically sitting on your nose, and the microphone is practically resting on your brow. And because of the nature of the medium itself, the director and editor (at their discretion) can make it impossible for the audience to look anywhere but at you and your face at an emotionally critical moment. In the motion picture theater, you become many times your real size, and every subtlety in your physicalizations is magnified. On television, your close-up filling the screen focuses all the audience's attention on your face, and again all the subtleties are seen and, to a certain extent, magnified.

Because you are so close to the audience in the film medium, it takes less to let them know what is happening, and because all their attention has been directed toward you, it takes very little for you to be effective. In addition, editing helps dramatize what is happening by sharply shifting the audience's focus from one person or thing to another. In a well-edited film, the cutting is motivated by stimuli. In most instances those stimuli are the ones affecting the person to whom the editor has cut. In itself, the editing is an articulation of the effect of the stimulus; you need not compound it by laying in your response with a sledgehammer, or the excess will be ludicrous. Therefore, the greater-than-life style necessary for naturalness in the theater is unnecessary—and even undesirable—for film. Moreover, anything you do that is dishonest in relation to what the character is thinking or feeling will be noticeable to the audience. The camera allows no deceit. Either you are truthful or you are not.

In a scene, for instance, a woman enters her home. Her husband tells her that her sister called to tell them that her beloved mother passed away last night. The audience will anticipate the emotional impact of this news by virtue of their own involvement with such a concept. When the director and editor force the audience to look at the wife by cutting to her close-up, they will share her feelings, whatever they may be, even if she does nothing at all. If she does something dishonest, she will destroy the emotions that have begun to well up in the audience, because they will not believe her response. If she does only what she would do in real life, or even does a shade less, she will be her most effective. The key is *simplicity without loss of passion!* (Passion, as I use it here, means emotional energy, not sexual energy.)

It is easy to accept the word "simplicity," but the quality is not easy to achieve. To be simple demands that you trust yourself. It demands that you are secure enough in your work as an actor to know that you are articulate, that the right thing and the real thing will happen, and that the audience will get it.

Why do actors live in such terror of the possibility that the audience will not understand what they are feeling? The audience is on your side, and does half your work. That's their "job"; they pay money to empathize with you. They've followed your entire performance up to this moment, so they know what you're feeling. They have turned on their television sets or gone to the movies in order to be moved. Therefore, they are not challenging you. They have feelings, all of which are universal, and if you are *truthful* they will understand what you are supposed to be feeling when struck by certain stimuli. They will invest you with the feelings they expect you to have! So you can trust being simple. You *must* be simple!

A wonderful story is told about this very thing. Greta Garbo was starring in a film titled *Queen Christina*. The story is about a beautiful, bright young queen who loves her country, and who is worshipped by her subjects. She falls in love with the emissary from Spain, and abdicates her throne so she can go back to Spain with him. She goes to his ship to meet him, only to find him dying as a result of a duel with the villain. He dies. This is the end of the movie. There was no dialogue written, no stage business indicated. She didn't know what to do. Nothing she thought of seemed right. If she said this, she would seem too cold. If she said that, she would seem too weak. Finally, Rouben Mamoulian, the very talented director, came up with an idea. He told her to say nothing, merely move slowly to the front of the ship and look out for ninety feet (one minute), and "don't even blink." She did; he moved the camera slowly in to a close-up of her, and held it for the required time. That was it.

He waited as the first audience came out of the theater at the end of the film. Some said she was "so vulnerable!"; some said she was "so strong!"; some said she was "so courageous!" The people in the audience invested her with the feelings they wanted her to have—and she did nothing to make them feel one thing or another. She dealt with her own feelings about the death and kept it simple! The audience *participated! They did their job!*

If you are genuinely listening with all your senses, and if you are at all responsive to stimuli, there is no way for an audience to escape being brought into what you are experiencing; there is no way for you to be lacking in emotional, as well as verbal, articulation. You don't have to try for even one moment to *act* and to say to the audience, "Look at me, ain't I feeling a lot?"

Remember, always, that simplicity is the essence of good film acting. Ed Asner brought a very appropriate quote to my attention: When doing *Ages of Man*, Sir John Gielgud was asked what the most difficult thing in acting was for him. He replied, "Making it simple."

Also, remember that "simple" does not mean dead. It means *simple without loss of passion*. If someone has killed your mother, you would *feel* the same whether it's for a TV screen or the Hollywood Bowl. All that's different is how you deal with it.

Which brings me to a common Hollywood saying: "Less is more." Nonsense. Less is less. I repeat: *the passion is the same; what you do with it is different for the camera than for the stage*. Perhaps the saying should be *"Less externalization is more* effective." Move that wonderful energy *inside!*

It will help you achieve the simplicity you need if you remember that on the stage you must work through the other actor to the back row of the theater—in other words, you work across artificial space, theatrical space. *In front of the camera, you work across real space*. You need not concern yourself with the back row of the theater; *you need only reach the other actor*.

In his book, *Confessions of An Actor* (Simon & Schuster, 1982), Laurence Olivier spoke of his early days in film, and the transitions back and forth between the theater and soundstage.

> At that time, stage-acting and film-acting were thought of as two entirely different crafts, even professions. We know now that this is not by any means a true assessment; the truth is infinitely subtler. They call for the same ingredients, but in different proportions. The precise differences may take some years of puzzling work to appreciate; in each case there are many subtle variations according to the character of the actor. It took me many years to learn to film-act; at least ten of these were appallingly rough

and ready, from sheer prejudice and ignorance. After that, *it was necessary to relearn how to act on stage, incorporating, though, the truth demanded by the cinema and thereby reducing the measure of theatricality.* (emphasis mine)

A final thought: on the stage, you can give a performance. In front of a camera, you'd better have an experience!

2

The Development of Film-Acting Styles

We have all seen movies made in the early days of motion pictures. People moved at speeds faster than normal because cameras were hand-cranked, and there was no accurate method of coordinating camera speed with projection speed. More often than not, actors were untrained people who looked good or were available at a reasonable fee. Because there was no sound, directors and actors felt that gestures and facial expressions had to be exaggerated to communicate the actors' feelings. There was a great deal of mugging and hamming. Theater acting was still not far removed from the days of melodrama, so even there the exaggerated style we call *hammy* was in vogue with many actors.

That style prevailed for many years, and audiences came to accept the conventions and allowed themselves to be moved by them. There was a gradual shift toward greater naturalism as we moved into the twenties, but still, acting was not comparable to the way people really behaved. It was not until the advent of the talkies in 1927 that things began to change. That's when things had to change.

Shortly before, when sound was first offered to the film industry, most Hollywood producers (filmmakers had by then moved to Hollywood from New York, where moviemaking had its origin) had rejected the idea that sound would be an advantage. On the contrary, many felt that even thinking about it was ridiculous.

The Warner brothers felt differently. They had a script titled *The Jazz Singer*, based on a Broadway play, and wanted to use a singer named Al Jolson in the lead. In the role, he had to sing popular songs and chant prayers as a cantor in his father's synagogue. The Warners took the big chance. They installed new equipment in the many theaters they owned, and shot the singing portions of the film in sound.

The result was electric. Audiences loved sound. There was no doubt that it not only would work, but would take over the entire industry.

There were serious problems, however. Many of Hollywood's biggest stars "couldn't talk." They had terrible voices. They lisped. They stuttered. None of that mattered when the pictures were silent, but when audiences listened to talkies, they laughed a number of actors off the screen. The studios began scrambling to find actors who looked good, who could perform, and who could also speak.

Directors and producers turned to Broadway, luring the more experienced stage actors into the movie industry. Performances became more realistic, but still were somewhat exaggerated for the most part. The early talkies can easily be identified by the artificial and theatrical acting style.

In the early thirties, things began to change. The depression had not disappeared, and the audience demanded escape films as an antidote to their unhappiness. The order of the day became musicals and dramas using attractive people in luxurious settings. There was a greater use of people with special talents but with little or no acting training, such as singers and dancers. Youngish, handsome men and women became stars, at the expense of John Barrymore, George Arliss, and Wallace Beery. Acting became simpler, since so many of the performers had no training or acting talent. They were best when they were not trying too hard.

By the end of the thirties, film acting had come of age. Improved writing made heavier acting demands on the performers. Movies starred Henry Fonda, James Stewart, Clark Gable, Spencer Tracy, John Wayne, Katharine Hepburn, Greer Garson, Claudette Colbert, Joan Crawford, and Olivia de Havilland—good actors who worked simply and honestly, bringing their own personalities to the work rather than trying to become characters. Scripts were tailored to their special talents and personalities, and little effort was made to change the actors, especially since the audiences were paying millions of dollars to see them as they were. Most important, performers began to look more like people and less like actors in a role, so audience identification became easier.

In the theater there was a parallel movement, based on Konstantin

Stanislavsky's work in Russia. The Group Theatre, in New York, was his principal exponent, and from the Group came the very naturalistic style of leading men exemplified by John Garfield and Franchot Tone, two of the few highly trained stage actors who managed to become film stars. Their style was essentially the same as that of Tracy, Gable, and other film actors, but their stage training was much more theatrical. A number of excellent character actors (including Roman Bohnen, Art Smith, and Morris Carnovsky) also went from the Group to films. Interestingly, few women made the transition.

The naturalistic style prevailed trough the mid-forties, when a single actor triggered an acting revolution of sorts. Marlon Brando did Tennessee Williams's A *Streetcar Named Desire* on Broadway, then as a film, under the direction of the realistic director Elia Kazan. Brando was super-naturalistic. His pace was deliberate; he took time to think and to smolder. He was passionate, but not bigger than life. Dozens of actors and actresses tried to imitate his style, but most were unsuccessful because Brando was unique. The resulting performances were even closer to total simplicity and realism.

In the early fifties, there was another revolution: television. Actors were brought into the home; they were only a few feet away from the viewer. The television screen was small compared to the motion picture screen, so the directors of such early TV dramatic series as "Studio One," "Philco Television Playhouse," "Kraft Television Theatre," and "Playhouse 90" got closer to the actors' faces than directors did in feature films. The extreme close-up (E.C.U.) became commonplace, and the small screen was filled with the faces of the performers. The slightest exaggeration of facial expression became noticeable and even unpleasant, so actors had to learn to keep their physicalizations simple.

Soon after, television directors such as John Frankenheimer, Ralph Nelson, Arthur Hiller, Norman Jewison, Delbert Mann, Mark Rydell, and Sidney Lumet moved into features, adopting the TV style they had been using to the feature screen. As television stars became movie stars, they took their approach with them, and soon all camera-oriented media used the same basic approach.

Being simple, being honest, being most involved with listening, became the dominant acting approach.

On the Oscar telecast in 1980, Sir Alec Guinness, upon receiving a special Oscar, said that when he started in films he realized he should do nothing, and he's been doing it for twenty-five years: being simple!

3

The Approach

Most acting teachers begin with exercises of one sort or another. They may be theater games, sense-memory exercises, emotion-memory exercises, imagination or concentration exercises, or whatever. Only after extended study in the so-called basics are the students given scenes to work on.

Having thought and taught that way myself for many years, I am familiar with the process and the rate of growth students experience, and I have come to the conclusion that those methods are not the most effective ones and are far too time-consuming. When students spend their first months, or in some cases years, on exercises, the exercises take on an importance all out of proportion to their functions; they tend to become the most important things to master. As a result, when the students progress to scenes, their focus is all too often on the exercises that will help them achieve the necessary sensory and emotional values in the scene, and the *listening* process becomes secondary, when in fact, *listening* is the all-important aspect of an actor's work. It then becomes very difficult for the actors to relegate those exercises to their proper place as *training tools* and to forget about them when playing a scene.

It's always very comforting to hear affirmations of the value of *listening* from actors and actresses I respect. In a CBS "Sixty Minutes" segment, Anthony Hopkins was being interviewed. He spoke of the first film he was in, *The Lion in Winter*, playing the son of Katharine Hepburn. As they were rehearsing and talking about his performance, Hopkins said, "I've got to do something! I should be doing something!" She said, "No! Don't! Don't do anything. Don't act. Don't act. *Acting is reacting. Just listen and react.*" (Italics mine—very few people speak in italics). *Don't forget: very often you are listening to yourself, your inner activity.*

An actor's emotions will be freed more quickly through scene work than through exercise work if the scene work is approached properly. When I can teach actors to listen with all their senses, and to work from themselves in relation to the stimuli and responses that make up a performance, the emotional wells are tapped much more quickly and effectively.

I do not mean to say that exercises are useless or unnecessary. When actors reach a plateau in their development, as most actors do, or when they find a moment in a role that they can't connect with, they need tools to draw upon; then those exercises are very valuable. But if at the start we work from scenes, and train the listening instrument properly, the exercises take their place as tools and do not intrude on the performance.

Teachers must be aware of a time factor as they train actors for the film and television industry. Someone decides to become an actor and enrolls in a workshop like mine. In a few months that actor goes out to find an agent and to meet casting people, and soon that young and inexperienced actor is getting roles. The reason for his quick success is that in the film and television media an actor's quality is often more important than his talent level. The intimate nature of the camera is largely responsible for that standard. It is not important that the actor move well, have a well-trained voice, or be able to play an in-depth characterization from O'Neill or Miller or Shakespeare; it is primarily important that he have the quality the director wants for the particular role. It therefore becomes our responsibility to help the actor develop that quality, and to free him so that he can give his natural talent its fullest expression. In this way he will be as ready as possible to handle a role when his special quality wins it for him. That is why I decided to approach training as I do, and why I use camera equipment from the very beginning to train students. If I even begin to doubt the approach, examples like the following quickly bring me back to reality.

An attractive, but not exceptionally beautiful, young woman came to study with me, right out of junior college. She was a fair actress, as a nineteen-year-old beginner goes, and she had a lovely personality. She was bright, cute, and intelligent. After she had been studying with me for three or four months, I heard that an actress was needed to play a role in a new series at Universal, and she seemed perfect for it. Not really expecting anything to happen, I sent her there, and lo and behold, she got a minor lead in the series.

A young man had been studying with me for a little less than a year. He was probably one of the least promising and stiffest young actors I had worked with in a very long time. There was a quality about him, however, that couldn't be ignored, as I saw girl after girl being intrigued by it. He left the Workshop, and just a couple of months after that he had a costarring role in a series that appeared on NBC.

I do not have a class for teenagers, but at the insistence of her grandmother I once took a fifteen-and-a-half-year-old into one of my regular classes. She seemed a bit of a mouse, but after two classes I realized what an extraordinary mouse she was. Shy and introspective, she had a wonderful ability to accept and believe in imaginary circumstances. Those qualities, coupled with a rich emerging talent, made her a very special actress indeed. In about six months she was signed by one of Hollywood's top agents, and very soon after that she was doing guest-star roles in major TV series.

It may seem that I have isolated three cases out of the hundreds and even thousands who have worked with us over the years. The truth is that countless students find themselves working professionally in a very short time. They may not get starring roles, they may not get many lesser roles, but they do get work. It's very unlikely that they're going to be asked to improvise or do an exercise in concentration or sense memory; therefore, I feel that the best and most important preparation for them is to work with scenes so that they will be prepared for what they have to do when they get that first call.

4

•••••••••••••••••••••••••••••••••

Acting Defined

There are many definitions of acting, each of them probably related to the approach of the particular teacher making the definition. But too many of the definitions are much too abstract. When I ask new students to define acting, I hear answers such as, "Acting is believing." "OK," I say, "get up there and believe." Do you know what to do? What the process is? Boleslawski, the famous Polish teacher-director, said, "Acting is the life of the human soul receiving its birth through art." OK. Get up and help the human soul receive its birth through art. Does this definition tell you *what to do*? I think not. As far as I'm concerned, if I can't *use* it, I'm not interested in it.

To define acting concretely, it is helpful to examine the structure of human behavior. In real life we respond to a series of stimuli, each one following the other and each creating in us some forward motion, whether it be a forward motion of thought, emotion, sensory experience, physical activity, or any combination thereof. *How* each individual responds to those stimuli depends on the kind of person he is and his state of mind, emotions, and body at the moment he receives the stimulus. *The important point is that humans respond to stimuli in a continuous action-reaction pattern.* Therefore, since acting is supposed to mirror true-life behavior, the actor in his role should also respond to stimuli from moment to moment. Responses create the thrust for the forward-moving life of a character—at least, they provide the motor energy in all areas of human behavior and actions. So to begin a definition of acting, say that *acting is responding to stimuli*, which may be real or imaginary. Example: You sit on a tack, jump, and yell, "Ouch!" That's a real stimulus-response pattern. Or you hear the words "I love you" in the imaginary circumstances of a scene, and your heart beats faster.

Obviously, not everyone who responds to stimuli is an actor. We all respond to stimuli continually; if we don't, we must be dead. Therefore, there must be other important factors involved. The most obvious is that in acting the circumstances are imaginary. So *acting is responding to stimuli in imaginary circumstances.* One step further is the need for imagination in acting, to enable you to *believe* in the imaginary circumstances. Then, additionally, responses must be enriched, so that they are not just simply truthful, but interesting and *theatrical* as well. So now you are *responding to stimuli in imaginary circumstances in an imaginative way.*

Since you are dealing in theatricality, whether you are acting for the theater or for any of the film or tape media, you must be concerned with the dynamics of what you are doing, so that there is rise and fall, change and interchange, in the work. If there isn't, the performance is monotonous, one-dimensional, and dull—the kind of performance one would expect from a layman but not from a professional actor. So the definition can be enlarged to state that *acting is responding to stimuli in imaginary circumstances, in an imaginative and dynamic manner.*

Of major importance is the character in the script who is responding to the stimuli, because the form of the response to a stimulus depends on the individual, and the character is the individual with whom you are dealing. You must consider all aspects of that individual: the time and place in which he lives, the way he dresses, the way he speaks, the way he moves. In other words, you must be stylistically truthful to the character. If you are, then the definition of acting does not change no matter what the form or style of the drama involved. You are, therefore, *responding to stimuli in imaginary circumstances in an imaginative, dynamic manner that is stylistically truthful to the character and his environment—true to time and place.*

Being stylistically truthful to the character is a very important point in this definition of acting. That element insures that the approach will always be *contemporary to its time,* since being stylistically truthful means taking into account the attitudes, mores, etc., of the time in which the drama takes place. Thus, contemporary drama will always have a contemporary look; it will always be truthful by current standards—and that's where the audience lives, isn't it?

The definition is not complete without taking into account the ultimate aim of the performance. Unless the responses communicate ideas and emotions to an audience, they are of no value, since the actor's ultimate obligation is to the audience.

The actor must, therefore, not only act, but *communicate*. The full definition of acting becomes this: *Acting is responding to stimuli in imaginary circumstances in an imaginative, dynamic manner that is stylistically true to time and place, so as to communicate ideas and emotions to an audience.*

If this definition is correct, then the first goal is to develop your body—your instrument—so that it becomes aware of all stimuli. Second, your instrument must be able to absorb all stimuli without blocks and without rejections. And third, your instrument must be free enough emotionally, sensorially, and physically to respond to the stimuli that are present.

The actor's body is extraordinarily complex. In virtually all instances an actor begins his training with an instrument that can be compared to a piano that has at least twenty or thirty inoperative keys. The function of the acting teacher and the actor is to free all those keys so they can be played upon easily and on demand—a difficult process indeed, and one that may take an entire lifetime to achieve.

Acting depends on two major elements. The first is a free instrument—one unhampered by emotional blocks, intellectual rigidity, or sensory dullness. Ideally, during the first months, perhaps years, of an actor's training he should concentrate almost entirely on attaining that freedom. The second, and equally important, element is the craft and technique of acting. Again, many years need to go into this training. Each element without the other makes for one-dimensional, undisciplined, or uninteresting acting; both are truly necessary for the full achievement of a role.

Remember that the audience has only two senses you can reach. They can't taste, touch, or smell you; they can only *hear* and *see* you. That is why physicalization is so vital if you are to communicate to an audience. Whatever you want them to get, they can only get through those two senses. You can think, or stare at your navel, until you're blue in the face; until you've given the audience something they can see or hear, you cannot communicate to them. And remember, physicalization refers to *anything, however subtle, that the audience can detect*. A pause, a movement of the eyes, delaying the intake of breath for an instant—these are as much physicalizations as throwing a chair across the room.

Now that you know what acting is, *be careful how you do it!* A young actor once approached Spencer Tracy, one of the finest film actors who ever lived, with a number of questions about acting, finally asking if there was any one thing he considered most important. Tracy looked at him for a moment and said, "Well, acting is fine, as long as you don't get caught at it."

5

Listening/Sensing

If I had to answer the question, "What is the most important ability for an actor?" there would be no contest. The answer would emphatically be *listening*.

To avoid any misunderstanding, let me define what I mean by *listening*. I am talking about listening with all the senses. In other words, listening involves more than what you "hear" with your ears: it involves what you see; *it involves the responses of all of your senses—touch, feel, sight, sound, smell*; and, very importantly, it involves what you perceive intuitively and emotionally and what you have experienced and perceived in the past.

The meaning of dialogue is enhanced by all the other things you "hear." You hear the sound of someone speaking; you hear the literal meaning of the words; you also hear the inflection and, therefore, the actual underlying meaning of what that person has said. You "hear" a headache or a toothache; you "hear" the heat or the cold; you "hear" the other actor's feelings and mood; you "hear" the smell of the other person, the walk of the other person, the manner in which the other person sits. When you are truly listening, you "hear" whatever you can perceive, and all the things that we "hear" affect us to some degree or other. So *listening is also sensing*. You "hear" your own thoughts, your inner activity, and you don't give all the things you hear equal weight. When you're "hearing" more than one stimulus at any given time, one will be dominant.

In an interview in the *Los Angeles Times*, Morgan Freeman, Oscar nominee for his wonderful performance in *The Shawshank Redemption*, said, "Most of acting is reacting, and you only react if you're listening. I think that if you have a talent for acting, it is the talent for listening."

It is difficult for actors to give themselves over to listening

with a full trust in the effects of that process. We tend to worry
about our next line or our next piece of business, and we tend,
therefore, to limit our involvement with the other actors—a very
dangerous procedure. The truth of the matter is, if you really listen, you're at least 80 percent of the way toward your ultimate performance.

We do a simple listening exercise in the classroom. I learned
it during a series of special sessions conducted by an extraordinary
psychologist, Dr. Nathaniel Branden. Branden conducted seven
sessions with a select group of our students, exploring some of the
techniques he uses in psychotherapy to see if we could find some
that would benefit actors without their becoming involved in
therapy. Out of these remarkable sessions this exercise stood out
above all the rest:

Two actors sit on the floor facing each other, as close as they
can be without touching, and get into any position that is comfortable for them. One actor is the listener; the other is the speaker. The listener has absolutely no obligation in this exercise,
except to look directly at the other person and to listen fully. He
need not make any responses of any nature whatsoever, but if he
feels he wants to, or if he makes an involuntary one, fine. If nothing happens, that's also fine. In other words, the listener should
have no need or wish to perform, just simply to listen.

The speaker is then given a series of incomplete sentences. In
each case, the speaker repeats the dictated first part of the sentence, then finishes it. Then he repeats the first part again with a
new ending, repeating the procedure until the teacher gives the
speaker another incomplete sentence. For example, the teacher
might say, "The good thing about being an actor is . . ." The speaker then might say, "The good thing about being an actor is you can
make a lot of money. The good thing about being an actor is it
gives me a chance for fame and recognition." The speaker continues until the teacher changes the incomplete sentence. The new
one is, "When I was a little boy . . ." and the speaker might say,
"When I was a little boy, I hated going to school."

Incidentally, the actors are told to invent an ending if no real
one occurs to them; the content doesn't matter as long as the con-

tinuity and rhythm of the exercise are not broken. Somewhere along the way, the speaker will consciously or unconsciously reveal certain feelings about some of the things he is saying. The listener, having no obligation but to listen, will in most instances perceive those feelings, however subtle they might be. And again, in most instances, the listener will begin to respond: he may laugh or smile; he may cry; he may shake his head with disbelief. *The listener learns that if he trusts to listening, he will perceive things that he would not otherwise perceive.* Most importantly, he will frequently *begin to feel,* because the process of listening in itself will generate emotion, and the actor's biggest problem in most cases is to generate genuine emotion in imaginary circumstances.

The listener also finds that he will have occasional impulses to physicalize (move, touch) as a result of the feelings generated in the exercise, and it is marvelous to learn that such impulses will be generated by *listening to the other actor.* This is a major part of the actor's work (and an all too often neglected part), since the other person is one of the most important sources of stimuli in virtually any scene of any screenplay or play. The actor is also responsive to the many stimuli within himself. In the long run, however, the best scenes are usually those in which the give-and-take between the actors is rich and full and imaginative and, above all, real—a result best achieved by listening fully.

Let's not kid ourselves; we are terrified that we will forget our next line, and the whole process involving remembering and saying the words not only takes our minds off what's happening in the scene, but makes it impossible for us to "hear" everything that's going on. One marvelous plus about film acting is that if it is wrong, it can be done again, and the director really needs only one good take. There is nothing terrible about a scene having to be done again (as long as again doesn't mean thirty times for something simple). And the listening in film acting is a hundred times more important than listening in the theater, because in film the most exciting close-up is often not the one of the actor speaking, but the one of the actor listening. If you watch the work of any good actors in a good feature film or television show, you will soon find that their best moments are those in which their lips don't move at all; where they are just listening to the other actor and allowing themselves to be affected by all the circumstances involving them at that instant. As a matter of fact, if, in your work as an actor, you are a good listener, you will attract the editor, who will be tempted to cut to your close-up. Need I say more?

The value of improvisation, when it is used as a classroom exercise or as a rehearsal technique by some professional directors, lies not in helping actors determine how clever they are as writers, but in helping them learn how well they can listen and how responsive they can be to what all of their senses have heard. How many times have you heard someone you cared for deeply say, at a time of travail or despair or grief, "I'm fine," and felt tears welling inside you because what you heard was exactly the opposite? How, then, can you trust the words that are spoken? How, then, can anyone say that the most important thing in a play or a screenplay is the dialogue? Nonsense. The most important thing is what is *under* the dialogue; it is what makes it happen. The *implication of what has been said*, what you hear with all your senses, is most important. Only when you hear with all of your senses can you know what the spoken words really mean, or whether it was necessary for them to have been spoken at all.

This is not to be taken as a license to change dialogue as you see fit because Tony Barr said, "The words are not important." A good writer's dialogue will be economical, articulate, and specific to the background of the role. It will have its own rhythm and its own emotional texture, and any changes could be very damaging.

Recently we were doing a scene in class in which a woman is disturbed because the man she is living with had gone to visit his child, who is living with his former wife. Concerned that he might want to renew his relationship with his ex-wife, the woman accuses him of wanting to do just that. The man loves this woman; he has no intention of leaving her. The scene becomes heated, building to a strong argumentative climax. At one point the man ad-libbed, "If that's what you think, fuck you!"

I stopped the scene. The ad-lib had given the scene and the relationship an entirely new texture. First, the woman could never have played the rest of the scene, following that line. She could not have said what the author gave her to say and still remain credible and sympathetic. Second, the line gave the man a characteristic that contradicted what had been set up, making the balance of the scene unplayable from his point of view as well. The actor had given himself over to a true feeling, but a feeling that was wrong for the scene because it was the way *he* felt, not the way the character felt. He had not yet totally "reshaped himself" into the role. (See Chapter 14 for more on reshaping.)

It is important to learn dialogue as written. If there is a line or a word that you have difficulty with, discuss it with the director, who may then either make the change or get the writer or producer to make the change.

Back to hearing with all the senses. That is the teacher's first concern since it is the most basic thing the actor needs to learn. The teacher should do simple scenes in the beginning, keeping the action simple. Even better, the teacher can let the actors just sit through the scenes, so that they don't have to worry about doing bits of business. All the teacher's attention should go to whether or not the actors are hearing and sensing the stimuli, be it dialogue, a look, or whatever. They should be stopped when something gets by them, and made aware of what they missed. This will help them become aware of the need to listen more closely. After they have learned to listen, the teacher can begin to work with them on giving the scenes a physical life as well.

This simple sequence will illustrate what I mean.

A man is interested in a woman.

HE

When will you be going home?

SHE

Right at the semester break.

These are not just words. The implication is that she will not be around for him to continue his pursuit. He will then be affected by her statement to whatever degree he is interested in her.

HE

I was hoping you'd go to San Francisco with me
next week to see the opening of a new production
of *Hamlet*.

The words imply an interest in her, and they also imply a
proposition. How SHE feels about those implications must be
dealt with before she responds.

SHE

Oh?

"Oh?" is only a word. But before HE can know how to
respond, HE must sense—from the look on her face and the way
SHE said the word—if SHE is pleased, hostile, eager, or amused,
for her attitude will determine where HE is emotionally at that
moment. (See Chapter 14 for further expansion of this process.)

It is important that actors take the time to absorb the stimuli
hitting them before they respond. That means that an actor must
not jump to his next line the minute the other actor has finished
speaking; he must not "pick up his cue" for the sake of speed. I
never use the word "cue" in my teaching. As far as I am concerned,
there is no such thing as a cue. They don't exist in real life—do
you wait for a cue before you speak? If they don't exist in real life,
why should they exist for the actor? Moments like this are normally thought of as a *thought pause,* which sounds like a dead
moment. In actuality they are very full and dynamic moments in
which the actor is processing the stimuli, and allowing them to
generate his response.

There is a bridge between stimulus and response. The actor must
take the time to hear the stimulus, absorb it, let it affect him, and
then respond—in other words, take the time to cross the bridge. It
may be instantaneous, or it may take quite a while, depending on
the circumstances, but the stimulus must be dealt with before the
response can happen, just as in real life. Remember that very frequently the stimulus hits you before the other actor has finished

speaking, and therefore you start—and even finish—crossing the bridge while the other actor is still talking, and you are ready to respond before he finishes. In that case, any pause would be wrong. And the director won't have to ask you to "pick up your cue."

There's a perfect example of the importance of the bridge in William Goldman's book *Adventures in the Screen Trade*. He tells about a moment in *Marathon Man*, in a scene between Roy Scheider and Laurence Olivier, where, in rehearsal, Olivier took a pause after Scheider says, "I know that sooner or later you're going to go to the bank." Olivier took a moment before responding with "Perhaps I've already been." The director wanted the pause eliminated, so Olivier suggested that the line from Scheider read, "I know that you're going to go to the bank sooner or later," so that he could deal with "bank"—the stimulus for his next line, "Perhaps I've already been"—by the time Scheider finished speaking, and the pause would no longer be necessary. It worked.

This probably seems quite obvious, but it is too often overlooked. The producer/director of a very successful television series recently told me that the greatest problem he had with new actors was that they were afraid to take their time. Could it be because the learning actor too often hears the director screaming "pick up your cues," when the real problem is that the actor is not really listening? Pauses are wonderfully dramatic and effective if they're the right length. They're bad if they're too short, and deadly if they're too long, because such a pause interrupts the rhythm of the moment, and everything stops while the actor indulges himself and "acts" all over the place.

How long is a pause? I don't know. It depends on only one thing: how long will it take you to get across the bridge from stimulus to response? That depends, of course, on the stimulus and how it affects you. If I ask you your name and you're cold sober, the bridge will be very short. If I ask you the product of 3,756 multiplied by 2,312, the bridge will be longer. In the earlier example, Laurence Olivier needed only a second or so to cross the bridge. In *Prizzi's Honor*, when Jack Nicholson is told by the Family leaders that they want him to kill his wife, he takes literally twenty-seven seconds before he responds. That's a long time for silence and no action. Rightly so; that's some bridge he's crossing! And the audience will wait while he crosses that bridge, because they understand how difficult a time he is having.

The audience won't go home if you take a pause, as long as it is justified. Trust yourself! Take the time to get across that bridge!

I have often said to my students that if I were to teach Shakespeare for the stage, I would start in exactly the same place—with truth, with honesty, and with listening as the base of the work, always remembering that the distance of communication is not *to* the other actor, but *through the other actor to the back row of the theater*, so adjust accordingly.

6

The Character

Character analysis and understanding is a very important part of the actor's preparation. The big question for me is, "What should it consist of?"

Throughout this book you will read that the actor must play moment-to-moment, and build his performance that way. I must make it clear at this point that taken together, all those moments comprise almost all of what is conventionally called "the character" and what the audience needs to know about him.

Most actors carry around a lot of cerebral information, derived from extensive intellectual analysis. They decide how the character would feel about this or that, and what made him that way. What he would say in this circumstance, and what in that. What we have here is an intellectual scenario designed by the actor. Not good enough, in my opinion. Sometimes actors go on the assumption that the author has written marvelous stage directions, and has written them in stone and they are thus unchangeable. Not so; the actor must bring parts of himself to the role, because it is the imaginative actor who makes interesting choices and breathes emotional life into the material. That's what makes a good actor's work unique.

I have abandoned the word "character" as much as possible in the classroom, and use in its place the word "role." And for good reason. When an actor thinks of playing a character, he places himself inside another person, an imagined one. He shoehorns himself into that other being in his mind, and loses sight of himself; he distances himself from the role. In my classes the actor is told that he is all things—that he was born with all feelings and senses and intuitions, but that many of those have been locked away by the demands of his environment and culture. Now, as an actor, those things must be freed. If you can accept that you are all things—and you must if you are to call yourself an actor—*then you must bring to the role those parts of yourself that are congruent with what is written*, so that *you work from yourself at all times, not from some imagined person whose skin you struggle to squeeze into*. Don't force the character on yourself; find the character in yourself.

This is a difficult concept to accept. It was for me. But isn't it true that you can only bring yourself to your work, after all? And are you not likely to respond more truthfully if you know that the expected response is what you are feeling, rather than what you think some imagined character is feeling? Once your preparation is complete, *and you have reshaped yourself into the role*, you will respond to stimuli honestly and as the author and director intend. You'll be working from yourself, but the audience will see the character; you will have shelved those parts of you that are wrong for the role and will use only those parts that are right. But it will be your real self at work, *being the character*, not *pretending to be*. Another reason to work from yourself is that the one thing you have that is unique and special is yourself. There's no one like you, and that makes you a very original and beautiful commodity. No one has ever been successful being another Tracy or Hepburn or Dean or Bancroft or Streep or Hopkins or Hanks or Ryan. Every truly successful actor has been unique, has worked from himself.

You must first study the role in depth so that you can thoroughly understand what feelings you need to experience. Then you must be able to empathize with those feelings, so that you can fully understand, appreciate, and feel what the character does in response to what happens to him and around him. Only when you can fully empathize with those feelings can you begin to feel them yourself, and that, of course, is your ultimate goal. As an actor you cannot be self-centered, selfish, indifferent to other people. If you are, how can you identify with anyone else? And if you can't identify with anyone else, how can you play anyone else? Open yourself up to other people. Try to understand how they feel. Put yourself in their place, and see if you can begin to feel as they might be feeling. I think that only when that process is easy, and comes naturally, almost by itself, can you really begin to effectively play a large variety of roles.

There is discussion in the book *about* the subconscious, and its place in preparation and performance. As I state in those places, since you can't use the subconscious, I don't see any point in working on it.

So where does an actor look for the necessary information? What does he work with? I believe the answer lies in carefully studying every bottom line; that is the basic need that drives the character through each scene. It is, the sum of all these individual bottom lines that make up what the audience sees as the character. Actors have to look at what other people say about them, of course, but what one person says about another person can be completely wrong, so it has to be used very judiciously.

Let's examine Hannibal Lecter in *The Silence of the Lambs*. What is the "character"? Well, based on how he behaves toward other people (this is in the writing, so it's not an uncertain quality), he seems to be in control, an important characteristic. The writing clearly tells us he is intelligent, a thinker of some stature. It also tells us that he is a very astute judge of people—witness the way he handles the Jodie Foster character. If that's true, he must take his time judging people—that's a good thing to play. He is unquestionably dangerous and evil, *but that's not what the actor plays, and not how he perceives himself.* He's cannibalistic to us, but to him he's a gourmet, and the rest of us are lacking in culinary sophistication. Taking a life, therefore, is no serious offense to him, since he's only doing what all living things do: eating other living things up because they need sustenance. The writing tells us pretty clearly that he is a proud and authoritative man. How does he walk? I don't know. Does it matter? The things determining that are his physical condition, and he seems normal in the writing, since nothing contradictory is indicated. Since he is an authoritative person, intelligent, cultured, there would probably be a certain pleasant bearing to his walk—and that seems to me to be a pretty good description of Anthony Hopkins.

It looks like we have found most of what we need to understand and play the character, with no suppositions and intellectual probing to find it, just using what is presented in the material. All that's required is that the actor be sensitive and talented enough to see all of that.

No big deal. You just need to be a great actor.

Don't jump all over me. Of course selectivity is important. Of course making the right choices is important, especially where none are indicated in the writing. But those choices should be based on what you already know about the role based on what's in the material. And of course actors and directors working together can make a character better than what was written. But look carefully and you'll see that those choices are almost always based on what is already in the material. Can an actor and/or director change a character completely away from what is written? Sure, but that's the exception, not the rule.

Now about the emotional structure of the character. Again, the material will usually give you that blueprint: hints about when you are hurt, when you are angry, when you are amused or when you are brought to tears. Add to that carefully selected parts *of yourself* that you bring to the role, and you will have a rounded emotional life to play.

For instance, in one of our classes we were doing a scene from *Rain Man*. The woman playing Charlie's girlfriend listens in astonishment as Charlie tells her that he is keeping his brother, Raymond, who he has taken from the facility where he has been living since the death of their father. Is she horrified? Yes. Can she play that? Yes. Is that the only thing she can play? No. Could it be that it hits her as being so ridiculous an idea that she laughs? I think so. The seriousness of it can strike her a moment later, so there can often be more than one possible emotional response to any given stimulus. Those possibilities are what come from *you*, and if you play from your *reshaped self* some parts of you will come into the performance. Let them! The worst that can happen is that the director will say, "I don't think that works." Or "Don't do that!" He won't fire you! It's much cheaper and less time consuming to say, "Don't do that!"

Since actors should work from themselves, it follows that if you give five different actors the same role to play, you'll probably get five different performances, all valid. Each performance will come from the actor reshaping himself into the role as he sees it, and then playing from his reshaped self.

Don't forget, 90 percent of all the answers you need will be found in the bottom lines you will use.

An important additional note: Don't be afraid to play *against* what is written. Iago must not play a villain at all times or Othello would be stupid not to notice. In *The Silence of the Lambs*, Anthony Hopkins did not play villainy, he played against it, which made him even more terrifying. Who's more dangerous, someone who is clearly a villain or sociopath, or someone who can walk at your side and not be noticed as being someone unusual? Playing *into* the character is very likely to lead into a cliché performance. Use your imagination!

7

. . . .

Focus and
Concentration

In simple terms, *focus* and *concentration* refer to where, and how intensely, you direct your entire instrument. You cannot be affected or responsive when you are giving only part of your attention to the major stimuli being directed at you. If, while playing a role, you are thinking about your troubles at home, or whether or not the audience will like your performance, you are clearly giving yourself only half a life. You are truly half dead; your senses, your mind, your emotions, are not totally there with you. You've created your little monster, and the poor thing is hobbling around with one leg, one arm, one eye, and half a brain. Certainly it will feel no emotion and will have dull senses. Give the poor thing a break; give it all your attention.

Chapter 5 covered the importance of listening, which is at the core of focusing. The ability to concentrate is essential for listening. You must learn to zero your attention in on the various elements in the scene if you have any hope of delivering an acceptable performance, let alone a great one.

The power to concentrate needs frequent exercise. Spend the time. Direct your attention to a specific object, a specific person, a specific idea—you name it, but see how long you can keep your attention directed on it and only it before something intrudes and distracts. It will help to investigate the person or object; to try to understand it, study its details. Keep doing this and you should find, as time goes on, that you can go for longer and longer stretches without being disturbed by extraneous influences.

The film actor has a great advantage over the stage actor as far as concentration span is concerned. Film is shot in bits and pieces; the nature of the medium demands that procedure. It is unusual to shoot a scene that runs longer than two or three minutes in a master shot, and it is extraordinary when a seven- or eight-minute master is shot without being broken up into bits and pieces. But that is about the extent of the need for prolonged concentration. When the director calls "cut," your whole system can crumble for the moment if that is what it has to do. It's better if it doesn't; it's better if you stay at least partly connected to the role and the material until the next take or the next setup. While you're on a take, though, your total concentration is needed.

It will help you set and maintain that concentration if you find a center of focus in the scene. From moment to moment you will be more concerned with some things than with others, and in all probability you will be more particularly concerned with one thing or person than with anything else. That object of your focus demands your concentration, and by focusing on something specific, you will help yourself find the energy you need to perform the scene, and you will help your instrument be responsive to the stimuli that strike it during the scene. You will also find it easier to call upon those very slippery, evasive, hidden little devils we call emotions.

There is no good acting without intense focus and concentration. Even the character who is supposedly relaxed and casual has something on which his life or lifestyle at the moment is centered. Find it, focus on it, concentrate. Remember, the camera is practically on your nose; it will know when you're distracted or unfocused much more easily than will the poor guy sitting in the second balcony watching your performance on a stage. He will miss the subtleties that betray you; the camera will not.

Although the actor must concentrate and focus for only short periods of time when he is working in film, there is another side to that coin: there is no isolation for the film actor. On the stage, particularly in the proscenium-type theater, the audience is in the dark, and the light directed to the stage helps give the actor a sense of being in the world represented by the set in which he finds himself. There are no distractions to speak of; everyone backstage is hushed, the audience is hushed (let's hope not during your funniest scenes), and everything possible is done to help give the actor a sense that the only world is the one onstage.

In film, however, there are innumerable distractions. There is no way for you to avoid noticing that there is a camera pointed at you and that there is an operator behind it. There is probably another man alongside the camera, fiddling with the focus knob. There is also a man with his hands on the handle of the camera dolly, ready to push it. He'll move the machine and the men on it just about the time you're ready to reach your biggest moment. Then there is a fellow off to one side, sitting on a wheeled platform that has a long tentacle sticking out of it. Dropping a few inches from that tentacle is a microphone, which the man swings and turns, directing it toward or away from you. Up above, on a platform nicely lit so that you won't miss them, are electricians who are focusing lights and putting in gels and screens up to the moment you're ready to shoot. And in the background, behind the camera, is a nervous first assistant director who is undoubtedly being told by the production office that the director is taking too much time. There is a director anxiously watching you; there is a cinematographer watching you, but probably only seeing the effect of light and shadow on your face. There are grips, a propmaster, and electricians standing around the camera (maybe munching on doughnuts), and very possibly a producer, an associate producer, a casting director, and a few friends of almost anybody involved in the production. All of these people are within fifteen or twenty feet of you, and unless you can obliterate the people and the machinery and focus on the other actor, the prop, the scene, your performance will be disjointed and ineffective.

Don't worry about it. Concentration is much like driving a car; after you've done it a lot, you'll find that it becomes easier and easier to block out all the distractions and create your own private world.

The ability to function in spite of distractions or disaster is something we must all learn. One summer, in Provincetown, Massachusetts, we were playing *Blithe Spirit*. In the third act, during the exorcism of the ghost of the leading man's first wife, our Madame Arcati was staged to find her way, in the dark, to the proscenium arch, then to lean on it so that when the lights came up she would be discovered triumphant after her very special victory. In the dark, however, the actress missed the proscenium arch.

I was the stage manager, and from backstage I heard a dreadful thump; our actress had leaned where the proscenium wasn't. There was a pause—obviously the actor onstage had also heard the thump, for soon a querulous male voice asked, "Are you all right, Madame Arcati?" Only a second elapsed before we heard the actress booming from the auditorium, where she had fallen from the stage, saying, "Yes, would you turn on the lights and help me, please." The lights came on, the leading man helped her climb back onto the three-foot-high stage, and without missing another beat our Madame Arcati continued the play. At least part of the audience believed it was all planned, she carried it off so well, and the play suffered very little.

Going up—forgetting one's lines—could be the result of any one of several things, but the most frequent cause is lack of concentration, which causes an interruption in the listening process. When the mind wanders out of the scene, the lines are likely to be forgotten. (This presupposes that the scene was learned properly in the first place.) One of the biggest challenges to the actor is to develop his power of concentration to the point where he can remain engrossed in the role, without interruption by a wandering mind, for as long as the scene demands.

A word about tension. Unless you are relaxed within the role you are playing, you will experience certain tensions, both physical and emotional. They are inevitable. Those tensions will interfere with the listening process; they will form a solid wall that stimuli and emotions will be unable to break through.

You must learn to relax—to trust yourself so completely that no tensions of any kind exist, except those that belong to the role. Only then can you be truly listening. And only then can the instrument be free enough to allow your most unique and interesting personal qualities to become part of the performance ("a consummation devoutly to be wished," to quote some obscure author).

How do you learn to relax? *Concentrate.* Most tension occurs because you are concerned with things other than the scene, usually with worry about the quality of your performance. The more intense the concentration—usually on the other person—on *listening*, the more relaxed you will become.

8

• •

Energy

Throughout all of my teaching years, I have been asked, "What is energy? How much do I need? Where do I get it? How come that actor seems to have enormous energy when he's not doing anything?"

I don't think there's much question that there are certain performers who walk on a stage and command your attention whether you want to give it to them or not. These performers invariably have a great sense of authority, even though they might be playing characters seriously lacking in authority, and they have a great deal of apparent energy. You expect things to happen. You wait for their responses. Their every look, their every physicalization, has meaning and impact, and yet they are just people. They have not been endowed with any special bodily organ to create that energy. (Authority is something we will get into elsewhere.) Where does the energy come from?

I believe that *energy is the direct result of how much you care about what is happening*. If the content of the scene—if what is happening in your performance life—is important enough, you will be listening with sufficient intensity, absorbing and responding with sufficient intensity, to create the necessary energy.

We have gone through a period (I use the phrase "gone through" because I hope it is over) in which "naturalness" was confused with reality. In the effort, then, to be natural, actors picked their noses, scratched their behinds, and spent great amounts of energy being careful not to spend great amounts of energy. They posed, they scratched, and they determinedly refused to allow themselves to care, except in deeply emotional moments, when anything less than throwing dishes and chairs around was absolutely unacceptable to them. Perhaps this kind of thing was the greatest misconception to come out of the Stanislavsky, or Method, approach. Montgomery Clift once said he learned that, in film acting, you had to *speak softly and think loud*.

If you watch a person listening or watching intently, your eyes will stay riveted on that person. Your focus will drift from the casual listener or observer; it is difficult to pull it away from someone who seems to care. An audience will have the same reaction when watching you in a scene. If you care, the audience will care. And if you care enough, there will be energy in the way you listen, in the way you respond, or even in the way that you choose *not* to respond.

You must never choose *not* to care about the stimuli in the scene. For example, a man and a woman are in a restaurant. After a short argument, the man says he is going to leave. If the actress chooses to play that she doesn't care if he goes, then she has de-energized the scene. She has made a choice that de-energizes her and bores an audience. Unless the material *demands* that you not care, *always choose to care about what is happening as much as you logically can within the context of the material.*

It is extremely important that the physicalizations reflect how much you care to the same degree. The inner energy, which is the result of how much you care, needs to be physicalized, since the caring must generate a physical response in order to articulate your feelings to the audience.

A good example of the importance of proper physicalization occurred when two of my students selected a scene from Edward Albee's *Everything in the Garden.* The scene starts with the husband having just opened a package in a plain brown wrapper, addressed to him, which contains a substantial amount of cash. The husband is stunned; he fumbles around for a cigarette, can't find one, opens drawers, and then finds another stack of money. Looking around, he finds another stack of money, and, unable to contain himself any longer, calls out to his wife. She enters the room speaking about the preparations being made for cocktails and guests who are about to arrive. He confronts her with the money. She finally admits she has sent it, or planted it for him to find. She then offers one explanation after another of how she got it, none of which he accepts. Finally, the truth comes out—she has been working as a prostitute in the afternoons to earn more money for the family.

The actress chose to make her entrance speaking casually of cocktails and guests and then allow the content of the scene to help her build toward its high moments. But she lacked energy, and the opening of her scene was down considerably from what it should have been. When we discussed the lives of the two people, it soon became apparent that if she planted the money for him to find and sent him an anonymous package, she therefore would be aware that the issue was about to be confronted. She would be concerned about his reaction to her becoming a prostitute, as most wives would be. Therefore, she must be well aware that when she comes from the kitchen, talking about cocktails and guests, she is going to be facing the question of the money, and so must have some sense of anticipation about what is going to be said and what is going to happen. If she cares about it, then her inner rhythms will be up; her inner focus will be less on cocktails and guests than on her husband, his reactions, and her own explanations.

The actress understood; we started the scene again, and her entrance now carried a completely different flavor, getting the scene off to a much more dynamic start, but leaving plenty of room for the ensuing dynamics to take place. What the actress did was to change her emotional attitude before her entrance; she cared about what was about to happen. The result was highly increased energy and a much more interesting scene.

The teacher can make this point clear quite easily by taking a strong scene and telling the actors that they are to take the adjustment that they do not care a great deal about the stimuli in the scene; that they don't care that the husband has found another woman, or that the woman has just miscarried and lost the chance ever to become a mother, or whatever. After playing that scene, the actors play the same scene with the adjustment that they care a great deal about the circumstances of the scene. The students can see the difference.

Let me add something with which all good teachers, good directors, and good actors will agree: in order to generate energy on any level, it is important that the actor's instrument be healthy. It is astonishing to me that actors who have only their own bodies as the instruments of their craft, as the only instruments available for use in a career to which they choose to give their lives, will abuse those instruments. Not only do they physically destroy them through excessive use of alcohol, cigarettes, or drugs, but they wreak havoc with the functioning of the instruments through bad sleeping habits, bad eating habits, refusal to exercise: in other words, doing with their own instruments what no intelligent musician would do with his clarinet, violin, or piano. Can you imagine a concert pianist leaving his Steinway out in the rain and snow until he's ready for a performance and then having it dragged up on the stage? Without even retuning it? Can you imagine a violinist doing the same thing with his Stradivarius? And yet, the actor will sleep badly, take drugs, eat badly, drink to excess, smoke to excess, become flabby and perhaps even gross physically, to the extent that his instrument comes nowhere near resembling the instrument with which he started, which he thought was going to be available all his life. What a terrible waste—and what stupidity.

Before you go away, let me remind you, I used the word "excess." Heaven forbid anyone should think that I said the actor must live the life of a monk. Forget it. That could be worse than going the other way. You do need to exercise all your senses; you do need new experiences, so that the instrument can touch base with virtually all things. So enjoy yourselves, but remember, in the next role you play, you might have to look and sound healthy. The actors who do take care of themselves look younger and more appealing, and generally they have a longer and more successful career.

9

● ●

The Emotions

The single most difficult problem the actor faces is that of generating real emotion. I am going under the assumption that to be moving (in other words, to affect an audience on an emotional level), a performance must be based, at least to some degree, on the actor's having the personal experience of real emotions.

Since the free expression of emotion is generally taboo in our culture, by the time we are young adults we have successfully locked our emotional instruments so that they are not responsive to stimuli. From the time we are little children, we are told "don't yell, don't cry, be a good boy, be a good girl," to the point where we begin to feel that it is wrong to cry or to get angry or—and this is the most tragic thing of all—to experience pure extravagant joy. We are so burdened with guilt for giving expression to the impulses we were born with that we very carefully padlock them in some deep corner and throw away the key.

All healthy children are born fully equipped with all their emotions and senses available and responsive. As infants, we need no instruction to cry because our diapers are wet and we feel uncomfortable, or because we are hungry and our stomachs hurt; we need no instructions about when or how to laugh when something pleases us; we need no help getting sore as hell when the breast or bottle is taken away before we're through with it. We are all born very free little animals, and what we must do when we decide to become actors is to learn once again to become an animal and then, through our craft and talent, to discipline that animal so that it is effective to an audience.

The senses will do a great deal toward freeing emotions—perhaps more than any other single thing except listening/sensing. That is why so many of today's good and great acting teachers involve young actors in what are usually called sense memory exercises.

It is not enough that the senses be reawakened and made available for the sake of performance; they must also be responsive, because they are in many cases a direct path to the emotions. If you recall very clearly the smell and the specific look of a funeral chamber, you are more likely to re-experience a sense of grief over the loss of a loved one than if you try to remember the loved one in general terms. It is the sound of the loved one's voice saying something, or the look on the face, which triggers the emotion; emotion is rarely released by thinking, "I loved my mother. I loved my mother. I loved my mother."

Don't forget that the emotional response is only one part of what is necessary. There must also be a physical response, an intellectual response, and a sensory response; in other words, the entire instrument must be responding. Emotion alone does not constitute good acting.

Speaking of physicalizing emotions, one of my favorite no-no's is the use of the face as an acting tool. Don't. Your face is so intimately connected with the rest of you that it is virtually impossible for it not to do things by itself, and without your help, when your emotions or senses are affected. Trust it; it'll do what has to be done, and more importantly, it will not do what is unnecessary. The face actor becomes unattractive in film, because the audience's focus is so directed, and the physicalizations are so magnified by virtue of either size or focus or both, that exaggerated facial activity becomes grotesque.

Don't take my word for it; watch your favorite and most successful actors and actresses. You will see that they do very little, and yet you know everything that is going on behind their faces and throughout their entire instruments. In an interview with Dick Cavett, Alan Bates said, "Thought does register on camera." That's almost accurate. Actually, what happens is that the thought causes some reaction, however subtle, and *that's* what is noticed by the audience. This very accomplished stage actor understands the special nature of film acting.

It boils down to one thing: play the truth. Don't exaggerate. Don't try to articulate with anything but what is honest. And be simple.

There are those whose faces in real life are animated. To them, a great deal of facial activity is natural and is absolutely truthful. It may well be; but real truth may not be good performance truth. As long as they play people characterized by a very mobile face, they're in very good shape. But that physicalization is not common to everyone. It therefore becomes seriously out of place with any other kind of person, and thus limits the roles those actors can play. You can always animate a face if that's what you want; it is very difficult to simplify facial activity if you can't do it in real life.

One of the most common failings of the poor or inexperienced actor is that the emotional level of his scene seems to lose consistency; it grows stronger or weaker depending on whether the actor is listening or talking, rested or tired, or more involved or less involved in the role at that given moment. In other words, the scene does not have a continuing through-line of emotion. Also, inexperienced actors will make sudden emotional changes, and those changes frequently give the lie to the truth of the emotions involved.

I use an analogy in my classroom: emotions are like a car going downhill. They will pick up speed and intensity as they move toward the bottom of the hill (or climax) unless something slows them down or pushes them in a different direction. If brakes are applied to a car going downhill, it will not stop immediately; it will continue to move, or at least skid, as it slows down. If the steering wheel of the car is turned, the car will not turn at right angles; it will turn in an arc so that there will be a time lag before it is headed in a new direction.

The same is true of emotions. If you are genuinely experiencing an emotion, it cannot stop suddenly with the pressure of a new stimulus; a certain amount of time is needed for a new emotion to take its place. You've all seen it happen: an actor laughs uproariously at something, then suddenly stops laughing and becomes serious. If you look around you, or better still, if you look at yourself the next time something really funny happens, you will discover that your feeling of amusement does not end suddenly, even after you've stopped making the sounds of laughter; the feeling continues even though some distraction (stimulus) has moved your mind from what caused you to laugh to something new. The word *transition* obviously means a change from one state to another, and if you remember the analogy of the car going downhill, you will make your transitions with honesty, and you will affect an audience with them.

Speaking of genuinely experiencing an emotion, *it should affect you all the way down to your toes.* If you are not that totally involved, you won't move correctly, and you won't respond to stimuli correctly. Your body language will betray the fact that you are not fully committed to what is happening at that moment, and believe it or not, even in your close-up something will be missing.

Every role is made up of many transitions from one emotion or thought to another. The actor is bombarded by stimuli that he must hear, then absorb, and then respond to. In time, however, another stimulus hits him, generating a different emotion or thought, and he must make the transition from one to the other.

Remember, there is a bridge from one feeling to another. You are on one side. Something happens that impels you to the other side. You must hear it; you must absorb it. It will then affect you and cause you to move across the bridge to the other side, which is where the new emotion awaits you. In order for that to happen, you must take the time to deal with the stimulus that strikes you, and which then moves you across the bridge—through the transition.

As I've pointed out, sometimes the bridge is crossed almost instantaneously. Most of the time, however, it takes a moment or two for the full process to happen, and you must not be afraid to take that time. The audience will not be bored if you are truly involved and caring about what is happening; they will actually work with you as you go through the transition, so there is no need to hurry. *Take the time to deal with the stimuli that hit you.*

Here's an example. You have just received a letter telling you that you have won a contest and as a prize will receive two all-expenses-paid trips to Paris for you and your loved one. You rush to tell your husband, thrilled at the prospect. Instead of reciprocating with joy, he sadly tells you that he is seriously ill, and cannot even consider a long trip. You must now cross the bridge from joy to unhappiness, despair, or fear.

That can't be done instantaneously. The stimulus (his state-ment) hits you; it affects you; the joy diminishes; the new emotion begins to well up, replacing the joy. All of that takes time, and you must take the time to allow it to happen. The audience has also heard; they empathize; they feel with you; and since in real life the transition would take time, the moment will not seem real if you don't take the time you would be expected to take.

Wouldn't it be silly if an actress wept bitterly, eyes tearing, nose running, because she thought her dog had been run over, then suddenly exclaimed with joy as the dog bounced into the room, and she had no residual effects of the tears, runny nose, heavy breathing, and other physical and emotional symptoms that accompanied her grief?

Incidentally, that brings me to what may be a digression, but one of my pet peeves is the dry weeper. I don't remember ever see-ing a living human being cry without shedding at least one tiny tear. Only actors and actresses make funny noises and sniffle while they dry-cry. The camera is much too intimate for that kind of baloney to be successful. If you can't cry, don't fake it, unless you can play the whole thing with your back to the camera or get the makeup man to spray something in your eyes to make them tear so that all of your sobbing and other gyrations may look at least a lit-tle real. If all else fails and you are in a position to do so, ask the director to have the makeup person put a couple of glycerin drops on your face for your close-ups so that it will look as if you have shed tears. The director can break up the accompanying master so that the close-ups and the master will match.

When you are through with that performance, I suggest you go get help. In our acting classes, I try to help the actor find the ability to cry if it is necessary. If that fails—well, maybe it will take someone outside of an acting class to help you. Learn how to free your tear ducts so that they are available to you when you need them as an actor. Maybe an acting teacher can do it for you; maybe it will take an analyst or a psychologist or someone else to give you a punch in the nose. But you had better do something about it so that the next time, the camera will look at something real happening.

There is another giveaway about crying that many people, surprisingly, have never noticed. Before most people cry, their eyes moisten, their faces change color, and their noses start to get red. There is no way I know of to fake those symptoms, and if they don't happen before you start to cry, perceptive people in the audience will know you're faking it. They will understand intellectually that you are supposed to be crying, but they will be unmoved, and our obligation is, of course, to move an audience. They may not know consciously why they are unmoved, but some part of them knows what happens when people cry, and they'll know that it is not happening to you.

One of the real causes of an actor's failure to cry is that the actor frequently *tries* to cry; he tries to play an emotion that a person in real life would almost always try to suppress or counteract. In real life, a stimulus makes you want to cry, and you try not to cry. As an actor you should do the same thing, for it is your struggle to keep from crying that makes an audience feel like crying. Then, when you lose that struggle and a tear appears, the audience will be likely to cry with you because you will have caught them up in your problem and they will be feeling it with you (but from their safe distance as an audience). The effort to keep from crying will cause feelings to be pushed down inside of you, and that suppressed energy will help you to get to the tears. Of course, this result presupposes an instrument that is free enough to accept the stimulus and be responsive to it: an instrument that will want to cry or be angry when given the proper stimulus so that there can be the struggle to keep from doing so.

Pushing for an emotion is a common acting mistake. The actor tries to tell the audience what he is feeling when he isn't really feeling it, by generating the symptoms of the emotion with nothing real making them happen. This deception doesn't fool the audience; they will simply not be moved by what is happening. Nor will the actor.

You must not try to convince the audience that you are feeling something. *You must convince yourself.* And you can't convince yourself unless it is really happening. If you are indeed feeling it, then the right things will happen, the audience will be convinced, and they will share that emotion empathetically and be moved by it.

It is very difficult to portray more than one emotion at any one time. However, we are frequently faced with a need to let the audience know that what is on the surface is not what is underneath.

In one scene we recently did in class, a young wife is deeply troubled because her husband has not been going to work. He has become obsessed by the need to receive mail and has been writing to people all over the world and even ordering magazines that he never reads. In the beginning of the scene she does not want him to know how troubled she is. She therefore must try to appear relaxed to him. Later in the scene they begin an argument, so what she actually feels can come out.

The problem for the actress is that if she only plays being relaxed there will be no underlying conflict—and there is an underlying tension. What must be done, then, is to find the way to allow the underlying tension to affect physicalizations early in the scene so that the casualness has an edge to it that can be seen by the audience but not by the other character. In her preparation, therefore, the actress must first find what her *true* feelings in the scene are by giving them full play during several rehearsals. Then, in the next rehearsals, she must begin to compress and contain her true feelings so that she can keep her husband from seeing how she really feels. This conflict will create certain tensions that will affect her physicalizations, letting the audience know that there is something *under* her seemingly casual attitude toward her husband's being at home when it is time for him to go to work. In the discussions on rhythm and interrupted physicalizations (Chapter 15), I cover some of the things that articulate most clearly to the audience this very duality of emotion. Examine that chapter very carefully.

The emotional build in a well-written scene is dependent on the series of stimuli presented to the character. Each of the stimuli must provide some new emotional drive in order for a build to occur; otherwise the "car" will soon reach the bottom of the hill and begin to slow down.

Problems arise when the actor is not fully aware of the significance of the moment-to-moment stimuli in a scene. If, for example, you have a need and you set out to fulfill that need and are unable to do so, that frustration generates an emotional response. If you continue to try to fulfill that need and continue to be frustrated, the emotion generated by the frustration will become more and more pronounced so that there will be an emotional build until another stimulus causes it to slow down in intensity or to change its direction.

Take the following scene as an example. A man and the woman he lives with are in the midst of an argument because she wants to become a cab driver, like him. He wants to talk her out of it.

INT. APARTMENT-NIGHT

NICK

You're gonna what?

TONI

I'm gonna start driving a cab.

(She presents an obstacle to his objective, or need. It frustrates him.)

NICK

You gotta be crazy!

(He presents an obstacle to her need. It frustrates and annoys her in turn.)

TONI

Why? Why is that so crazy?

(Again, she doesn't give in.)

NICK

Because you're a woman!

(Nor does he. This pattern applies to most of the balance of the scene.)

TONI

What does that mean? I'm not good enough to drive a cab because I'm a woman?

NICK

No, dammit! It means it's not the right kind of job for a woman.

TONI

There are women driving cabs right now!

NICK

That's right! But they're not you! And I don't care about them. I do care about you, and it's too dangerous!

TONI

I can take care of myself.

NICK

Not with a gun at your head or a knife at your throat. Not with some guy who weighs three times what you weigh.

TONI

I'm gonna do it.

NICK

No, you're not!

TONI

I am!

NICK

You start driving a cab and this arrangement is
over.

TONI

Meaning what?

NICK

Meaning we ain't livin' together if you start
hackin'.

(This stimulus has a new direction. It motivates a new action from
her.)

*She stares at him for a moment, then storms to the closet, reaches in,
and takes out a suitcase. During the following, she packs angrily, with
NICK paying no attention to what she is packing, as he continues his
harangue.*

(Her packing is further rejection of his cause. It continues to frustrate and anger him.)

NICK

There are guys who weigh two hundred pounds
who have been taken apart by some bruiser who
wants their money. Guys who have gotten
creamed by some jerk who rammed into them
and then blamed them for the accident. They
come out of their cars with a jack or a baseball bat
in their hands and come at you. What the hell are
you gonna do when that happens? Huh? What?

[She says nothing, just continues to pack]

Dammit, talk to me. What are you gonna do if
some guy grabs you and tries to drag you into an
alley someplace? He'll tell you he lives out in the
boonies someplace, and when you get out there,
there ain't no house or anything and the guy's all
over you and you're screamin' and nobody hears
you. What are you gonna do then, huh? Huh?

[*No answer as she packs*]

Now listen to me. I love ya. But I really mean it—
no livin' together if you start drivin'. So you can
just get the idea out of your head right now, and
stop packin' your clothes because we both know
you ain't goin' through with it. You ain't drivin'
and you ain't leavin'.

TONI
[*Finished packing, she slams the suitcase shut, closes the snaps*]

That's right. You are.

[*She slams the suitcase into his gut*]

(This is a new stimulus. A turnaround point in the scene. The
straight drive of the scene to here now shifts course.)

NICK
What?

TONI
I was packing your clothes, not mine.

NICK *looks at her, speechless, as she goes to the kitchen, slams
around getting the coffeepot, and starts to make some coffee.
NICK throws the suitcase down, storms over to the couch, and sits,
staring at the TV, which has been on during this whole scene.*

(His action stimulates new feelings from her. Her course has shifted now.)

TONI looks over at him, realizes that he isn't going anywhere and that she is going to have it her way after all. She suppresses a smile, walks over to the couch, and sits next to him.

We have come full circle to the matter of *listening with all the senses,* because only when all the senses are aware of the stimuli and their implications can the actor be responsive.

Anger sometimes presents an interesting problem. Recently we were doing a scene from Neil Simon's *Chapter Two* at the Workshop. In it, George is deeply troubled because he cannot commit himself fully to his new bride, Jenny. A bitter scene ensues, in which he becomes very angry, apparently at his new wife, but in reality at himself, because he feels guilty that he is still grieving over his recently deceased wife. When the scene was over, one of the students, who was not familiar with the material, asked about the relationship between the two, because George seemed so deeply angry with her that it appeared he hated her.

It was an interesting point, since what we have in the scene is an *indirect anger,* the kind in which someone lashes out at another person, but that other person is not the cause of the anger. The actor had played the scene looking directly at Jenny, giving full vent to his rage as he looked right into her eyes. I had him do the scene again, this time directing his eyes away from her; into the suitcase he was unpacking, to start with. Now the scene had a different texture; the mere fact that he couldn't look at her told us that he was not angry at her—or not only at her—but at something else as well. Because the audience knows the material to this point, having seen it, they can then correctly conclude that he is angry at himself.

This kind of indirect anger occurs very often, in life as well as in drama. It is good to remember that when that happens, we do not look at the other person as much as we would if the other person were the primary cause of the anger. It is even better, when playing such a scene, for you to become involved in the material to the extent that you will be unable to look at the other actor because your anger is largely directed at yourself. In other words, do it because you feel it, and not because it's a technique you once read about.

I am always asked how one knows where to look. As a general rule, one's visual focus and emotional focus are the same. In other words, if my emotional focus is on you because I'm angry with you, then I will look at you. If I am angry at someone or something else, my emotional focus will be on that person or problem, and therefore I will be more inclined to look away from you, probably into some activity I will find or invent. Obviously there are other factors. When we feel guilty, for example, we don't want to look the other person in the eye, so we look away—again perhaps inventing an excuse to do so. In general, however, if you are fully focused and involved in the moment, your visual focus will take care of itself.

What you must not do is break visual contact for no reason. Remember, every time you look away from the other actor you are breaking the connection between the two of you. If you have a strong need to get some point across, that looking away causes you to lose strength. Watch how seldom good actors look away from the other actor without reason, and how seldom they even blink— something which also breaks the connection between you and the other actor.

Emotions are often difficult for the actor to achieve, because in real life he is ashamed to reveal that he is capable of experiencing them. One good exercise is to stand in front of a group of people and say to each one at least once, "I have a right to cry," if being unable to cry is your problem, or "I have a right to get angry," or "I have a right to be happy." (You may find that that is the toughest one of all; don't be surprised if you do.) This exercise is really connected to some of Dr. Branden's work, which was mentioned in Chapter 5. Many times we do not express an emotion because we have been taught it is wrong to do so, and we need to learn to believe that all emotions or sensory responses—whichever and whatever—belong to us and are part of us, *and we have a right to experience and express every single one of them.*

No part of you calls for shame or guilt. If you want to be an actor, it is important that you recognize that you are a whole and separate person made up of all human parts and that your expression of those parts, particularly in performance, is good and wholesome and natural. If you want to be an actor, it is important that your total instrument be available to you and that you be able to tap it with complete freedom, comfort, and joy.

We talk a great deal about emotion in acting, but it is important to know that emotionalizing is not acting. The most difficult scenes to play are those in which there is little or no apparent emotion; yet these scenes are necessary, and frequently quite telling. Don't be afraid of a scene that is simple. You'll get a chance to scream and tear your hair out sooner or later. Emotion is a vital part of a performance; overemotionalizing is not.

10

· ·

Spontaneity

No other art form demands the appearance of spontaneity that acting does. You will notice I emphasized the word "appearance," because what the audience is looking at is something that has been rehearsed. The end result of all the actor's preparation and repetitive efforts is to make his work look as if it's happening for the first time. I don't think any definition of acting or any acting teacher will disagree with that.

Differences of opinion will come from the definition of *spontaneity*, however. Many believe that the actor's only responsibility is to open himself up to whatever feelings are generated in a performance (not just rehearsals) and respond spontaneously. By definition that means that the actor is responding as himself, not as his self "reshaped" in the role, and that his responses may vary from performance to performance or, in the case of film, from take to take.

You might ask, "Why would the performance vary? We're dealing with the same human being, aren't we?" Well, the answer is, "No, we're not." The way you respond to any given stimulus at any given moment in your life is not only a function of what you are as a total person, it is also a function of what has happened to you in recent moments, because you are affected from moment to moment by new stimuli. Therefore, the way you respond to any given stimulus might vary from moment to moment.

Let me be more specific. Suppose you are doing a scene in a film and you have just shot the master. You slept well the night before and felt good when you woke up. You arrived at the studio and everybody was pleasant to you. You went to makeup, had a nice cup of coffee and a pleasant chat with the makeup person, then reported to the set, where you were treated like royalty. The director came in and praised your work of the day before, and you sailed into the master scene on a cloud. Having finished the master, the director, the cinematographer, and the crew now begin to set up for your close-up.

While this is happening your agent comes in to tell you that the remaining portion of your role has been cut in half because the star demanded the lines you had! Certainly you do not feel the same as you did before your agent arrived with this terrific news.

Now you must go do your close-up. Can you react spontaneously? Of course you can't, because the way you would react to stimuli, feeling as annoyed as you do at this moment, would be totally different from the way you reacted to stimuli in the master. Your so-called "spontaneous reactions" would be absolutely different in each setup, making editing the scene impossible, because only part of your performance is truly related to the role.

The point that I'm making is that *spontaneity does not mean your personal spontaneity*; it means the *character's spontaneity*. Therefore, in order for your behavior to be truly spontaneous and correct in terms of a performance, your preparation has to be such that you are believing as the role demands, feeling as the role demands, and sensitive to stimuli as the role demands—not as you personally might respond. That means sensitive in a way that is determined by the earlier circumstances of the life you are playing, as well as by all the facts and conditions that have been set up by the script.

Spontaneity, therefore, is only true and real when you are *totally* immersed in the role. That means there must be some parts of you that you have put in a basket somewhere so they won't be involved in your performance.

I can hear the screams from some actors that we're keeping them from being themselves. But they're wrong; they'll have to go on screaming. Because the truth is that it is the character who is alive on the screen, not the actor. And, as much as the actor must bring himself to the role, he must always remember that the end result of the merger of self and role is the creation of a new self, or character.

All of this doesn't mean that you should lock down your responses. Don't forget that there will probably be more than one take for each setup. Your performance may vary somewhat each time, but that's OK if what is happening is that you are responding to the stimuli given you. A director needs only one good take!

....

TWO

Working on the Role

11

Preparation

Here are some solutions to the problems I just raised in the chapter on Spontaneity.

Very few things are more important to the actor than his preparation for a role. A reading and rereading of the script to develop an understanding of the material in its entirety is vital. A reading and rereading of the script to determine how the role relates to the author's overall meaning and intent is also vital. How you then decide to approach a role cannot be purely a matter of your own taste in acting and how you would like to come across to the audience; you must make your broad selections on the basis of what the author is trying to say. An actor can destroy a perfectly good piece of material by playing a role in such a way that the validity of the material is affected; that has happened many times when stars insist on playing roles their way, instead of as the author and director intended.

If you carefully examine what other people in the script say about you, you will learn a great deal about yourself and how you affect the world around you, as well as gaining some insight into your relationships with those people. And if you examine *not the words you utter, but the implications of those words*, you will begin to get a true idea of yourself in the role.

As important as anything you say is what you do, because the *doing* tells the audience far more than any words can tell. If you carefully examine how you respond physically to the stimuli presented, you will begin to gather great insights into the makeup of your role.

One very important question you must always ask yourself is, "Why am I saying or doing this at this particular moment? Why not an hour ago or two speeches ago or three speeches from now? What is the specific stimulus that made this happen *at this time?*"

When you examine responses in those terms, you will begin to nail down the exact moment-to-moment thread that keeps the entire person you must become connected and alive.

No responses happen in limbo; no response happens just because the author wrote the words. A response can only happen when the conditions and stimuli are such that the response is *inevitable* at that moment. That includes the line you say, the look you give, or the piece of business you do.

Make sure that you have carefully examined the stimuli that cause a given response. The line-by-line exercise described in Chapter 14 is vital for such an examination, particularly for beginners. (It would be a great exercise for professionals, as well, to remind them that there is a lot of connective tissue between stimulus and response that they sometimes tend to gloss over.)

Preparation immediately preceding the performance is a much more important and difficult process for the film actor than for the stage actor. Once you have achieved your general preparation (as described at the beginning of this chapter), the performance on the stage offers lengthy rehearsals and a good deal of preparation time before the curtain goes up, after which there is continuity of performance. In film, the situation is quite different. Scenes are shot in short sequences, and even out of sequence; the actor must find ways of bringing himself to the necessary physical, sensory, and emotional levels in a very short period of time. You will not have an hour before each scene to put on your makeup, walk around in your costume, finger the props, and so forth. There are times when you will have only a few seconds or minutes between setups, and your concentration will frequently be interrupted by technical needs or the activities of the crew, executives, and others on the set. It is essential, therefore, that you find those tools that generate quick and full responses in you.

Rhythm is an important tool. Obviously all your other tools should be available and should be used, but if they all fail, the one thing that will be extremely helpful in almost every case is to *move in the rhythm required by your sensory and emotional state as demanded in the upcoming take.* If you know what emotional level is demanded at the beginning of a scene, then you should also know what rhythmic level is demanded, since they go hand in hand (see Chapter 15). If you take just half a minute of preparation by walking in the proper rhythm or by working with a prop in the proper rhythm, you will help generate the necessary emotion and build it to where it is supposed to be when the director says, "Action." In that way you should be able to reach a proper level of inner activity as well as physical activity, even when the take is beginning in the climactic moment of a scene, as is frequently the case when a director does pick-ups.

You must search diligently for the tools that work for you, and you must always be aware that the scene starts when the director says, "Action." You do not have five minutes of Act I exposition to get you going.

An excellent manner of preparation is to study the scene immediately preceding the one to be shot, so that you will know exactly where you were emotionally. Then you will know exactly where to start at the beginning of the new scene. If the take were to begin anywhere other than at the beginning of the scene, add a quick, private reiteration of the moments immediately preceding the start of a take. In that way you will be able to lift yourself to the necessary level so that your entire performance will flow in a continuous line, with proper rise and fall. Each moment will be at the correct emotional level. Each physicalization will be part of a logical series of physicalizations, properly connected emotionally, physically, and sensorially.

Read the script carefully; that will help you understand what those values are. See what the author is trying to say, then examine the various characters to see how they relate to the theme and how they help to articulate it. Assuming a well-written piece of material, you should be able to distinguish those elements quite easily.

Now examine your role in particular. How can your performance help to articulate the author's ideas? Suppose the play is an antiwar play, and the author lays much blame on the military. You are playing a commanding officer. If you select to play him warm and compassionate, are you fulfilling the author's intent? It may be—but it also may be that what the author really wants is to make the military look guilty through this character, and you have taken the sting out of him. Maybe you have selected an approach based on how you want to be seen, and not on what is necessary to make the material effective.

In several instances major stars have changed the interpretation of a novel and screenplay by twisting their characters to their own personal needs, distorting the material beyond recognition. In most such cases, the films fail.

Find the structural pattern of the script. The material will rise and fall; scenes will build to a climax and then decrease in intensity. Find those dynamics; if they are not easily visible, dig deeper, or even try to add them to the material through your performance. If you can, all the scenes will be more exciting, and the author and director will be grateful.

Some time ago, Karl Malden appeared at the Workshop as a guest speaker. He told a story about himself that helps explain why actors and directors, as well as the public, hold him in such high esteem as a performer. He had been signed for a role and had several weeks before shooting began. In his customary way, he read books and articles on subjects related to his character's profession and spent hour upon hour thinking about the man, his background, his wants, and so forth. One morning he went to his garden and began to putter around the greenery. He suddenly realized that this was completely unlike him, since he rarely got involved in the gardening, and for a short while he couldn't figure out why he was there. However, it soon dawned on him that his character was the kind of man who would enjoy puttering around in the garden. It was his involvement with the character that brought him to a behavior pattern unlike his own, but like that of the character he was about to portray, *which then became his own*. This kind of thoroughness in preparation is what leads the actor toward the ultimately desirable goal: to be so immersed in the role that all of the spontaneous reactions are role-spontaneous and not just personal-spontaneous.

In your preparation for a role, avoid the temptation to play the end of the material in the beginning. For instance, by the end of the play, Romeo is, by all standards, a tragic character with great sensitivity and tremendous emotional depth. At the beginning of the play, however, he and his friends are just a bunch of horny teenagers looking for a party. If the mood of tragedy were to be played all the time, then the fun written into the beginning of *Romeo and Juliet* would not be there, and the play would have nowhere to go.

Design your role on a moment-to-moment basis, making sure that each moment and each selection is carefully chosen so that when all are added together they will form a complete picture.

Actors tend to try to play all the facets of a role all the time, thinking that this will show the audience how wonderfully deep and profound they are as actors. Obviously that's wrong. In real life we are never involved with all the facets of ourselves; we are usually only involved with what's driving us at any particular moment.

Let's say you want to build a house. You buy a lot. (That's you.) You hire an architect, discuss the kind of house you want, and he prepares a set of blueprints for you. (That's the script). Do you have a house? No—just a lot and some blueprints. Now you proceed. A truck comes along and dumps a lot of bricks on your lot. Got a house? Nope. All you've got is a lot, blueprints, and a lot of bricks. Another truck comes along and dumps a pile of bags of cement on your lot. Got a house? Nope—just a lot and some stuff. Now a pile of sand is dumped on your lot, and some wood. Got a house? Nope—just a lot, blueprints, and a lot of stuff. So what do you do? You build a foundation. That's your preparation. The foundation determines the kind of house, the shape, the size—all the basic facets. Have a house? Nope—a lot, a foundation, and a lot of stuff. So what do you do? Do you throw a whole bunch of bricks on the foundation? No. You take one brick—just one—and put it in the right place. Got a house? Not yet. A lot, a foundation, one brick in place, and a lot of stuff. So you take another brick, and put it in the right place. Still no house—just a foundation, a couple of bricks in the right places, and a bunch of stuff. So you put another brick in place, then another, and another, until, *one brick at a time*, you've put all the bricks in their proper places. When you're all through putting each little brick in its proper place, and added the wood and glass, you step back and what have you got? A beautiful, many-faceted multidimensional mansion. How did you build it? *One brick at a time!* You cannot build the entire house with every brick, and you shouldn't try. The shape of a house, the true quality of a house, becomes apparent only when all of the various kinds of materials have been carefully placed, one at a time, into their proper niches.

The same is true of building your role. Play one moment at a time; each moment will make its contribution to the whole. The whole cannot be played all the time; it will be clearly visible to the audience when the entire performance is over. If you try to play all the values at once, the result will be confusion and dullness.

How do I play a character I dislike? That's a question that keeps cropping up in classes. During one session, one of my students was doing a scene in which he never quite got a sense of reality into his work. I gave him a number of critiques, none of which seemed to work. For some reason I was unable to spot the real difficulty, and it wasn't until he muttered something like, "this guy's really rotten," that the bulb lit over my head. He apparently hated the character and, therefore, was unable to justify anything he did.

Obviously you cannot editorialize on the role you're playing while you're playing it. You cannot condemn yourself (and it must be you!) and expect to do and say things with conviction. A character does not hate himself: Hitler believed in what he was doing; Richard III believed in what he was doing; Lucrezia Borgia believed in what she was doing; Hannibal Lecter (*The Silence of the Lambs*) believed in what he was doing—and none of them hated themselves while they were doing it.

If you expect the audience to suspend disbelief, then you must do it first; you must believe in who you are. You must find valid reasons for doing the things you are doing or saying the things you are saying, reasons that you accept as right and as rational. The rule, then, is to accept who you are and to like who you are; only then can you begin to be convincing and to be dimensional.

How can you do that? Find the things the person you are playing likes, loves, has sympathy for, or at least understands. (Every person must be striving for some goal that is positive for him.) There must be some things the character likes that you as a person can also like. And there must be some things the character dislikes that you as a person can also dislike. Finding things in common will help you to understand the character; *understanding* is the first step toward acceptance. Having accepted the character, you can now believe in his goals and his methods and play them with conviction.

Preparation is exactly that: for preparation, not for performance. You must absorb the preparation, let it shape the kind of person you are, then discipline yourself to put aside the thoughts of the preparation when the scene begins so that you can devote full attention to listening. If the preparation is valid it will determine how you will respond to the stimuli you receive in the scene. In other words, *you can work from yourself, reshaped, rather than trying to be someone else, the "character." It's the reshaped you all this is happening to.*

....

Remember: ALWAYS WORK FROM YOUR-SELF

....

1. What kind of person are you (as mandated by the material)? In other words, validate the material with your preparation. Are you volatile? Arrogant? Submissive? Argumentative?
2. What else is there about you that you can infer from the material?
3. Have you ever been involved in a situation like the one in the material? If so, how did you feel? What did you do? How did you react? If not, put your imagination to work: how would you feel if you were really involved in that situation? MAKE YOURSELF BELIEVE IT WITH ALL YOUR HEART! COMMIT YOURSELF TO IT!
4. Where are you emotionally at the beginning of the scene? What has happened immediately before the director calls "Action"? In life, we are always doing something until we finish it or move on to something else, or something interrupts us. However, many actors do not come to life until they hear the first line of dialogue.

Where have you been? What were you doing just before the scene began? Choreograph thirty to sixty seconds of activity to get you involved in the reality of the situation before the first line of dialogue is spoken.

5. What is *driving* you through the scene? In other words, what do you need to accomplish? Make it positive; make choices that energize you. Always choose to care as much as you logically and credibly can in the circumstances.

The Rocky Principle: Even if Rocky fights for the Police Athletic League and a $20.00 trophy, he fights as if it's for the World Heavyweight title.

6. Where are you emotionally at the beginning of the scene? What is the rhythm of the emotion? Faster than normal? Slower? Normal?

7. What is (are) your obstacle(s)?

External: Who or what is standing in your way? Study the other person's lines; you will sensitize yourself to the kind of resistance you are facing. It is important to understand not just what is being said, but also what is not being said. For example: the body language; the look in the other person's eyes; the pause that shouldn't be there, etc.

Internal: What ideas, vulnerabilities, or recent experiences are making it more difficult to accomplish your needs?

THE BOTTOM LINE

It's important that the actor keep every moment in his work as clear and articulate as possible. That means the work must be simple at any given moment, with all the "simple" moments adding up in the end to a rich, fully dimensional characterization.

The quickest and best way to achieve that is to find the *bottom line* of the scene. By bottom line I refer to that which is driving the scene—*what the scene is about in terms of what you need to accomplish*. Look for the most basic driving force. For example, this driving force might be that you need to persuade someone to lend you some money; or that you need to avoid talking about something painful; or that you need to make a girlfriend give up another lover, etc. If your preparation is good, that's all you will need to make the moment work. That's all you should play, until another strong stimulus shifts you to another bottom line.

Of course, there are many facets to a character, but in a well-written piece of material those facets are articulated one at a time throughout the entire piece, so you don't have to play all of them all the time. Build your role one moment at a time, just as you would build a house one brick at a time. Remember? If you do that, your work will be clear, strong, and dynamic.

NOW BOTTOM-LINE THE SCENE. In the simplest terms possible, decide what is the major force driving you through the scene. WHAT DO YOU NEED TO ACCOMPLISH AT THIS MOMENT IN YOUR LIFE? Make it a verb form. For example, in *Kramer vs. Kramer,* in the scene where Ted goes to meet Joanna, who has called him two years or so after she left him and their son Billy, the bottom line for her in the scene is made clear by the line, "I want Billy back." Her bottom line is then, "I need to get him to give me custody of Billy." For him, that line from her establishes his bottom line, which is, "I need to keep her from taking Billy away from me." For each of them, that constitutes the "trunk" of the scene. Later dialogue takes what are apparently different directions, but those are only branches coming from the trunk.

Once you have bottom-lined the scene, let that drive you through it. Don't think about the preparation elements you used to get ready for this moment. *Just play the moment.* It is possible that another stimulus might come along that will change the bottom line. When it does, move to that one and *let it drive you.* You will soon learn how to do this quickly and with ease.

Remember: Fight the temptation to overintellectualize your work in an attempt to make it look deep, or profound. Don't add elements that are not part of the moment in an effort to "enrich" the performance. This advice is especially valuable when you are auditioning for a part, and you've only had a little time to prepare for the reading. Playing the bottom line will give you focus, it will give you energy, and it will help you get to the emotions you need more quickly than anything else I know.

In other words, you can't win an Oscar in just one scene or one part of a scene, so don't try. Keep it simple; play the bottom line, and the rest will take care of itself.

In an interview, Sydney Pollack, one of film's very best actor's directors, said, "I tell actors, 'Watch "Candid Camera," then flick the channel to something else, then turn back. You'll see how phony the acting looks because real reaction so often means doing nothing.' It's always simple. The tendency with actors is to think that if you're doing more, you're doing more."

MARKING YOUR SCRIPT

There is a simple and wonderful method of marking your script that will magically help you in your preparation. Usually actors grab the script and highlight their speeches. Wrong! Study the other person's speeches and business; *find what triggers your next response—the stimulus—and highlight it.* Now study your responses as they relate to the stimuli, to what makes those responses happen. You will be learning the role as you do this, in a conditioned-response pattern, much like Pavlov's dogs. You will "hear" a stimulus, it will affect you, and you'll begin to "salivate." And there's your next line! No more nightmares!

12

Facts and Conditions

I have spoken of playing moment to moment, rather than trying to play a scene as a whole. I have spoken of playing from yourself, and not some imaginary character. It is important to remember that the author has laid out certain facts and conditions that you must understand and utilize as you prepare to play moment-to-moment, since they determine where you are at any given moment emotionally, intellectually, sensorially, and physically. Those facts and conditions cannot be ignored.

In *Hamlet,* for example, can we ignore the fact that Hamlet's father has recently died, and Hamlet suspects he was murdered? Can we ignore the fact that a ghostly figure has appeared on the parapet in the first scene? Can we ignore the fact that it is cold on the parapet? That Hamlet loves his mother? That Hamlet hates his stepfather? How you, playing Hamlet, will respond to any given stimulus is determined in a very important way by those facts and conditions.

Take a situation in which a young man and woman have returned from their honeymoon the night before the scene starts. It is 7:00 A.M. They are deeply in love, and last night was a night of magnificent lovemaking. Now the man must return to his job.

SCENE

HE

Good morning.

SHE

Good morning.

HE

How do you feel?

SHE

Great.

HE

I'm sure.

SHE

What do you want for breakfast?

HE

Whatever.

SHE

I'll fix you some scrambled eggs.

HE

Fine.

SHE

You going to work this morning?

HE

Have to.

SHE

Oh.

HE

Do you want me to stay home?

SHE

It's up to you.

HE

Can't.

SHE

Like I said—it's up to you.

Now take the same scene with new facts and conditions. They are married. The man came in about 4:30 in the morning, clearly having had an affair. The couple fought bitterly, and he wound up sleeping on the couch. Now they are up, and he must go to work,

SCENE

HE

Good morning.

SHE

Good morning.

HE

How do you feel?

SHE

Great.

HE

I'm sure.

SHE

What do you want for breakfast?

HE

Whatever.

SHE

I'll fix you some scrambled eggs.

HE

Fine.

SHE

You going to work this morning?

HE

Have to.

SHE

Oh.

HE

Do you want me to stay home?

SHE

It's up to you.

HE

Can't.

SHE

Like I said—it's up to you.

A very different scene! So much so, that the first time I tried this in class, one of my students insisted that the dialogue was different. It wasn't. But the circumstances behind the dialogue so colored it that the scene seemed to be made up of different lines.

Each scene has to be studied carefully to find which facts and conditions are stated and which are implied. Then they must be absorbed and made part of the actor so that his responses are flavored by those essentials.

If you're not yet convinced, play the scene with a third set of facts and conditions: yesterday afternoon the man and woman learned he has a terminal disease.

SCENE

HE

Good morning.

SHE

Good morning.

HE

How do you feel?

SHE

Great.

HE

I'm sure.

SHE

What do you want for breakfast?

HE

Whatever.

SHE

I'll fix you some scrambled eggs.

                              HE

Fine.

                             SHE

You going to work this morning?

                              HE

Have to.

                             SHE

Oh.

                              HE

Do you want me to stay home?

                             SHE

It's up to you.

                              HE

Can't.

                             SHE

Like I said—it's up to you.

A different scene? Of course.

A single line like "You going to work this morning?" can be a sexual invitation, an angry challenge, or a compassionate search for a way to help a dying man. *The implications of the dialogue are important, not the dialogue.*

Try the same dialogue with the following facts and conditions:

1. HE is alone in his apartment. SHE enters. HE has never seen her before, and has no idea who SHE is.
2. HE is in bed with a woman. SHE is his wife, entering as the scene starts.

3. HE has spent the night in SHE's apartment. Now HE can't find his false teeth, and doesn't want her to know HE wears them.

Try the same exercise with another scene:

                    SHE
What time is it?

                    HE
It's early.

                    SHE
You just wish it were.

                    HE
Don't you?

                    SHE
I'm trying not to think about it.

                    HE
Let's pretend it's last night.

                    SHE
Last night we were in a different world.

                    HE
There's a spot on my shirt.

                    SHE
Send it to the laundry.

> HE
>
> I did. They couldn't get it out.

> SHE
>
> Shirts are not a priority right now.

> HE
>
> That's for sure. What time is it?

> SHE
>
> It's early.

Take the following sets of circumstances:

1. HE is about to leave town for an indefinite time to start a new job. SHE won't join him until HE has been able to find them a new home.
2. SHE is leaving town on an extended European trip, as part of her job.
3. SHE is leaving town on an extended European trip as part of her job, and SHE is accompanying her playboy boss.
4. SHE is about to go to a hospital for a breast biopsy.
5. HE and SHE are about to leave home for court, where their eldest son is being tried for murder.
6. Do the scene with two men, and set up your own set of circumstances.

Here's another "neutral" dialogue scene:

> HE
>
> Which tablecloth do you want me to use?

> SHE
>
> The new one.

HE

The real silver?

SHE

Don't you think we should?

HE

I don't know why.

SHE

I'd rather.

HE

Well, if you'd rather. . .

SHE

And set out the silver-rimmed wine goblets.

HE

Why not some champagne?

SHE

You're catching on.

HE

Maybe I should wear my tux.

SHE

Hm . . . No, that would be just a touch too much.

The circumstances might be:

1. It is the first anniversary of a very loving marriage.
2. A real estate agent is bringing a very rich buyer who is inter-

ested in buying their home at an outrageously high price.
3.   HE was just fired.
4.   They have agreed on a divorce.
5.   They have just agreed to divorce, and his boss, a believer in
     conjugal tranquillity, is due to arrive for dinner with his wife.
6.   SHE has just been promoted at work and has become his high-
     er-paid superior.

You will find that with some very minor adjustments, you can
use any of the sets of circumstances with any of the scenes.

This may seem obvious and too simplistic, but there are actors
who ignore some very important facts and conditions. Believe it or
not, there are even some teachers who teach that they are not
important, and that the actor should work only from his personal
feelings at any given moment.

I've spoken about "words" quite a bit in the preceding pages,
but I have one more important thing to say about the little devils.
Actors fall in love with words. They play them as much as they
can, because they're so tempting. If "The wind is howling," they
want to howl as they say it. If "I love you" is what's written, they
want to wax romantic. But what if those three little words happen
as in the story told about a wealthy cereal king who married a
number of times, and on the wedding night of his last marriage
said to his wife, "Look—I love you, I've loved you from the first
moment I saw you, and I'll always love you. Now let's not hear any
more about it." How do you say that romantically?

We do not speak in words. *We speak in ideas.* Words are only
tools we use to express those ideas. So never mind the words. If
you are speaking in ideas, the words will take care of themselves.
Those that need to be accented will be accented because you can't
get your ideas across *without* accenting them.

I often tell my students to "throw the words away." Trust me;
they don't get lost. They're the tools you need to communicate
your ideas, and they will be there when needed. *Don't speak words;
speak ideas!* The rhythm of your dialogue will be better, and your
whole performance will be more clearly articulated. *However,*
none of the preceding means you don't have to learn the lines and

deliver them as written. You do. But once you've made them your own, they become the perfect words to use at that moment. If you have a serious problem with the dialogue, talk quietly to the director and enlist his help in making changes. If he won't or can't, you're obligated to use them as they are.

Words are not important; it's what's under the words, what's making them happen, that's important.

13

• •

Imagination

In going over the original edition of this book, I realized that I had not given enough attention to one of the most important aspects of the actor's craft: imagination. What a great word! Without imagination the human species would still be in the trees, and there's not much theater or filmmaking there.

In case you haven't noticed, we are constantly putting our ability to imagine to work. When we read a book, our imagination helps us to visualize what we are reading. We listen to music, and our imagination helps us build a path from the abstract to a very real image compatible with the music. We imagine ourselves successful. Wealthy! Appealing! Intelligent! Of course, most of us know we are those things anyway!

When we read a script, we must be able to see the locale and characters in our imagination. We must be able to empathize with the characters in the script by using our imagination to identify with them. We must imagine the whole thing to be a truth, so that we can eventually play it effectively.

Much as I would prefer to use a film script to examine here, in the interests of general awareness of the material being used I'm going to talk about *Hamlet*. Everybody knows that one—or should.

One person's imagination says that Hamlet is a dutiful son who loves his mother in a purely filial way, and hates the fact that she has married his uncle, Claudius. Another person, using the same material, says that Hamlet is a son obsessed with his mother's beauty, and loves her as a woman in true Oedipal fashion. Another might say that Hamlet doesn't really care that much about his mother either way at this point in his life, but cares only that she is being unfaithful to his beloved late father. My imagination tells me that the first is true, because Shakespeare was a very articulate writer, and if he wanted us to believe either of the other two, he would have made it clear to us in the writing. But then your imagination may say my imagination is way off target here.

So, what's the answer? Make your choice, and go with it. If you can validate that choice throughout the performance, fine— it's a choice. There's no way an author can spell out everything you need to know about the role you're playing. He can give you lots of hints, but you then have to take those, put your imagination to work, and come up with what you—and the director— think is right.

You may certainly have to put the old imagination to work to make yourself believe that the ghost of your father is real, and that you're not a nutcase having a bizarre hallucination.

When you study *Hamlet,* and your reading has put everything in the play into an initial focus, your imagination must really go to work. Are you a terribly depressed, listless young man? Are you suicidal? If so, where is the pointed dialogue to Claudius coming from in your opening scene? Maybe you're an angry young man, and this opening scene is much more alive than you thought, and you are a much stronger, more dynamic person than the depressed state would indicate.

Why do you hate Claudius as your mother's lover? Your imagination can visualize him making love to her, doing things that are abhorrent to you. See the dirty pictures, and you have to hate Claudius!

How do you move? Do you see Hamlet in your imagination pacing the floors, walking the parapet, or sitting on a stool and brooding, moving only when absolutely necessary?

How do you feel about Ophelia? Nowhere in the play is there any direct reference to a physical relationship, but is there one in your imagination? Perhaps there should be, especially if you think that will help you relate to her in a way that will strengthen your relationship with her, and make her death all the more tragic to you. You and your imagination can decide.

What do you imagine your relationship to the soldiers to be? Are you friendly drinking buddies, do you chase girls together? Or are they kept distant from you because you are a prince, and therefore you mustn't hobnob with common soldiers? They admire you as a soldier and courtier, so does that help you decide? Put your imagination to work. Imagine what happens out of your sight and hearing with Rosencrantz and Guildenstern. Actually, you have to, if you expect to get to where you are emotionally and intellectually in the first scenes you play with them. More often than not, such use of the imagination is absolutely necessary as part of your preparation before each scene you play.

"Aha!" some of you will say. "You're having us do things that complicate the moment-to-moment simplicity. You're having us use things we can't communicate to the audience!" Nope. They are things you might be thinking about *while you're playing the moment*. They're things that drive you through the moment. If anything, they will get you focused even more strongly on the moment.

Don't take anything for granted. Let your imagination roam all over the script; play with the people until you really get a solid fix on them. Let your imagination find a clear understanding of where Denmark will be if the tyrant and murderer remains in power, and goes unpunished in both the here and the hereafter. That could be a big help in forming your opinion of Claudius, and make more intense your rage at your inability to kill him.

At the risk of being put into a straightjacket, try imagining yourself as other people for a little while each day. Play games with yourself, and let your thoughts, your feelings, your physicalizations, all be affected. It's really fun. More importantly, you'll always be stretching the instrument a little, and becoming a richer and more versatile artist—and person.

Only a vivid and effective imagination can put you in touch with what other people are feeling. You need that in order to make contact with the person you are playing—to get yourself inside that other person. Practice it; play with it; have fun with it. Makes acting a lot easier.

14

· ·

Learn the Role—
Not the Lines

The actor's recurrent nightmare is that he will one day find himself in front of an audience—or in front of a camera—and he will hear a cue and not be able to remember what to say. Olivier said that every night was torture, because he was afraid he wouldn't remember his next line. My sister was in one high school play; that was the extent of her theatrical experience. Yet, to this day—and she has just had her eightieth birthday—she still has a recurrent nightmare that she will not remember her lines.

There is a famous old joke about memorization that I will mention only because it helps demonstrate the danger of just learning lines without any connection to stimulus, character, and so on.

As the story goes, three elderly men who hadn't worked in some years were all hired to do a play in summer stock. Having less than a week in which to learn their roles, they crammed like crazy until opening night. On that night everything went well until the middle of the third act, when suddenly all dialogue stopped. The stage manager, who was also the prompter, threw the next line out, but the actors ignored it. One of the old men went back a few lines, picked up the scene, and carried it to the same point—and silence again. Once more the stage manager frantically threw the line out; one of the other men went back a few lines and brought the scene to the same point, where it stopped again. The stage manager climbed into the fireplace and whispered the line straight up at the third old man, who was leaning on the mantel. That old man looked the stage manager straight in the eye and said, "We know the line, damn it, who says it?"

Learning lines is the simplest of procedures if you want to go about "learning lines." But in fact, you should never "learn lines."

As I've said, *the words themselves are not important; it is what makes the words happen that has significance.* If you learn lines, you are responsive to a cue instead of to a stimulus. The sad result is you will learn a series of words that you will utter when the right cue words are thrown at you, and they will lack connection and depth.

Let me repeat: the words themselves are not important; *it is what makes the words happen that has meaning.* If, therefore, the actor connects properly to the stimulus that causes a verbal response, is aware of the real significance of that stimulus to him, and responds to the consequences implied, the proper verbal response will be inevitable. That applies whether the stimulus is what someone says, what someone does, the state of the weather, a toothache, or an emotion or thought. The procedure of high-lighting the stimuli that make your lines happen instead of high-lighting your lines is a great help in the memorization process.

Certainly there will be little danger of forgetting the lines if you have learned, through all your senses, the connective pattern between the stimuli and the responses that they generate. Also, if you have conditioned yourself to respond to stimuli instead of cues, you will be more receptive to what the other actor is *doing* as well as saying; you will be more responsive to the inflections and intonations of his lines, and you will also be aware of subtle phys-icalizations that will reveal what he really means by those lines.

It is what a person means when he talks to us that is of conse-quence, *not what words he says.* For example, if someone is looking deep into your eyes and says, "I love you," certain feelings are gen-erated. Your feelings about those words will not be the same if he now says them as he's looking off at someone else or as he's look-ing at his watch. Think, too, of the many variations on those words, from anger to ridicule to disbelief, and so forth.

In other words, if you are open to all the stimuli that are reaching you at any given moment, you will absorb them; they will affect you; and your responses, certainly your verbal responses, will come to you without any difficulty. Obviously if you are nervous about your lines and thinking of your next one, then you have shut off the ability to receive stimuli, and your work will be flat, unimaginative, and (worst of all) truly unresponsive to the other actor. Ultimately, a great performance lies in the proper stimulus-response patterns of the actor in the role.

In films the response mechanisms are not given the chance to work in the same way they do on the stage. You may be doing a scene with an actor in a master shot, and everything works very well. Then, in your close-ups, the other actor might not even be there; his lines might be read by the script supervisor or the director, in which case you must be responsive to what the actor did in the master shot and in his close-ups, if his close-ups were done before yours. You cannot be responsive to what you would have liked him to do or what you vaguely remember he did; you must bring his performance to yours, and that is not easy.

In case there is some question about why all this is necessary, just remember that when the editor, the director, and the producer get through putting together the pieces of film, the audience is going to see the other actor saying his lines or doing something; then they will see you responding to that. If you are not correctly responsive to what the other actor said and did, you're going to look like you're in a different movie.

We do an exercise at the Film Actors Workshop that perfectly demonstrates what I've been talking about. It also demonstrates the proper way to learn a role. As I said, I use the phrase "learn a role" instead of "learn your lines" because you should never sit down to learn lines, since they are connected to a role, which includes the whole person, the stimuli, the significance of the stimuli, and the lines as well.

We take fifteen or twenty lines from a scene and put each line on a separate card, also including significant stage directions. I give each actor all of their lines. The actors might have read the material once or twice or not at all; the exercise can work in either case.

The actors are briefed so that they know in broad strokes who the people are, what their relationship is, and what each character's needs are. The first actor then looks at his first card, which might be merely a stage direction. Let's say it reads, "He approaches the apartment door, looks at it a moment, starts to knock, then decides not to. Instead, he slowly reaches for the handle, turns it, and to his surprise the door swings open. He looks inside, sees the girl, and speaks."

Then the actor is asked to tell us what stimuli he "heard." He might say, "Well, I 'hear' that this is not my home, since there is some hesitation before I knock on the door. I know that my ex-wife lives here, so I must assume that it's okay for me to go in. Also, since I didn't knock, I 'hear' that I have a certain brashness in myself. These things make me feel a little cocky, so I might say, 'You ought to keep your door locked.'"

Then the actor looks at his line to see if he has guessed correctly. If he has, then he has put his finger on certain character qualities that come to him easily, either because they are similar to his own or because he understands them on an intellectual basis. If he has guessed wrong, it might even be better, because in guessing wrong, he will become aware that his own personal responses are different at that moment than those of the character, and, therefore, there is a part of him that he knows will not work in this role—a very important thing to know. But there is also a part of him that *will* work, and it is that part he must work with as he plays the role. This weeding-out process continues throughout the exercise, so that the end result is that the actor has discarded the parts of himself that are not congruent with the role and is using those parts that are. *In other words, he is reshaping himself into the role.* The actors are not expected to guess the lines. The exercise is only designed to see if they respond on a personal level the way the character does.

Next the actor reads the line. In this case, it reads, "You shouldn't leave your door unlocked. Somebody could kidnap you and hold you for a terrific ransom." He was "in the ballpark" with his answer, which is good.

The actress repeats the actor's line exactly as he said it. It is important that she not change the reading; in other words, she should not editorialize or comment on his line, but read it exactly as he said it so that she gains some insight into the significance of the line beyond the words themselves. Was there sarcasm? Was there anger? Was there love? She repeats the line aloud, then says out loud what she "hears." She might "hear" that he's still handsome; that he's still cocky. She might "hear" that she still loves him. She tells us that it makes her feel excited that he's there, and that she'd like to put her arms around him, and kiss him and say something very simple, like, "Hello, Harry."

Next, she looks at her card and reads the line on it. The card reads, "She stares at him for a moment, then says, 'Next time I'll make sure that the door can't be opened unless I want it to.'"

Obviously, the actress guessed wrong. The character is hostile to the man; she is angry because she hasn't seen him for so long. The role, then, is that of a woman who is more volatile emotionally, more easily hurt and sensitive than the actress herself, so the actress must change her orientation to the role in a very important aspect.

Next, the actor repeats the actress's line and states what he "hears." "She is not glad to see me. She feels hostility, and I am not welcome. That makes me feel that I need to ingratiate myself in order to make her feel better, in order to insure my welcome, so I think I would say something like, 'You look terrific in that blouse.'" The actor looks at the card, and the line is, "I just wanted to see the kid."

The actor, then, guessed wrong, which is good, because apparently the character is not as willing to compromise as is the actor. The character is aggressive and hostile and either lacks the social graces or does not want to exercise them, perhaps for fear of seeming weak. So again, we have zeroed in on a very important personality aspect that is different from the actor's true life personality. (Remember, each of us is capable of all feelings and attitudes. What we are in real life has been determined by conditioning, but with proper training we can make other feelings and attitudes that the role requires our own.)

The actress repeats the actor's line and articulates its implications to her: "I hear that he is still hostile; I 'hear' he is still unpleasant. I 'hear' that he doesn't want to see me and feels no love or even warmth towards me. All that makes me angry, hurt, and I think, therefore, that I would want to get rid of him and I might say something like, 'Close the door on your way out.'" Then the actress looks at the line, and it reads, "Kids are goats. Marilyn's not a goat, she's a child.'"

In general, the actress's observations were accurate. She sensed the lack of warmth and the hostility, and she attacked, so that even though the words were wrong, the impulses, feelings, and sensitivities were right, so it was a good guess.

In class I follow this procedure with some fifteen or twenty speeches, by which time we will have zeroed in on any number of major character specifics, at the same time differentiating the character's reactions from the actor's reactions. We will thus very quickly arrive at a broad and accurate role portrait.

Next we repeat the entire exercise without verbalizing the thought process, but taking the time to think it through silently. The actor speaks his line, the actress repeats it in her mind as it was delivered, there is a pause while the actress speaks in her mind what we are now going to call the *subtext*, and then the actress speaks the response out loud. In other words, she will receive the stimulus, she will repeat it, she will absorb it, she will allow it to affect her, and only then will she respond. We do the fifteen to twenty speeches this way, then go back and do the same exercise in real time, as if reading for the job.

Finally, we put away the cards that have been used up to now (after the first time through, the actor looks at the cards when he is ready to speak so that he speaks the correct line). Without the cards the actors try as best they can to create the scene. Astonishingly enough, in almost every instance, 75 to 100 percent of the scene has been learned without anyone ever taking the time to memorize lines. Most importantly, what has been learned is the entire sequence of stimulus, absorption, effect, and response, so that the actor is beginning to respond on a conditioned level. At the same time he is conditioning himself to be responsive as the role demands. From this point on, the rest of the material becomes much easier to understand and respond to. The results achieved through this procedure are where the performance lies.

Again: The words are not important. What is important is what causes them to be spoken. The same is true of any response, whether verbal or physical, and the actor must make sure that he undergoes the complete process and never merely responds to a "cue."

The stimulus for a response could happen in the middle of the other person's speech. The actor, therefore, might want to respond long before the other person is through talking.

For example, let's assume that in the above scene the girl's last speech was, "Close the door on your way out; I have to pay the utilities. It's chilly, and gas is very expensive." He would have received his stimulus at the very beginning of the speech, when she said, "Close the door on your way out," because that is the rejection to which he responds. He is not interested in the price of gas in the apartment and whether or not she pays the utilities. Therefore, his absorption of the stimulus "Close the door on your way out" and his crossing the bridge to his response might occur long before she has finished her speech. He might try to interrupt her, or at the very least, he would not need a thought pause to absorb the stimulus after she was through speaking. In other words, he would be ready to speak immediately when she stopped or paused. In this case the actor's need to respond will cause some physicalization, even though he may not, in fact, speak until the other actor stops speaking—a delay that the actor must justify. (See Chapter 5, Listening/Sensing.)

In terms I do not like to use, he would be able to "pick up the cue." I say I do not like to use that term because, as I have said, *you do not pick up cues; you respond to stimuli*. If a scene is well written and if your absorption and response processes are accurate, there will be no problems of pace or the need for the director to yell, "Pick up your cues." The tempo will be right, and any pauses will be filled with inner activity that will be dynamic enough to hold the audience's attention.

I'm going to be repetitious because it is extremely important that you remember: *never learn lines, always learn the role*. This means that you must learn the full stimulus-absorption-effect-and-response pattern. In this way the lines will be memorized, and they will be memorized in such a way that you will not forget them.

The exercise I have outlined is at first tedious and time-consuming. I know that. You will know it in a very few minutes, but the results are worth it, and after you have done it forty or fifty times, you will find that all of the processes involved will happen very quickly, and eventually you will be able to do the entire exercise without thinking about the fact that you are doing an exercise. All of the process between the receipt of the stimulus and the response, verbal or otherwise, will be done in real time. Transitions will be clean, clear, and articulate for the audience and for you in every way, and your performance will be completely honest. There will be a few pauses, but they will have significance, and they may be the most articulate moments in the entire scene.

Let's take another scene. A young woman has decided she wants to be a cab driver. She knows that the dispatcher does not approve of women driving cabs, but he has hired her anyway because she was clever enough to make him feel she would cause trouble if he rejected her because of her sex. She reports for duty and finds him standing near a dilapidated old cab. Her first line is "Good morning."

She is not the person he is most anxious to see. He would rather he didn't have to see her at all. The actor feels that he would like to tell her to get lost. He looks at his line; it is "Yeah." His feelings are right.

She "hears" the rejection, which is what she expected. The actress would like to tell him off. She checks her line. "Where's my cab?" Since it is not an effort to make friends or be funny, she was not far off target. The character is sidestepping her real feelings, dodging the possibility of starting her new job with an argument.

Her question reminds the actor that she is going to drive one of his cabs; his stomach sours. He'd like to tell her there isn't one, but he can't, since he hired her. He checks his line: "You sure you want to do this?" He's right on target.

The actress is aware of his feelings, of course. She again would like to tell him off. Checking her line, she sees that what she does say is, "What's wrong with me wanting to drive a cab?" She was right in her guess about how she would respond.

He doesn't like her question, which gives him a chance to try to discourage her once more. "You're a broad, and broads don't belong driving cabs."

A hostile and insulting remark. Now the actress really wants to tell him off. Her line is, "No? Where do they belong?" The line is a kind of attack, so she is right on target again.

The question annoys him even more. She asked a question, and the actor wants to tell her what he really believes. He reads, "In the kitchen. . . ."

As he says it, the actress knows the rest. Her mouth wants to form the words that are coming next. As a matter of fact, the script calls for her to say them at the same time he does— "And in bed." The line really annoys her, and she wants to attack further. Indeed, she does. "Myerson, you're a chauvinist. You keep your wife chained to the stove? Barefoot and pregnant?"

Now she's insulting. The actor feels he doesn't have to take that from her, especially since he didn't want her working there in the first place. He's right. "Don't get smart," he says. "I hired you, I can fire you."

The actress would like to attack even further. She checks her line. "You wouldn't do that. I'm too cute." This time the actress was wrong. Her role is written for her to take command here by turning the argument off through humor. An important point: she has humor.

He doesn't want to buy humor. He still doesn't want her here. His line is, "You're too smart-ass, that's what you are. Here's your cab." He points to the pile of junk they are standing near.

Now the actress would really like to tell him off, but since the character has decided not to continue the argument, the actress wants to respond with a smart crack. Checking her line, she reads, "Pick of the litter, huh?" Exactly right.

In the preceding scene, the actors have quickly understood who they are, and what their relationship is. It is easy for them to understand how they feel about each other, and how they feel about the circumstances in which they find themselves. As a result, they can accurately guess what happens moment to moment in the scene.

Do the exercise first with simple scenes, with scenes in which the exchanges do not depend on specific knowledge of subject matter such as complicated medical speeches or political speeches. You'll find eventually that even the most complex material will avail itself of this approach, and that although the lines will not be verbatim, the correct thought processes will be there; the correct drive will be there; the correct intentions will be there; and the correct physicalizations will be there. You will have found those parts of yourself that validate the material, and you will be able to work from your "new self"; in fact, the performance will

find its way into the work, even though the lines may not be verbatim. Then, with rehearsal, the lines will come into place.

Will you ever have to memorize by rote? Of course, when
there is complicated technical information or an extremely long
speech, you will have to sit down and memorize it. But, again, if
you truly steep yourself in the role, the information will also
demand research, and soon, if you are truly thinking like the character, the information will begin to come all by itself and not as a
pure rote process, which is the worst possible way for an actor to
learn to articulate the author's ideas and emotions.

There is another very important value to the approach outlined in these previous pages. And I'm going to repeat something
I said in the discussion on character (see Chapter 6), because it is
important. In my classes I use the word *role* more than *character*.
There's a reason for that. When an actor thinks about playing a
character, he will be trying to be somebody else, and will have
some little person in the back of his brain doing things a split second before he imitates that person as he gives his performance.
You can't be somebody else; you don't have anyone else's instrument. You have only your own.

As I've already mentioned, if we are normal, we are born with
all normal capabilities—physical, intellectual, emotional, and
sensory. But when we are children, we disown those parts of ourselves that don't win approval, and lock them in a closet somewhere. We become the adults we are. Now, if we are to be actors,
we must let all those nasty little animals out again, so we have
them available for the roles we play, because not too many roles
are going to fit us perfectly as we are. In doing the line-by-line
study approach to the role, we find parts of ourselves that fit the
role when we guess right about what's coming up, and that's great.
But we also find parts that *don't* fit the role when we guess wrong.
When that happens, we have to leave behind the parts that don't
fit, and replace them with the parts that do, so that by this process
of elimination we are left with only what belongs in the role. In
other words, *we must reshape ourselves into the role, so that we can
then always work from ourselves, reshaped.* No more trying to be
somebody else.

Station Break

● ●

If I had only a limited time to spend with a student, this is as much material as I would attempt to cover. If the student has learned to listen with all his senses and to fully focus on the scene, and if he has freed the emotional instrument so that it is fully responsive, he has learned the most important things he must know to be a successful film actor. If, in the study process, he has learned to trust himself so that he doesn't feel compelled to "act," but only *listen* to give himself over fully to the stimuli that strike him, he will have achieved what very few actors manage in a lifetime of work. The techniques discussed so far are the most effective and quickest ways to get the necessary results. If your performance is based on the ideas on the preceding pages it will be real, it will have energy, and it will be moving.

What follows are tools for the actor, to be used only when a tool is needed. There is a danger that the tools will become crutches on which the actor leans, replacing the greater reality of simple listening and trusting in the responses. When that happens, the actor is thinking of the tools as he works, and is therefore always one step removed from the circumstances of the scene. The result is a lessening of the reality that is so essential to the intimate medium of the camera.

THREE

Tools

15

Rhythm and Change

If there is any one thing to which an audience cannot refuse to respond, it is rhythm and rhythmic changes.

At the very root of our survival is the beat of the heart and the changes in its rhythm as we are affected by emotions. As a consequence, rhythm is the most basic recognizable and the most effective phenomenon at our disposal. If we anticipate that the next number to be drawn at a lottery may bring us a prize of a hundred thousand dollars, our pulses quicken. And this rhythmic change in heartbeat and pulse accompanies every response we feel to any significant stimulus. When we become angry, our pulses quicken. When we are sad, they slow.

Rhythm is so basic to our makeup that we even attribute rhythms to inanimate objects. A crown implies a rather slow, stately rhythm; a typewriter implies a rapid, staccato rhythm; an easy chair implies a slow, calm rhythm. Even such abstractions as the seasons carry a sense of rhythm: summer, slow; winter, fast; spring, moderate. In the same way, emotions imply rhythms: joy, anger, and terror imply a fast rhythm; sadness, a slow one.

Every person has a basic personal rhythm. From that baseline, a person will move slower or faster, talk slower or faster, think slower or faster, depending on the stimuli affecting him.

In the majority of instances you will be hired to play roles that are rather close to you in most respects. When this "typecasting" happens, it makes it unnecessary for you to change your basic personal rhythm. What is necessary, however, is that your physical instrument be free and responsive enough to change rhythmically with the various stimuli that hit it. If the physicalization resulting from a stimulus is not rhythmically congruent with that stimulus, you will not convince the audience that what you are feeling is real.

For example, when you become angry, you move faster; you "move angrily." When you are sad, you move slower than you normally do. When you are acting, therefore, it becomes imperative that you *respond to each stimulus in a rhythm that is compatible with the logical emotional effect of the stimulus.*

I have found that beginning actors do not understand these relationships. They will become very angry in a scene, but will not change the rhythm of their walk. The result is that the performance may look excellent from the neck up, but the rest of the body reveals that it is a lie. The real reason is that the actor is not truly involved emotionally, or if he is, his instrument is not responding freely.

In real life you almost always respond rhythmically, changing the speed of your movements, whatever they may be, depending on how you feel, the climate, and so forth. When there is a disparity between the rhythm of a person's emotion and the rhythm of his movements, the cause lies in the fact that there is a conflict of some sort; perhaps the person doesn't want to reveal (or can't reveal) that he is angry. He will, therefore, try to avoid doing the very thing his body cries out for him to do: that is, to move swiftly. The result of this kind of conflict is tension, which will cause other physical changes that will be apparent to the camera. Remember that the internal rhythm and the external rhythm are married and cannot be separated without a struggle.

If this kind of control and conflict is a proper part of the role you are playing, you must articulate the conflict through some physicalization or rhythmic change, or both. The tension may cause you to handle your cup of coffee or cigarette differently. It might cause an interrupted movement. Something will happen that the audience will detect, and they will know therefore that you are angry, but that you are controlling your anger. Thus, the fact that your rhythm has not changed with the stimulus is in itself an articulation of conflict.

A change in rhythm is only one of many possible physicalizations, but it is probably the most effective one. If you are walking and you suddenly do nothing more than change the speed of your walk, an observer will believe that you have been struck by some stimulus; in other words, that something has happened. In purely physical terms, if you walk rather rapidly, then slow down for a couple of steps, then start to walk rapidly again, it is inevitable that the audience will draw the conclusion that there is some uncertainty in what you are doing, only because they draw conclusions based on rhythmic changes. Even a pause is a rhythmic change.

For reasons I've never been able to understand, it is very difficult to convince young actors of the importance and singularity of rhythm as an actor's tool. I suggest that you carefully watch people and see for yourself how their basic rhythms frequently give insight into their personalities, and how rhythmic changes will tell you things about a person even though you might not know that person. It is not hard to guess the nature of a conversation several tables away in a restaurant if you can detect rhythmic changes in the people talking.

One of the foolproof methods of letting an audience know that you have been affected by a stimulus is to interrupt an action. Let's suppose that you are washing dishes and your husband is three hours late. As you are wiping the dishes, the front door opens. If you stop wiping the dish for only half a second and then start again, the audience will know that you heard the door open and that it has significance. If you do not stop wiping the dish, the audience will assume either that you did not hear the door open or that you are not concerned about it.

Remember, it is *change* that is most apparent to an audience. Rhythmic change is clearly and immediately evident; a vocal change is certainly evident; and even a change in the direction of your visual focus is evident. Again, if you are washing dishes, the door opens, and you turn toward the door and wait, the change in visual focus, perhaps coupled with the change in the rhythm of the dishwashing, will tell the audience that the opening of the door is significant.

In performance, the clever actor will make sure that, if it is appropriate, he has a chance to turn his head and change the direction in which he is looking when something truly important happens or is said. For instance, an actor who has been looking out of a window while playing a scene with another actor, will give great importance to the words, "It's time we talked," when they are spoken to him, simply by turning and looking at the other actor before responding. The smart actor knows when something important has been said, and he will give himself the chance to change his visual focus when he gets that stimulus. The great actor will do it with no conscious use of the device. His craft is so well developed that these things happen by themselves.

It is important to the film director for you to remember this, because, as I mentioned, the most important shots on film are frequently of the listener who is reacting, rather than of the speaker. If the director can cut to your close-up as you turn, the director will have a more dramatic moment. But for you, the actor, it is important to remember that this is one of the ways you can articulate the important moment for the audience, and that is, after all, your primary function as an actor: to *articulate*, so that you can *communicate ideas and emotions to an audience*.

The word *articulate* is used in its broadest sense, not only in its verbal meaning. A gesture, a raised eyebrow, a pause, a change in rhythm—all these things articulate ideas and emotions—so when I use that word, I am referring to anything that makes something you are experiencing clear to an audience.

Two of my students prepared a scene from *Tea and Sympathy* in which the wife berates her husband for treating a sensitive boy very badly. She says to him that she wished, the night before, that she had helped the boy prove to himself that he was a man, and then finishes the scene by telling her husband that she is leaving him.

Obviously, at the beginning of the scene the woman is deeply troubled. The actress, however, was bringing little of the underlying turbulence into the scene. I suggested that she start her preparation by walking rapidly around in the set and think about the circumstances in the scene which were driving her. Then, after she had done that for a short while, begin the scene.

She did exactly that. After she had been moving quickly—angrily—for a few moments, her color began to change slightly. Soon after that she began the scene, keeping in motion all the time, and was unable to keep back the increasingly heavy flow of emotion that began to generate as the scene progressed. That was the perfect emotional state for her to be in, and the *simple expedient of moving in the rhythm of the emotion helped to generate the emotion.*

The actress herself was startled at what had happened, and later realized that she had learned several very important lessons. One was that it is important that the inner emotional activity and rhythm be at a proper peak at the very beginning of a scene. Another was that *one way to help achieve an emotional level is to physicalize with a rhythm that is congruent with that emotion.* She learned that you can work from the physical to the emotional— the outer to the inner—but the inner truth and feeling must ultimately be real.

An exercise we do with beginners to demonstrate the effects of rhythm on behavior is to take two people and say to them, "You are both people with very slow inner rhythms." We then try to define what that would mean in terms of how the people would respond and move. The results of the discussion are always essentially the same: the people move slowly and are not quick to respond on an intellectual or emotional level to stimuli, however important they may be. I then give the students an improvisation in which the husband, coming home from work, tells his pregnant wife that he has found another woman and is leaving her.

With both husband and wife accepting slow personal rhythms for themselves, the wife's response is usually on the order of, "Well, I wasn't happy with the marriage anyway, so it's okay." (The actress usually likes that because it demands very little from her on any level.)

Then I tell the wife that she is a person whose rhythm is fast. That redefines her character; she is volatile emotionally, she is quick to think, and she moves quickly. Now when her slow-moving or slow-witted husband comes home, the scene becomes totally different; generally the wife is outraged and accusatory, and the husband calmly and quietly tries to cool her off.

When we do the scene a third time and change the husband's rhythm so that his is also fast, the same two people have a totally different scene—usually one that becomes a very interesting dog-and-cat fight. The improvisational base remains the same; the only things that are changed are the basic rhythms of the characters. But those basic rhythms are so connected to emotional, sensory, physical, and intellectual responses that the entire nature of the characters' lives changes. This is a simple illustration of a profound tool.

Let's see what happens in the following scene:

The setting is the study of a middle-class family. There is a desk and chair, which tells us that this room probably is the office of the man of the house.

We hear a door open offstage. HE *calls out:*

HE

I'm home, Betty!

The door opens, and HE *comes into the room. His gait is springy, and he is obviously feeling quite cheerful.*

HE *hums as he crosses toward the desk, swinging an imaginary tennis racquet as* HE *goes. Then* HE *stops, takes several swings as* HE *re-creates the big moment of the match* HE *just won. At that instant* SHE *enters the room.*

SHE *is also cheerful.* SHE *enters briskly, stops as* SHE *sees him playing out his game.*

SHE

Jimmy Connors couldn't have handled that last
one!

HE *turns to her.*

HE

You're right. And neither could Lester. Caught
him flat-footed.

[HE *moves to her, gives her a happy kiss, then moves to the* desk. HE *starts sorting through the mail.*]

Where are the kids?

SHE

Tommy's at Little League, and Meredith's in bal-
let class.

HE

They sure live full lives, don't they?

Suddenly HE *stops.* HE *stares at a letter in his hand, then slowly moves to the chair and sits.*

(Up to now, both people have been moving rather brightly. Their rhythm is up, on the fast side, congruent with their good spirits. Now HE is apparently shocked by the letter in his hand. His mood changes; so does his rhythm. It was fast; now it is slower.)

SHE *notices the change in him.*

SHE

What's wrong?

(Concerned, SHE takes a tentative step toward him. But her rhythm is slower now, too, as SHE waits for his answer. Her antic- ipation of a problem has probably caused her heart to beat faster, but SHE might control that, and move slowly to avoid a sense of panic. We will see this conflict of inner and outer rhythms mani- fest itself in some form of tension in her body.)

HE

Nothing.

SHE

Please, Jim. There's something in the letter.

HE

It's nothing.

SHE

(*Annoyed*)
You always do that to me! Let me in on what's
bothering you for once, will you, please?

(Because SHE is annoyed and no longer controlling her feelings,
her rhythm should be faster again. When SHE moves to him, we
will see that it has indeed changed.)

HE

(*Also annoyed*)
This is not something for you to be concerned
about! Let it be!

(Both rhythms are up now.)

SHE

No! I want to know what's in that letter!

HE

It has nothing to do with you!

SHE

Everything that affects you has something to do
with me! I'm your wife!

HE *looks at her for a long time. Then* HE *nods.*

(HE has made a transition. HE sees that HE must tell her. The decision worries him, and saddens him. His nod is slow. His speech slows down a little.)

HE
It's from someone—in jail.

SHE *stares, shocked.*

(Her rhythm will now slow down because of the shock that greets his statement.)

SHE
In jail? Who?
(HE *hesitates.*)
Jim—who?

HE
My first wife.

SHE
What?

HE
My first wife.

SHE
What first wife?

HE
I never told you. I didn't think it was necessary.
No—I was afraid to tell you when we got married,
and then it just never seemed the right time.

SHE
You were married once and never told me?

HE

I'm sorry.

SHE *rises angrily, paces the room.*

(Angry now, her rhythm is up once more. In anticipation of what
lies ahead, his rhythm is also up, his pulse beating fast, as it would
in these circumstances. But HE wants to appear in control, so HE
fights the impulse toward fast rhythm and seems to maintain his
calm for a while. This conflict—the impulse toward faster rhythm
that is held in check—generates tensions in him, which the audience will be able to detect, whether in his movements, his speech
pattern, or both.)

SHE

Sorry? You tell me you were married before and
now all you can say is you're sorry?

HE

What else can I say? It was over fifteen years ago.

SHE

I was entitled to know!

HE

You were. And I was a fool for not telling you in
the beginning.

SHE

Thank you! At least you acknowledge that much!

There is a pause as SHE *fights to regain her composure and* HE *waits
for the rest of the storm. After a moment,* SHE *takes a deep breath, and
turns to him.* SHE *speaks slowly.*

(SHE may speak slowly, but her heart is beating very rapidly. Again we have the conflict between inner and outer rhythms, and we will see that conflict manifested in some form. It may be in clenched fists, or head held too rigidly, or whatever, but we will see it if the actress is truly involved.)

SHE

Why is she in jail?

HE

She says for armed robbery. She says she was wrongly identified by a witness.

SHE

Why is she writing you?

HE

She has no one else.

SHE

I see. And what does she want?

HE

[Pause]

She needs someone to post bail.

SHE stares at him.

SHE

How much?

HE

Twenty-five thousand dollars.

Her calm breaks. SHE *whirls, crosses away.*

(Now SHE will be moving in the rhythm of her inner pulse beat. SHE will be moving faster—angrily—because of what SHE feels.)

                        SHE
        No.

                        HE
        I'm sorry. I have to help her.

                        SHE
        No!

                        HE
[*Losing control*]
        I have to!

(Now HE has let down the controls, and his rhythm is faster as HE follows his inner rhythm without restraint. HE will move more quickly as HE moves to her.)

                        HE
        Listen to me. She saw me through law school.
        She took care of everything until the day I got my
        first job. Now she needs me, and I have to help.

SHE *accepts this.*

(With this acceptance, SHE will feel calmer. Perhaps resigned is the word. In either case, her rhythm will slow down. HE will notice that, and his rhythm will slow down as a result.)

                        SHE
        All right.

Pause.

One question.

HE

Yes?

SHE

Have you—been seeing her?

HE

I haven't seen her since the day she left me.

SHE *nods, moves to him. They embrace.*

(They are both relatively calm now. Their rhythms will therefore be slower as they move; the pace of their dialogue will be slightly slower as well.)

This scene has more dynamics in it than most. You can see that there are many rhythmic changes caused by the emotions the people feel. Also, as one person's rhythm changes, the other notices it. That causes some response in the second person, because, as I have pointed out, a change in rhythm is one of the most articulate ways of communicating an idea or emotion to an observer. In this case, both the other actor and the audience are affected by the many changes in the scene.

Watch people around you. See if you can get an idea of how they feel by the rhythm of their movements. I think you will quickly see how closely emotions and physical rhythm are connected.

Be aware that the performances as I've outlined them are only one way to do the scene. Any scene can be played a number of ways, depending on the characters involved and the director's interpretation. Pray for a good director to help you make the best choices.

16

$\bullet$

Dynamics

A good scene (and, needless to say, a good screenplay or teleplay) has within it some change, or dynamics. In most instances, there is something different at the end than there was in the beginning; otherwise, there is little point in the scene's having been written and played. The best scenes are those in which there is some rise or fall in emotional energy—some movement toward or away from a climax. Very few scenes can work if the emotional level and the energy level remain on a plateau.

Change constitutes dynamics. It is not always true that a scene must reach a dramatic peak; exposition is necessary, and there are certainly moments in the lives of the characters when they are contemplative, depressed, or at a high emotional level from beginning to end of a short sequence. However, other changes can occur within the scene and give it a sense of dynamics. If you can find a shift in attitude or feeling so that you are not exactly the same person and in the same state when the scene ends as when it started, you have found a dynamic. Many times the choice is the actor's to make. Given a choice, you are always better off to seek out the shifts and changes within the scene, however subtle they may be, because *the shifting and changing command audience attention and cause them to be affected. They also give the material a sense of motion and thrust.*

Study any good script and you will see that the characters at the end of the material are substantially different as human beings than they were at the beginning. The characters have dynamics, as does the scene or the play.

You must search out the dynamics within the role so that you can offer the audience all the dimension, excitement, and interest it is possible to bring to your work. Look for changes; look for stimuli that can cause changes. Once you have found them, don't be lazy—even though the easy thing to do, and the one that demands the least energy from you, is to stay on a plateau. Dedicate your-self to finding the things that will demand harder work from you; dedicate yourself to selecting responses that cause a change in your attitude, feelings, or thinking. Remember, *change gives us dynamics; dynamics give us drama.*

At this point, I'm sure I can hear voices screaming, "No, no, it's conflict that gives drama!" I won't argue with that; conflict is a prime mover in a drama. But conflict can be very subtle as well as very big and energetic, and conflict alone cannot build toward an impressive climax unless everyone involved—actor, director, and writer—is aware that dynamics are an essential part of the conflict. Conflict has a beginning, a development, and (usually) a resolu-tion. Thus, it is part of the dynamics. A conflict that remained on a single level would become boring in a very short time.

Suppose a stimulus causes a change in you. This change alone could bring with it a sense of drama. Certainly, inner conflict is as dramatic as external conflict, provided that the inner conflict is real and that the actor has physicalized it in some way so that the audience knows that it is happening.

It is also true that there can be drama *without* conflict. For a love scene to be dramatic do the lovers have to be making love angrily or be at odds about how they should go about it? I don't think so. But the love scene will be more dramatic if there are *changes* in intensity, in dynamics, in one direction or another.

To repeat: whenever possible, look for change, whether it be a change in physicalizations, a change in your emotional state in the role, or a change in your way of thinking. Find all the possibilities for change and bring them to your performance.

Not long ago I was watching an episode of a television series I was involved in at ABC. In this episode an undercover narcotics agent was ordered to partner with one of the leads. The undercov-er man did not want a partner, since he had always worked alone. The episode dealt with his resistance to working with a partner as he desperately tried to get to the top man in a narcotics ring.

An exciting role was far less effective than it should have been because the actor chose to play (or was so directed) only one dimen-sion of the character: the intensity. As a consequence, in the absence of some humor, some lightness, and some changes in his levels of intensity, almost everything in the piece evoked the same kind of response from him. This gave us a performance that was on a continually high plateau, so that the truly meaningful moments had no chance to stand out. The end result was a one-note performance that was not necessarily bad, but that should have been exceptionally good and wasn't.

Always make sure that your rhythm and your dynamics are your own. All too frequently a strong actor will pull everyone else into his orbit, with each of the others in the scene losing their individuality. That danger is always present. Don't let a star overpower you; maintain your own rhythm, your own attack on the moment. Your scenes will be stronger, and your performance more impressive.

17

....

Movement

In a recent class, two of my students did a very intimate scene in which the man and woman were both examining their rather tortured feelings toward each other, tortured because of the circumstances surrounding their affair. When the scene was over, the actor said to me that he felt that he should have moved somewhere during the performance. I asked him why, and he said he didn't know; he just felt that the scene was kind of slow, and that it might have helped if he had added some movement.

First of all, we need to recognize that there are two kinds of movement. First, there is physical movement. Second, there is what I call emotional dynamics—or emotional shift and change—that can be as effective as physical movement and can frequently take the place of physical movement. If something significant is happening emotionally between two people, there should be a sense of movement, even though physically both partners were relatively static.

Physical movement should always come out of either some need within the character, or for the purpose of furthering the story. It should never be the result of an actor or director feeling that the scene is boring without it. Indeed, if the scene is boring, then the actor or the director is to blame, assuming that the material itself is interesting to begin with. In that case, resorting to extraneous movement will only obscure the real problems that need to be addressed.

If you move without sufficient motivation, then the move is arbitrary and distracting, and will confuse the audience, even though they cannot articulate what it is that's troubling them. Boiled down to its essence, what it comes to is that no move should ever be made unless it is inevitable because of what is happening in the scene. If it is the result of a physical need such as to

go get a cup of coffee, to go mix a drink (a common piece of triv-
ia), or to run to the phone to call an ambulance, that's fine. If it is
the result of a need created by a strong feeling, that's even better.
What I find with most young actors is that even though the feelings may be genuine within a scene, the entire instrument is not
free enough for the body to respond fully and credibly to the needs
those feelings generate. It is very difficult to stand still when one
is angry. It is difficult to stand still when one is suffering a deep
anxiety or great joy. There are many feelings that make us want to
move, and the actor's whole instrument needs to be free enough to
make the movement those feelings demand.

Economy is a very important concept in relation to acting. If
the movement is not inevitable, it shouldn't happen. This means
that properly motivated movement is not only desirable, it is
mandatory. Improperly motivated movement is not only undesirable, it is destructive. The solution for the actor in determining
when and how he should move lies in our very basic concept of
acting; that is, to believe in the imaginary circumstances, to give
himself over to those imaginary circumstances, to "hear" the stimuli coming at him, whether they're internal or external, to absorb
those stimuli, to let them affect him, and then do what is required
because of that effect.

All too common in the average TV episode, two actors either
stand still and talk through an entire scene, or sit and talk through
an entire scene, whether the scene is one of simple exposition or
major argument. In some instances no movement might be right,
of course. In other instances, movement is demanded, but there is
none.

The principal reason is often a simple one. Discounting the
possibility that the director has no sense of movement, or that one
or both actors involved do not have the capability of walking and
talking at the same time, the most common reason for the sta-
tionary nature of the scene is that TV makes devastating demands
on directors because shooting time is so short. It becomes simpler
to stage and shoot a scene in which there is no movement at all,
than to block and shoot movement. Therefore, many directors
will take the easy way out and direct virtually every scene the same

way, with the people involved in static positions throughout.

On the other hand, I have seen shows in which a director, faced with the usual time problems that plague TV series, moved the actors and camera in a way that was not only necessary because of what was happening in the scenes, but interesting as well. The movement gave the films visual dynamics as well as emotional dynamics. It is not impossible for a director to stage at least his most important scenes with some movement; it just takes imagination and energy—and talent. Again, the director has to be careful that such movement is not arbitrary and done for its own sake, but rather is demanded by what is happening in the scene.

18

The Need

"Intention," "objective," and "need" all mean the same thing. However, "intention" and "objective" are basically intellectual concepts, and I prefer actors to be driven by feelings, so I will use the word "need."

From moment to moment in life we move from need to need. We set out to accomplish something and then move on to something else when a new stimulus hits us. Our need might be to tie a shoelace; then it might become to understand why the baby is crying; then to soothe the baby, and so on.

In the same way, any role that an actor plays has a major need in its lifetime and any number of lesser needs that carry it from moment to moment, and ultimately carry it to the fulfillment of the role's major need, or *spine*, as it is often called.

Let's take an obvious example. Almost everyone has the same basic need: to find peace of mind. However, what constitutes peace of mind is different for different people. Let's suppose that for me it is to own a million dollars. (It is important to always pick a dynamic need in order to give thrust to the character and the scene. Always use the infinitive; always make the need "to accomplish something.") But "to own a million dollars" is too general; I must break it down to something specific I can play on a moment-to-moment basis.

There are any number of ways I could set out to get the million. My need could be to break the bank at Las Vegas; it could be to build up businesses; it could be to marry a millionairess.

Suppose it is the last of these. In order to marry a millionairess, I must first meet her, so I gear a number of my life actions to the "need to meet a millionairess." Having met her, my problem is to get her to marry me, now my need becomes "to win the millionairess." In order to do that, I might have to select the need to "flatter her" or "to amuse her" or "to seduce her" or "to insult her" or any number of other possibilities, depending on what kind of woman I'm going to marry. Let's assume that I decide to focus on the need to seduce. I have now found a series of playable needs, such as "to amuse," "to flatter," "to disarm," "to intoxicate"—ultimately winding up with a simple and direct need that will lead to the fulfillment of the major need: "to find peace of mind by getting a million dollars." What you play is the last, or smallest, need.

Any good role you play will be structured in essentially the same way. You will have a major need or needs, but from instant to instant, you will have minor needs to fulfill. It is important, therefore, that you know what your immediate need is at any given moment, and then set out to fulfill that need.

You cannot play *all* your needs at the same time; as I point out elsewhere in the book, you must build the role one small brick at a time, just as you build a house. Ultimately, when all the bricks have been put in place, one at a time, the entire structure becomes visible and identifiable. If you try to play several needs at once, or if you try to play several emotions at once or several life attitudes at once, you will be presenting yourself with an insurmountable problem.

Most scripts offer the chance to experience the various dominant emotions; all the actor need do is look for the appropriate moments in which he can focus on one or the other. For example, let's take a scene from *I Never Sang for My Father*. In this scene a brother and sister are arguing over what just took place with their bereaved father. Their mother died a few days ago, and their grief is very real. The argument is the result of their different attitudes toward their dominating father; it is quite heavy at the beginning of the scene. If the actors play the grief throughout the scene, the argument will lose its strength, and the scene will lack impact. However, the actors must find a moment in the scene, if possible, where the grief can be expressed clearly, without weakening the argument. That moment comes at the very end, when the sister says, "Suddenly I miss mother so!" Until then, the argument can dominate the entire scene. With that single moment at the end, the audience is reminded of the grief, without any loss of impact. As a matter of fact, the moment is all the more moving because it has been contained.

Being aware of your need from instant to instant is one of the most important facets of your work. It will give you purpose, and it will give every scene an emotional thrust. Most of your energy will be a consequence of how strongly you play the need *and how important it is to you that the need be fulfilled.*

As an exercise you might want to break down every role and every scene so that you are aware of the major need and of any secondary needs that drive you through it. Once you are ready to perform, however, such intellectualization *must* be put aside. Remember: we are driven by needs, we set out to fulfill those needs, and it is the effort to fulfill those needs that helps give thrust and dynamics to the drama. Obstacles cause reaction; reaction causes something to happen, giving us dynamics. So look for the obstacles and frustrations; play off them and you will generate exciting moments.

Remember, also, that in setting out to fulfill a major need, you will probably have to use several lesser needs as illustrated above. This is particularly true if your first efforts are unsuccessful. A real-life incident that occurred at the time of this writing will illustrate the point perfectly: A woman had climbed out on the ninth-story ledge of a building, intending to jump. All efforts to dissuade her failed, until finally a minister climbed out to her. His major need was "to get her to come back inside." His first lesser need was "to convince her that life was worth living." That met with no success. He then tried "to make her feel guilty about leaving her family." Again, no success. He tried every other need he could think of until finally he decided "to make her laugh." He told her she would be arrested if she jumped, because it was against the law. She looked at him and asked, "On what charge?" "Littering," he said. She laughed, and said, "All right, Reverend. You win." With that, she climbed in from the ledge.

A major intention, or need; a first lesser, or subneed, unsuccessful; a new secondary need, or approach, unsuccessful; finally, a need that worked. How much more interesting your work will be if you can bring this kind of shift and change into your work as you strive to fulfill your needs! Change and dynamics are magic words, and they are yours to use as you select your needs and subneeds.

Back in the early days of television, I was working at CBS. The network had just made its deal for "Perry Mason," which was to be a filmed series, and actors and actresses were being tested for the leading roles. To save time and money, the tests were being made electronically and kinescoped rather than with a film camera, and I was helping the producer direct the tests, since he was unfamiliar with the live television booth and the multiple camera system.

There was only one female role that needed to be filled on a continuing basis, the role of Perry Mason's secretary, Della. One of Hollywood's best-known agents arrived with an actress I had never met before, but one who was clearly wrong for the role.

I couldn't believe that she was seriously being tested, but since the decisions were not mine, we staged the scene, watching in awe as she played one single need: to seduce. This was in a straight expository scene with Perry Mason, her boss, and seduction had nothing to do with it. However, this obviously was the only thing the young lady understood. The actor testing with her stared at her incredulously through the entire scene, and I wish we had preserved the kinescope for posterity.

The need to seduce is a terrific one to have at your fingertips. But it certainly isn't the answer to everything.

Need is frequently determined by a sensory or emotional state. If in the scene it is cold, for example, *you do not play to be cold; you play to get warm.* You play *against* the stimulus, and it is that struggle to overcome a discomfort or obstacle that makes the moment real. You don't play to have a headache; you play to *relieve the pain.* You don't play to cry; you play *to keep from crying. It is necessary to create the real feeling or sensory problem first; then to do what is necessary to overcome it.*

Need may also be conditioned by the other actor. What you have planned as your need at some given moment may not work because of what the other actor is giving you. So remember to remain open and responsive to everyone and everything around you.

Suppose you are going to do a scene in which you are scolding your wife for spending too much money on clothes. You are going to shoot the scene in the morning with an actress you've never worked with before. The dialogue as written makes it appear to you that she will be defensive, and even hostile, when you begin your attack, so your need to scold will remain very strong throughout the scene.

That's the plan. Now you arrive on the set and begin rehearsals. Instead of her being defensive and hostile, her nose gets red, her eyes moisten, and her whole demeanor is one of apology, not attack. Won't the way you approach your need change? It very likely will.

Probably the most used word in the actor's vocabulary is *motivation*. There is always a reason for what we do; there is always a *motivation*. One may be motivated by greed, love, hatred, revenge, lust, fear, anxiety, or by any number of other emotional needs or attitudes. The motivation is an inner stimulus, which is the catalyst for a need, and it is that need that the actor must play, rather than the deeper, and sometimes subconscious, motivation.

You have no money and haven't eaten for twenty-four hours. You see a twenty-dollar bill lying on the sidewalk. You are very hungry; your need is *to get the money*, so you move toward it. The thought occurs to you that the owner may be somewhere near, looking for his money; that thought is another stimulus. You put your foot on the bill, covering it; your need is *to hide it from sight*. Again, the verb form, "to hide it from sight."

Let's take another example. You sit on a tack. You jump up. Your need is to get off the tack. Your ultimate need is to stop the pain. You certainly don't want to take the time to process the idea that you "need to stop the pain, so maybe I'd better get off the tack." Play the immediate need; it's much simpler, and as a result, faster.

You must never do anything without a reason, whatever you wish to call it. You must always know why you do or say something. Sometimes the reason is clear; sometimes it is hard to define. If you're not sure of your need (or motivation), ask the director. In most cases, he'll try to help you.

You will notice that I said, "in most cases." Sometimes you ask the director what your motivation is, and he answers, "Your pay-

check. Just do it." That's not as unusual as it sounds. Directors
have been plagued with actors who are too lazy to do their homework or too lazy to do their own thinking or, worst of all, actors
who are obsessed with "motivation." Many directors hate to hear
the word. If a director wants you to make a cross at a given time,
it is your obligation to do it. He may need the movement for pace
or to get his camera into position for what will follow your cross.

Does that seem an odd thing to tell an actor? In film, directors
have very little time, under the best of circumstances. Actors are
supposed to be able to work out their own performance, based on
the material and the director's wishes. The director will expect you
to be able to do that. If he must spend a lot of time in discussion
with you about every move you make, he will have no time left to
direct. And he will get very, very impatient and lose his enthusiasm for you as an actor. Need I say more?

On rare occasions, you may find yourself in a situation in
which the film or TV director has time for rehearsal and for
detailed examination of the script with the actors. Those moments
are wonderful, and when they happen, you need have no fear of
discussing needs or any other aspect of your role. Those situations
are rare, however, so you'd best be prepared to handle your own
problems with little or no outside help.

19

•••••••••••••••••••••••••••••••••

Selectivity

In real life, we are continually bombarded with alternatives. Basing our choices on who and what we are and what our needs are, we make each choice and proceed to execute it. It may be simple, such as having whole wheat toast instead of white toast; it may be complicated, such as quitting a job and moving to a new career; or it may be extremely traumatic on a personal level, such as the decision to seek a divorce.

Since the actor is obligated to take an imaginary person and make a living person out of him, the actor must be aware that the person has to make selections. Even more important than that, the actor has to be aware that some selections are more interesting and more effective than others.

I remember an episode of the television series "The Man and the City," starring Anthony Quinn. Quinn is one of the most imaginative and inventive actors I have ever seen at work, and to watch his efforts in dailies, where we had a chance to look at all the selections before they were edited to a final film, was truly an experience. One moment in particular stands out as a demonstration of the man's ability to be spontaneous and to make immensely effective selections.

In the scene, Quinn, in a hurry, as usual, to conduct his business as mayor of the city, drove up to City Hall. At the curb in front of City Hall was a sign on a stand that said, "Reserved for the Mayor." However, someone had parked in the mayor's spot. Angry, Quinn honked his horn as he sat there double-parked for a moment. He looked around, and then, with great annoyance, left his car double-parked and started up the steps of the City Hall. Up to that point, Quinn was doing exactly what had been staged and exactly what had been expected of him. However, at that moment in the take, Quinn made a selection: he turned back down the steps, picked up the sign, and put it on the seat of the improperly parked automobile. Then, with great satisfaction, he stormed up the steps of the hall. (The camera operator got it all because he had been alerted to follow Quinn and to be ready for the unexpected.)

He could have done any number of things when he decided to come back and reprimand the owner of that car. He could have kicked the tire or the door, or spit on the windshield—or stood there and just fumed for a moment. But what he did made its point with great humor, did not demean his stature as mayor, and left the audience with a very good feeling.

That's what I call selectivity. And if you watch any really good actor's performances you will find him doing things that are rich and unexpected and carefully designed to build his character a brick at a time through his very careful selections—many of them spontaneous, but spontaneous in terms of the role.

Selectivity can frequently make the difference between an acceptable performance and an interesting and brilliant one. Anthony Hopkins' performance in *The Silence of the Lambs* was brilliant, because he chose to *play away from the obvious insanity of the character*. As far as he was concerned, he was normal; certainly not the kind of man you would run away from if you met him on the street.

The truly imaginative and intuitive actor knows that there are numerous possible responses to a stimulus, and he has learned, consciously or through his developed intuition, which choices to make.

I'm going to digress for a moment and talk about intuition. It is a long-held theory among many that talent can be destroyed by studying acting and that an actor should depend on his intuition. The common statements are "Either you got it or you ain't." and "Actors are born, not made."

Intuition is a lovely thing to have on your side. It is also a very treacherous thing, because sooner or later you are going to turn to it for help and it's not going to be around. At that point, you'd better have some know-how and some craft available to help you get through the rough spots facing you—to help you find your performance when intuition has failed.

It's also true that an actor's intuition is not necessarily something with which he was born. The term "intuition" is frequently used when the process at work is actually conditioned response. As you learn, your experiences become part of you. Since you will call upon them without thought, they will appear to be intuitive responses. It's fine if you want to call it your intuition, because the semantics don't matter. Be aware, though, that this intuition is a growing thing that is becoming more beautiful and more fully developed as you gain craft and experience. It's not getting older, it's getting better.

Now let's go back to selectivity. When you read a scene you immediately form some idea about how that scene ought to be played. Although I encourage actors to follow their impulses, the first impulse may not always be the best one. That's why I have the students in my advanced classes do an exercise in which they work on a scene with more than one basic adjustment: emotional, intellectual, or personality. First they rehearse the scene as they see it and find out where that approach takes them. Then, if there is any uncertainty, they try a radically different emotional or personality adjustment to see where that takes them. After rehearsing two or more adjustments, they consciously look at the possible responses to major stimuli in the scene and try rehearsing with a number of those. During this process, it doesn't matter if you settle for the wrong choice, because the teacher will (we hope) know that you have settled for the wrong choice, will discuss it with you, and will guide you toward an unerring ability to make the right choice.

Ultimately, obviously, final selections will have to be made, but in the long run, this approach accomplishes two very important things. First, it helps develop selectivity. Second, the performances will be richer, more interesting, and more moving, because it is inevitable that some choices will be found that might not have occurred to you in the beginning.

You can rehearse this way in a classroom situation. *When you're working professionally in film or television, there is usually no time for this kind of experimentation. It must be done at home as part of your preparation or purely as an exercise.* And when you are working, once you have made your choice, believe in it with all your heart. Go for it with all the authority you can muster. Believe it to be the only logical and inevitable way to play the moment. If the director insists on another choice, *that* must become the only logical and inevitable way to play the moment.

If you are ever bored with rehearsing, the chances are that there is something wrong with your approach. One sure way to end the boredom is to do what I have described above. Don't "lock down" your rehearsals, repeating verbatim every move and every line reading that you have been using. Find some radical shift in the character, select something different and open your instrument to the new factor or factors. Rehearse freshly and freely that way; see what happens. You might make some marvelous discoveries. Or maybe nothing more will happen and you will find that your approach all along has been exactly right, and that none of the new things make sense. Even that should be a great comfort to you, so it ought to be worth the effort.

Don't be afraid of looking foolish when exercising your selective powers. You can't look foolish when you're experimenting on an intelligent and reasonable level. The things you do may not work; they may stand out sharply as being absolutely wrong for the scene, the role, or both. But rehearsal time is the time to reach and stretch and make mistakes in an effort to find the optimum values in the material and to stimulate yourself so that you can deliver the best you are capable of delivering.

The menace that prevents some actors from ever becoming more than competent is laziness, for which there is no excuse. It takes energy to feel things; it takes energy to analyze and think; it takes energy to rehearse again and again and again in the search for the best performance, but I don't know any other way to make a professional out of an amateur.

Following are some specifics to watch for as you make your selections.

Play against the dialogue. If the author has written a scene in such a way that the character's feelings and intentions are clearly stated in the dialogue, see if you can play other values. In other words, play against what has been written. You can often afford to do that, because if the statements in the words are clear enough and certain enough, playing directly into them may exaggerate them, make them corny, or make them dull. Playing *away* from them might give the moment more interest and give the character greater dimension.

If a love scene is being played, and the dialogue unquestionably says "I love you" even though those may not be the exact words, the actor does not need to play the romantic aspects of love; he can play any number of other elements and get involved in any number of pieces of business or other physicalizations. Thus, he can give the scene more fun, more interest, and more dynamics.

Let's say a man and a woman are eating dinner. The man says, "I never knew what love really meant until that time we spent in Hawaii. I suddenly felt things I had never felt before, and knew that I had finally experienced the meaning of true love." Now, must he gaze romantically into her eyes as he says those lines? Of course not, but that would be the way most inexperienced actors would attack the scene. The words are dangerously close to being corny; if the actor says them gazing dreamily into the actress's eyes, he could easily push the moment over the line. It could be much more interesting and moving if, for example, the actor played the dialogue with warm laughter, as if pleasantly amazed at the discovery—or even while continuing to eat, allowing the way he is eating to be slightly affected by what he is saying and feeling.

In Neil Simon's *The Gingerbread Lady*, there is a scene between Evy, the lead, and one of her friends, a homosexual actor. It is very clear in the writing that he is gay; that characteristic is not totally dependent on the actor's finding effeminate postures and speech patterns.

Since there is no doubt that the character is gay no matter how he plays the role, that element in his character need not be accentuated. There will probably be some degree of effeminacy in his physical attitudes, but it need not be overstated. In fact, if it is, there is a danger that the role will become a caricature and lose its necessary sense of reality. Instead, the actor can and should play what the scene is really about: he is shattered because he was fired from a play during the rehearsal period and replaced by an actor he considers inferior. The fact that he is homosexual has virtually nothing to do with the real problem in the scene, which is that after many not-too-successful years as an actor, he feels that he is a failure and that his career may well be over. That is a devastating thought, and it is that thought, that fear, which drives him through the scene. If the actor plays "homosexual" through the scene, he may well make the scene a campy joke instead of one of deep pathos. He will also probably lose the one element that offers something with which the entire audience can empathize.

Don't go into reverie because you're talking about the past. A very dangerous trap is the impulse to romanticize or move into reverie when the dialogue is about the past. In *Jaws*, for example, Robert Shaw, in a story-telling session with Richard Dreyfuss and Roy Scheider, begins to tell about one of his wartime experiences. He starts relating it to the other men, but as he gets deeper in the telling, he is drawn back into the horror of the time when he and hundreds of other men, afloat in the ocean after their ship was sunk, were surrounded and attacked by a large group of hungry sharks. His focus goes back and forth from the listeners to himself, until he is almost entirely immersed in the horror of the past. It's not until near the end of the story that he forces himself back to the present—to the other men.

In this case, falling into reverie would be absolutely wrong, because Shaw is talking about the past for reasons specifically related to the present. Therefore, *the same emotional energy and drive that brought the past to mind would continue through the telling of what happened,* at least in the beginning. It might be acceptable for the emotional direction to shift if, in the telling, the character becomes more deeply moved by the events of the past than by the motivating events of the present. If that started to occur, the character would struggle against those feelings so that he could continue the drive that started the speech. He then might or might not be overcome totally by the new feelings being generated.

To repeat: don't romanticize, and don't fall into reverie. Remember the need; remember that *you bring up the past for rea-*

sons related to the present, and not simply to have a chance to spend a few moments in reverie or sentimentality.

Find humor in drama, and drama in humor. Actors tend to play serious drama very seriously, and that can be a mistake. You should try to find humor even in the heaviest drama. It will make the role you are playing more interesting, and will give the audience a moment of relief, so that they will more easily be moved by your more dramatic moments—they will be more and more receptive to them.

A close examination of any good drama will reveal that the author has written some humor into the material. *Hamlet* is a perfect example. The second act scene with Polonius is full of humor, yet it occurs in the midst of Hamlet's grief and frustration. Hamlet jokes with the old man, then soon after jokes with Ophelia, before the start of the Players' performance.

Even the witches in *Macbeth* are allowed to be funny. It is to your advantage to learn to laugh at your own disasters in your role; your dealing with them will be more palatable to the audience, and you will have greater strength.

When I was a little boy, my parents attended a theater in St. Louis where a company performed a different Yiddish play every Sunday night. Most of the time they were plays with music, and I suspect that much of the material was a combination of original material, familiar Yiddish material, and probably stuff that was stolen from current Broadway shows. I found that my mother had the magic formula. She used to say, "If I can't laugh and cry in the same evening, it's not a good show." There really is magic in those words.

Think about it. The best dramas have their moments of humor. The best comedies have their moments of warmth, their moments of "schmaltz," and their tear-jerking moments. So you, the actor, should try to find the humor in your dramatic roles and the heart in your comedic roles. These can be critical selections. Obviously, I'm referring to roles where you would have the chance to make such selections. If the role is written to preclude this kind of an approach, you must stay with the author's interpretation.

Don't play the subconscious. Because we have become a world of armchair psychiatrists, the actor, in particular the "method" actor, will try to invent a deep psychological background for his character. Many feel that is a proper procedure. However, that often leads the actor into trying to play the subconscious he has invented.

That is a very serious mistake. The subconscious, *by definition,* is not available to us. So how can we play it? People do not respond to stimuli on a moment-to-moment basis with their sub-conscious drives; they respond on a conscious level. Therefore, what the actor needs is to determine how the character would behave on a *conscious* level, and forget about the subconscious entirely.

Let's take an example: suppose a woman had a very bad rela-tionship with her father, who beat her as a child. The father left home when she was quite young, so that she has very few, if any, specific memories of those terrible incidents. What she does have is a deeply rooted hatred of men. But growing up in a society where the male-female relationship is a desired one, she is not consciously aware of such hatred.

In her relationship with men, her moment-to-moment selec-tions might well be those that emasculate her male partner to one degree or another. If the woman were to be told that she hated men, she might stare with great incredulity, because as far as she knows, she loves men and loves sex. She has had many affairs to prove it. On a conscious level she believes that she is fond of men and that most of her actions are a consequence of that feeling. The truth, however, is that her actions are emasculating and destruc-tive, and the result of a love-hate relationship with her father.

Let me repeat: *you cannot, you must not, play the subconscious drives* of the character; you must play the *moment-to-moment con-scious drives.* Doing a deep psychological profile of the character can be a monumental waste of time, and could lead your perfor-mance seriously astray. Also, if you spend a great deal of time and thought designing a subconscious life, it will probably intrude on the performance because it will be extremely difficult to block it out. You aren't convinced? OK. When was the last time you thought of a white bear? Never? Good. Now for the next thirty seconds, *don't think of a white bear.* Gotcha!

Ultimately, the way you behave on a conscious level will tell the audience what you are subconsciously. Trying to play the subconscious involves you in inner activity that has meaning only for you; it leaves the audience in the dark, because you can't communicate a subconscious drive. Furthermore, if you are involved with the subconscious, you can't be involved at the same time with the conscious world that the audience is viewing and in which you, in your role, are living.

If you take the usual interpretation of Edward Albee's *Who's Afraid of Virginia Woolf?* you will decide that George is masochistic and Martha is sadistic. If the actor consciously plays George as a man who wants to be punished—in other words, plays his subconscious drive—the performance will fail, since he consciously denies that he enjoys the punishment Martha delivers to him. When she says to him, "You married me for it," he is absolutely outraged. The degree of his outrage is excessive because of the subconscious truth. Any person who was not masochistic would be more likely to laugh at the ludicrous nature of the statement than to be outraged by it. It is George's *excessive outrage* on the conscious level that tells the audience that there is *something under* the conscious level that confirms Martha's statement—that and the fact that he stays married to her.

When talking about this matter of the subconscious to my classes, I always use *Fatal Attraction* as an example. In this film, Glenn Close played a woman obsessed with Michael Douglas. Do you know why Glenn Close was the way she was? The answer almost has to be No, because in the film there are only the subtlest references to her father. You can guess; you can build whatever scenario you wish to explain it, but who cares? She does what she does because she wants Michael Douglas—that's it. Chances are she *wouldn't know* the real reasons because they would be in her subconscious, unless she has spent years in therapy. But if she had, and it was successful therapy, she wouldn't do what she did, and there would be no movie.

If the actress chose to invent reasons for her behavior, and it helped her give the wonderful performance she did, fine. I believe in using whatever works. However, since there is no way to articulate those reasons to the audience, because there's nothing in the script that describes them, all that busyness running around in her head could just as easily clutter and confuse the performance, rather than help it. If you can't articulate it to the audience, why bother? The work must be kept simple if it is to be effective. You must play the moment, remember? One brick at a time! Your preparation should be based on what is available in the material, on what you can play that the audience will understand.

You must realize that in real life, at any given moment, we are almost always thinking of and involved with only one thing at a time. Whatever stimulus is dominant at the moment, especially in emotionally charged moments, is what gets our focus. To illustrate this, I will take some change in my hand while I am talking to my class, jiggle the change, then toss it up in the air and let it fall to the floor. Then I ask the class if they were thinking of anything other than the change when I let it drop. The answer is always that they were not, because it was unusual, and therefore it got their attention away from everything else. Which is what a strong stimulus should do when you're performing. Try it.

Avoid self-pity. If you feel sorry for yourself, nobody else will; that is a cardinal rule. In an effort to create deep emotion, actors frequently get very weepy. This kind of emotional indulgence weakens one, and it is important to remember that the best way to avoid being victimized in this way is to select a dynamic intention to play.

In Chapter 18, I spoke about using the infinitive form when you define your need so that what you are trying to achieve has a dynamic base to it. If you play the need to solve the problem as opposed to playing being overwhelmed by it, you will minimize the dangers of becoming self-pitying and thus weak (unless this is what the role demands, of course).

Communicate through props and actors. Remember that the actor's responsibility is ultimately to communicate to the audience, not simply to the other actor in the scene or to himself.

One of the most effective ways of communicating to the audience is through the use of props. The way you handle an object, the changes you make in the way you handle an object, the way you relate emotionally to a prop—all are enormously effective in communicating ideas to an audience, because they are things that the audience can see.

If a woman in a role has recently lost her husband and is grieving over him, the actress playing the role must make that grief real for the audience. If she is able to relate to it and experience a real sense of grief as she plays the role, the audience will no doubt be aware of how she feels. If, in addition, she can strengthen the articulation of that idea in some way, that's all the better.

Let's suppose she is cleaning out her husband's desk. She finds his pipe. She stares at it for a long moment, then gently strokes her cheek with it. She sits slowly, holding the pipe to her face, smelling the familiar aroma, remembering. The audience is likely to be moved more by this kind of prop use than by any line of dialogue the author might write. More importantly, the actress may find that in handling the prop, she will start a surge of emotion that will make the moment more real for her and thus more effective for the audience.

What you do can be far more revealing than what you say, because *what you do* tells the truth about what you are feeling much more accurately than the words you utter. We lie a lot with words; we tell the truth with our body language.

A side note about the use of props: All too often actors will smoke or drink in a scene where smoking or drinking is not a necessary part of the moment. These activities are real, certainly, but if they become a crutch for insecurity, it would be very wise to try working without them. When props are used, the actor must be careful that the use of the props enhances the moment and does not stop the flow of the scene.

Suppose a man has a speech such as this:

MAN

You just implied I lied to you this morning! I have
never lied to you, but you have always mistrusted

what I have told you, and for no reason! I'm going
to say it once more, and then I'm never going to
mention it again!

You can readily see what would happen to this speech if the
man stopped to light a cigarette after his first line, "You just
implied that I lied to you this morning!" The flow of his dialogue
would be interrupted for a meaningless act—it has no bearing on
the scene, nor is it needed to help the man work through a transition. The speech is a single outburst; it requires few, if any, thought
pauses, and thus any interruption of the rhythm of the outburst
would be jarring to an audience.

While we're on the subject of interrupting the rhythm of a
speech, let me point out that there are times when you might have
a series of speeches that are actually a single speech broken up by
dialogue from another character. Take this exchange:

MAN
You just implied that I lied to you this morning!

WOMAN
It's time to leave.

MAN
I have never lied to you—

WOMAN
I only know what Jim told me.

MAN
—but you have always mistrusted what I have
told you, and for no reason!

WOMAN
I've never mistrusted you.

MAN

I'm going to say it once more—

WOMAN

I don't want to hear it!

MAN

And then I'm never going to mention it again!

The woman's lines are not a stimulus for what the man says. His stimulus is the feeling inside him; that is what drives him. If he plays the scene waiting for his cues before he speaks his lines, the scene will be jerky—the rhythm will be off. If he treats the scene as a series of speeches instead of one, he will lessen the impact of the moment. If, on the other hand, he considers his lines to be a single speech, and delivers them that way, the rhythm will not be broken, and the energy will remain high.

The woman must break into the man's speech; it is *her* responsibility, not his, for his speech to be interrupted. In real life he would not wait for her to speak, or expect her to speak; he would want to say all the things he is given to say here. If she didn't interrupt, he would go on.

We must get that feeling here. He should actually interrupt her lines just as she reaches the end of each one, so that there is a slight bit of overlapping dialogue throughout. What she says is not important; if we lose a little of her dialogue, it won't matter. What is important in this scene is the feeling between the two, which supplies the dynamics that drive the scene.

Another important manner of communicating ideas to the audience is through physical contact with the other actors. It is surprising how many young actors and actresses will be reluctant to touch. I suppose one of the major reasons is that in our culture we are not always encouraged to do so. However, early in our Workshop training we strongly encourage physical contact and try to break down any barriers our students may have that inhibit its free use. Making physical contact with other actors helps build the emotional relationship that is a necessary part of a performance.

We were quite surprised the first time we tried a touching exercise in a class some years ago. I gave the students scenes to memorize and perform, which they did in the usual way. Then I had them sit with their partners and explore each other's hands, arms, neck, face, and hair with their eyes and fingertips as they asked personal questions of each other (not related to the scenes). One actor did this for about five minutes, and then they reversed roles.

Now they did their scenes again, and the effect was pronounced. There was greater emotional depth, and there was a greater sense that the people really knew each other as husbands and wives, lovers or friends. And there was much more realistic physical contact between the actors.

Touching a person (or not touching a person) can be extremely significant, and the particular manner in which contact is made can tell far more about a relationship or about how a person is feeling than the dialogue can.

20

· ·

Personalization

Many acting teachers believe that the truest and surest way to get to an emotion is to recall something that happened to you that generated that emotion sometime in the past. This may have value as an exercise early in your training; it does help to release emotions that otherwise might not want to come to the surface.

The problem comes about when an actor decides to incorporate the exercise into a scene. For instance, he may decide that the way to cry in a scene is to remember the death of his mother. I suppose if he concentrates properly on this personal tragedy, the tears will come, but what happens to the relationship with the other actor and to the specific stimuli the actor is receiving, which have nothing to do with his mother or any member of his family? What if he's crying because his boss fired him?

If there is no other way to get to the tears, I suppose we have to accept "personalization" and "emotion memory" as last ditch tools. However, *listening* becomes much more difficult because the actor's focus is on his inner self, directed at something unrelated to the scene, thus shutting out the stimuli he should be receiving from the other actor.

There is no question that the truly great actor has an instrument that is free enough to *respond to the stimuli presented by the material and the other actor*. If you can't identify that closely and respond accordingly, then there might be something missing in your very basic training, and you owe it to yourself to go to a good acting teacher.

There could be a very valuable transference of the personal and real to the imaginary life of the role. Ultimately, however, the only sure way is to be certain that the responses will happen in performance as a result of the true stimuli existing in the material, and not as a result of thinking about an unrelated personal experience. If you once wept over a lost dog, and are now playing a scene in which your dog is killed and you weep, certainly you can give the imaginary dog some, if not all, of the attributes of the real dog without harm to your performance. It's when the dog becomes your mother that I begin to wonder about the validity of the approach.

The real value in the use of your own experience lies in the fact that you have a firsthand awareness of certain emotions, certain feelings, certain hungers. It is important for the actor to experience as much as possible, so that his instrument is aware of all the keys that need to be played. This doesn't mean you should go out and kill someone in case you ever have to play a killer. Obviously, as with all creative work, you must use imagination and exercise taste and judgment along the way.

Here is a perfect example of a personalized transference that is necessary: since you cannot actually kill somebody to know what it feels like, you must call upon the feeling of *wanting* to kill, and that feeling is one almost everyone has had at one time or another. If you can't consciously recall when you had such a feeling, you should be able to imagine a situation where you would want to kill another human being.

We've had students who have said they could never kill anyone, but after a few minutes of questioning, we've always been able to create an imaginary circumstance in which the student will reluctantly say, "Well, yeah, I'd kill him." As with all other emotions, the killer instinct is in all of us; we need only to find it.

Remember, the use of "personalization" to generate emotion is primarily to help free the instrument. It will be unfortunate if you must use it as a crutch all your acting life.

21

· ·

Animate and Inanimate
Object Images

One of the most popular jokes about what goes on in an acting class goes something like, "Today the teacher told me to be a willow tree, and there aren't too many demands from the casting offices for good willow trees."

It's true; if you are a good-looking willow tree and that's what you're getting out of the exercise, you won't have much of a career. However, I owe it to the exercise—I owe it to a tool that is enormously valuable—to spend a few minutes talking about it.

There are a number of purposes for the use of what have generally been called *images* (although that term is not an accurate one), all of which have great merit. First of all, they stimulate the imagination. Second, as I will soon explain, they are the quickest, most effective tools you can find when it becomes necessary to make major changes in a performance with only limited time available.

What we look for when we use an image is the essence of that image. For example, we have heard it said about people, "he's a bear"; "she's a cow"; "he's a mouse." Obviously no one means the person referred to is literally any one of those things. What is meant is that the person has the *qualities* of the animal referred to.

Just as animate objects have qualities, so do inanimate objects. As we noted in the chapter on rhythm (see Chapter 15), the word "crown" generates specific ideas in the mind of the person who has heard it. Certainly it implies a rhythm of its own, quite different from the rhythm implied by "typewriter" or "electricity."

The same is true of the rhythms of animals. Surely the rhythm of "cat" and the rhythm implied in the word "mouse" are very different.

Objects and animals also imply certain emotional and sensory attitudes. The emotional volatility or stability of the cow and the rabbit are very different. They would move differently, think at different speeds, respond to stimuli at different speeds, feel things differently, and have widely different emotional lives.

What happens then when an actor adopts an image? He will look for what I call the essences: the rhythm, the emotional freedom, the intellectual capacity, and the sensory and physical attitudes. Those essences need to be absorbed into the actor's system so that the actor becomes not a rabbit, but a rabbitlike person; not a bear, but a bearlike person; not a crown, but a royal person. The result of the complete absorption of the essences is that the actor's rhythms will change, his physical attitudes will change, the time and manner of his stimulus-response mechanism will change, and his emotional output will change. In effect, everything about the actor will be affected when the image is adopted.

If you were to try to make all these changes singly, it would be a horrendous task, and every change would very likely get in the way of the focus needed for the fulfillment of every other change. But with the simple use of a concept—the *image*—the entire instrument can be affected simultaneously without the need to concern yourself with a hundred details. You breathe without thinking about it, but if you tried to make the breathing mechanism work on a conscious level, you might very well lose the ability to breathe at all.

The image is an extraordinary tool. However, it is only a tool; it is only one of many tools. And it needs to be used in such a way that nobody in the audience will say, "Oh, look at him; he's a typewriter!"

Remember, too, that objects and animals mean different things to different people. There is no absolute in terms of what "rabbit" means; it is quite conceivable that you and I might have radically different ideas about the essence of rabbit. Therefore, it is important to remember that images are highly personalized tools. If the director says this character is a bull, and you use bull as an image but the results are not what the director is seeking, by all means get some specifics from him and then find the image that generates the necessary results. It doesn't matter to anyone but you which image you choose. If you are using it correctly, no one in the whole world will know what you are using. Have a box full of them available for emergencies.

Let's say that you have come to the studio well rehearsed in your own mind, with a very definite idea of how you plan to approach the day's work. You see yourself in the role as bouncy, full of humor, quick to laugh, quick to move. Your thought processes are fast, because you are a quick thinker. You choose to adopt a slightly hunched physical attitude to give the feeling that you are like a boxer—light on your feet, up, lightning-fast with your responses.

You rehearse once, and the director calls you aside. "What you're doing is very interesting, and quite good for what it is," he says—and you wait for the "but"—"but it's not the feeling I need for the role, especially in this scene. You're moving too fast; you're picking up cues too fast; you're hunched over a little, so you're losing strength; you're responding without giving yourself time to deal with what's hitting you"—and he goes on.

If you have to work on each of those items separately, you'll be a basket case when he calls for another rehearsal in a couple of minutes. After all, it took you most of last night to build what you brought in to rehearsal. What do you do?

You use an image. You need to (1) slow down, (2) avoid picking up cues too fast, (3) stand straighter, and (4) be stronger. What if we take "crown" as an image? Its essences are (1) slow rhythm, (2) deliberate thought, which will slow down response to cues, (3) upright, or stately, bearing, which eliminates the hunched-over look, and (4) a sense of strength, inherent in the idea of such power. If "crown" means those things to you, as it does to me, then absorbing the one idea and allowing it to affect your instrument will answer all your needs quickly and without too much strain.

Whenever I talk about using images correctly, I'm reminded of an actor who was one of our major film stars, but who shall remain anonymous for the purpose of the storytelling. We were doing an episode of a live television series in which this actor starred, playing a dual role. The author, who was a close friend of mine and a rather droll person, was approached by the actor two days before we went on the air. The actor, with a worried look on his face, said, "I don't know what I am. What am I?" A little stunned that this question was being broached two days before performance, the author facetiously replied, "You are a rutabaga." The actor nodded seriously and slowly walked away, absorbing this magnificent piece of imagery.

When we were doing the telecast, the author was watching from the sound booth, which was next to the control booth. Somewhere during the hour the actor blew his lines. The author, unable to resist it, came tearing out of the sound booth and into the control booth, leaned over, and whispered to me, "See! I told him I wrote a rutabaga and he's playing a radish. No wonder he can't remember the lines!"

22

•••••••••••••••••••••••••••••••

The Nonsense
Exercise—Unorthodoxy

Somewhere in this book I have said that we can forgive a bad actor who is doing the best he can, but we cannot forgive a dull actor. One of the things that make an actor interesting is an ability to do the unexpected. An interesting actor will respond in a surprising and yet still truthful way to a stimulus; he will do things in an unorthodox way.

I remember watching an actor work in a Western years ago, and almost the only thing I can remember about that scene was that he picked up a cup by holding the upper rim and the bottom of the cup instead of the handle and drank the hot coffee in that way. Nothing spectacular, but for the moment an interesting kind of life came into the scene. (The actor went on to have his own television series.)

We all tend to do things the safe way, the orthodox way. In order to stimulate imaginations and to give the actors in our classes a chance to become familiar with unorthodoxy, we take a scene that has been performed as a regular classroom exercise and have the actors perform it again, doing everything in the most unorthodox way they can, even if the context of the scene is adversely affected. They don't sit on chairs, they sit on the floor or they sit on the back of a chair with their feet on the seat or they lie on the floor and put their feet up on the chair. They light cigarettes any way except the usual. All props are handled in any way except the usual, and we encourage the use of props that were never before part of the scene, but whose presence is surprising and unorthodox. The result is that we often see a scene that is largely nonsense, but we also see actors freed of convention—actors who have used their imaginations to breathe interest and specialness into a performance. Every now and then we find that something has been brought in that is not only interesting and unorthodox, but also appropriate for use in the final performance of the scene.

Let me give you an example. In a scene from Manhoff's *The Owl and the Pussycat*, the actress chose to bring in an eyecover for the nonsense exercise. When she reached the point in the scene where she angrily said "Goodnight!" to the man in the scene, she pulled the eyecover over her eyes as a gesture of finality. (Surely a terrific way to say "I don't want to talk to you!")

The actor was stuck; he had no substantial way to communicate with her, since he could not reach her eyes. He paused for a moment, then went over and lifted the eyecover and delivered his next barb. She responded with great annoyance, hit him with her next line, and covered her eyes again. The business actually brought a marvelous new moment to the scene, but it would never have been discovered if we hadn't gone to the exercise.

The most important effect of the exercise is that the actor has been dragged out of his rut and pushed into being inventive. Enough work on scenes this way eventually results in an actor to whom interest, imagination, and unorthodoxy are second nature. What a joy it is to watch that kind of actor!

23

Comedy and Drama from the Actor's Point of View

It's almost axiomatic that the person who can play comedy well cannot play drama well, and vice versa. With a few exceptions, that rule holds.

A lot of people I know have tried to put their finger on what makes the difference between comedy and drama. We know there is a difference, and I want to point to some of the things that are apparent to me.

First and foremost, in order to play comedy one needs to be the kind of person who thinks funny. If you can see the funny or ironic side of an issue that is serious to everyone else, it will be easier for you to play comedy.

Although comedy must be based in reality, the *consequences* of an action in comedy do not seem to be as real as the consequences of a similar action in drama. For example, Hedda Gabler's suicide is tragic, and nowhere in the moments preceding the act itself, nowhere during the moment when Hedda decides to take her own life, do we experience anything funny. The consequences of her action are unquestionably real, and the problems that caused her to take the action were unquestionably real and important. On the other hand, in one of the funniest scenes ever written, the third act of Manhoff's *The Owl and the Pussycat*, the people talking about suicide do not seem to regard it as ultimate and total. They act as if they were discussing something as trivial as whether or not the girl can accompany the man on a trip to San Diego. The characters' evaluation of the act of suicide does not carry the sense of danger and totality that the real act actually conveys.

Suicide is an extreme example. The same lack of finality applies in one degree or another to most moments of real consequence in comedy. Death doesn't seem completely final; bankruptcy doesn't seem to be a total disaster; separation and divorce never seem to be permanent and heartbreaking.

Perhaps it is an oversimplification to treat comedy in this way, but I don't believe so. I have found in our classwork that when I give the actor an adjustment that is somewhat less than serious and final, a comedy scene is much funnier than if it is played with the same adjustments with which that scene would be played in a drama.

It is vital that the energy level in comedy be higher than in drama. Vocal energy needs to be up, physical energy needs to be up, and the energy of the dynamics of the scene needs to be up.

The term "pace" is familiar to anyone who has ever been near comedy. Basic rhythms must be faster than in drama. Thought pauses—crossing the bridges—must take only a fraction of the time they would take in drama. Responses to stimuli in general must occur in a fraction of the time they take in drama. Yet it is just as dangerous to "pick up the cues" without thought as it is to take long thought pauses between every line, for comedy, like drama, demands that you respond to the stimuli where they happen. The best comedy writing, in fact, places the stimuli *before* the end of the line when fast pacing is needed, so that bridges can be crossed while the other person is speaking.

So far I have talked about three major differences between comedy and drama. Here I have added a fourth:

1. Energy in comedy must be higher.
2. The consequences of a serious situation in comedy must not be given the same reality or finality that they are given in drama.
3. You cross the bridges between stimulus and response faster. In other words, all the basic rhythms in comedy are slightly faster than in drama. You move faster, and you think faster. You do not talk faster! Whatever is going on, you must be understood!
4. A fourth difference lies in the maturity of the responses. Comedy often depends on the fact that the people are responding on a

less-than-mature level to certain stimuli; if they responded with maturity as you and I understand it, the sequence would be dramatic rather than funny.

A perfect example, right to the physicalization, is the moment in *Born Yesterday* when the dumb blond, Billie Dawn, challenges the extremely successful but crude multimillionaire junk-dealer to define a peninsula. Without thinking, he stands erect, feet together like a schoolboy; then he recites the definition he learned in elementary school. The response is funny; if he had answered in his customary mature, angry way, it would have been only a definition.

In the suicide scene in *The Owl and the Pussycat*, the fun lies both in the unreal aspect of the consequences and in a very healthy degree of less-than-mature responses. A funny example occurs when the man and woman agree that they will commit suicide together by jumping from the restaurant at the top of the Mark Hopkins hotel. She suddenly cries out that she can't do that because she's wearing a pair of torn panties, and she's not going to jump wearing ratty panties!

In a hilarious scene from *Lovers and Other Strangers*, by Joseph Bologna and Renée Taylor, a woman climbs into bed with her husband, expecting sex to follow. However, he does not respond to her perfume, her filmy negligee, her roving hands, or her most sensual efforts. He tells her, "I owe you one." She replies, "You owe me three already." The responses are juvenile, and thus very funny.

Some emotions are too real to be funny. Anger and hatred, fully and truly expressed, are not funny. When such emotions seem to be called for in comedy, it is necessary to think in other terms: to use feelings like annoyance and frustration instead.

Another very important thing to remember in comedy is that the responses to stimuli are frequently much bigger than they would be in drama. In other words, stimuli of minor consequence will generate very energetic emotional responses—bigger-than-life responses—in comedy. *These responses must be made truthful, ultimately*, but they will probably not be the kind of response that you and I give in our saner moments.

In the scene from *Lovers and Other Strangers* just referred to, the woman responds to her husband's lack of enthusiasm about sex at that moment with great annoyance. It is only because she is annoyed rather than truly angry that the scene begins on a funny note. In true-life situations, or in a dramatic situation, the rejected wife might feel that she is unwomanly and respond in a deeply turbulent emotional way, which would be anything but funny; or she might accept the fact that her husband just doesn't feel like making love this night, but there will be other nights, so there is no problem. It is the overreaction to the rejection and the selection of a less-than-mature response that helps make the moment funny and keys the entire scene.

There are elements in the writing that are comedic, of course, such as an unexpected response, a bizarre character, or cartoon humor (physical humor such as slipping on a banana peel or getting a pie in the face), but here we are only concerned with the actor's adjustments that enhance the comedy material. "Seinfeld" is a very funny TV series. One of the things I marvel at in that show is how so much is made of something trivial. Entire episodes may spring from some very inconsequential thing but the overreactions to the trivial make for wonderful comedy.

A joke is made up of two basic parts. First the *feed*, and then the *punch line*, or joke. For example, "Why does a chicken cross the road" is the feed, or *setup*. "To get to the other side" is the joke. If either of those—feed or joke—is not clear, there will be no laugh. That's why an actor must be very careful about moving during either of those, or overlapping either of them with his dialogue. The feed may be a line of dialogue, a gesture, a look—anything. But it must be very clear to the audience. The joke may also be only a look, or a movement, or an interrupted movement. Again, it must be in the clear, or it will be missed and the laugh will be lost.

There is very little margin for error in comedy. Good comedy lines have their own rhythm, their own stresses, even a carefully determined number of syllables sometimes, believe it or not. That's why *you must learn the lines verbatim* when doing comedy. In drama, a word changed may not hurt anything; in comedy, it very likely will.

My first day's work at CBS as a stage manager was on the "Burns and Allen" show; my second on "The Jack Benny Show." Many times rehearsals or readings would be stopped while they tried to find the word that would be funniest, or a way to say what needed to be said with fewer words or syllables. Sounds strange unless you've been there, but it really makes a difference.

For those who are not aware of it, you should know that perhaps the most effective device in comedy is surprise. Most good comedy lines are funny because they surprise us. If we expect the line we will anticipate the joke, and there will be no laugh. An example: a classic Jack Benny joke is the one where he is walking down the street alone, when a mugger with a gun stops him, saying, "Your money or your life!" Benny stares at him, then looks around to see if anyone else is in the area. The mugger then impatiently repeats, "Your money or your life!" and Benny says, "I'm thinking! I'm thinking!" We don't expect it; we're surprised by the idea, which is absurd—and we laugh. Check the next time you see a comedy or laugh at a joke. You'll undoubtedly find that *surprise* is a very common element.

A cardinal sin in playing comedy is trying to be funny. *You must not try to be funny when doing comedy.* If you do, the audience will perceive an actor doing strange—not funny—things, and you are less likely to surprise the audience, because you'll be tipping them off to everything. The result will be that the laughs won't be there. Comedy must be played as truthfully as drama. You can't be funnier than the material. Don't try to be. If the script isn't funny, you're dead anyway; just do the best you can, take your paycheck, and go home.

If you ignore the advice I just gave you, you may be asking for the same review that a very famous and successful actress once received in a film comedy in which she starred. The critic, after lauding her performances in previous films, said that while watching her in this film, he wasn't sure if he was watching *funniness or the impression of funniness*. The audience really doesn't want to see an actor giving an *impression* of a character in a film. *The audience wants to see a person having experiences.*

One characteristic that gets in the way of our ability to play comedy is the tendency to take ourselves much too seriously. We should take our work seriously, and we should take our values seriously, but I have a sneaking suspicion that if we took ourselves less seriously, we would be better actors, both in drama and in comedy, and there is no question in my mind that we would be better and happier people.

Comedy is undoubtedly much more difficult to play than drama. There is a story about Edmund Gwenn, a wonderful English character actor, that makes the point. It seems that when Gwenn lay near death, he was visited by a director who had worked with him several times and who adored him. They spoke for a while, and when it came time for the director to leave he said, "I must go. Before I do, there is something I would like to ask you. It's difficult, and I hope it doesn't offend you, but I would like to ask it."

"What is it?" asked Gwenn.

"Is it hard?"

"Is what hard?"

"Dying."

Gwenn thought for a moment, then said, "Yes. But not as hard as comedy."

24

· ·

Cold Reading and
Auditions

The audition is a necessary evil. How else are the producer, direc-tor, and casting director to determine who is best suited for a par-ticular role? You would like to believe that after you've done one or two roles, however small or large, they will be as aware of your excellent talents as you are. Alas! They probably won't be. They will want to meet you, talk to you for a few minutes to get a sense of your basic quality, and then have you complete your audition by doing a cold reading.

Cold reading is really a misnomer, since it implies that you will be asked to read for a part without being given a chance to study the material first. That almost never happens.

The first thing you need to do is study the scene you are about to read without regard to the fact that you are in it, so that you fully understand it. Then bottom-line the scene. Focus only on that, and *work to fulfill the need* that the bottom line represents.

One important thing to remember when you go in to audition for a role and you are asked to do a cold reading is to look at the person with whom you are reading as much as possible. Hold the script in such a position that your face is visible and your eyes need to do only a minimum amount of traveling from the other person to the page. Look at the other person for as long as you can as you listen, timing yourself so that a glance to the page will give you your next speech, which you can then deliver without interrup-tion. This way you can maintain a sense of pace and a sense of proper rhythm for the scene, even under cold reading circum-stances. Look and listen to all the stimuli as intently as you can. You'll become very adept at this if you practice.

It's also important to find a physical position that will give the impression of physical involvement. If you read a highly emotional scene with your legs comfortably crossed, your body is going to contradict what is happening in the scene, and although you may read the lines well you will communicate a sense of only partial participation.

In a cold reading you should also indicate the necessary physical actions, such as hitting someone. (Don't hit, but take a partial swing with your hand to show that you know it must happen.) You may rise, sit, or move a step or two toward or away from the person with whom you are reading.

Use physicalizations unless you have been specifically instructed otherwise, so that the director and producer will know that you understand all aspects of the scene. If your reading partner gives you nothing, react as if he did what was required. For instance, if you were supposed to have been hit, move your head as if you had been.

Get a clear idea of your needs in the scene. If you are unsure of what they are, pick something definite out of the possibilities you see. You can't read well if you're uncertain about any part of the scene; make your choice, and believe in it with all your might.

Work from yourself. Don't try to second-guess what the people auditioning you want. The best thing you can give them is yourself. If it isn't right this time, they will at least know what you bring to a role, and you will have brought your best.

Wear the right clothes. If you're going to read or be interviewed for a Western, don't show up in a low-cut cocktail gown or a flashy sport coat and turtleneck. If you're auditioning for the role of a vice-president of a bank, jeans and sweatshirt would be wrong. Dress right because you want the casting group to recognize immediately that you can look the role, so that all their attention can be devoted to your performance and to your personal quality.

Don't go in to an audition saying, "If they can't judge my talent regardless of my clothes, the hell with them!" That's really a cop-out. After all, you're the one who wants the job. And casting the right people in the right roles is difficult. I really believe that actors who resent having to read for a role, or who refuse to do so before they become major stars or supporting players, do so out of fear.

"I'm very talented; I'm just a lousy reader," you might say. No one will accept that. No one is likely to say, "Well, fine. In that case, I'll just give you the lead in my new feature." My advice is that you work your tail off learning to become a good reader. Your career will probably hinge on it. Take a speed-reading course. At the very least, read aloud from any source for at least fifteen minutes a day, taking your eyes off the page as much as you can without interrupting the flow of your reading.

When you go in for an audition, leave your personal problems and any personal unhappiness you might be feeling outside. No one wants to be forced to share your misery, and that's what happens if you wear an unhappy look when you are with others. Whatever the role you're after, be up when you make your entrance. Make everyone feel that they will enjoy having you around. Let them know that you're happy to be alive and happy to be an actor. Let them know that the audience will enjoy looking at you, even if you're going to play the role of a downer.

Does that last one sound like a contradiction? It isn't. The role of a downer should not be a downer to watch, any more than the role of a bored person should be boring to watch. The audience should feel that there is a ray of sunshine under all those clouds.

Remember that every scene should have some changes and dynamics in it. If you can't find them, invent them.

To recap:

1. Study the scene carefully.
2. Bottom-line the scene.
3. Look at the other actor as much as possible, except when your feelings or the moment demand that you look away.
4. Listen intently with all your senses.
5. Find what you need in the scene, and go for it.
6. Find the dynamics and the conflict in the scene.
7. Care as much as you reasonably can about all the circumstances in the scene that affect you.
8. Dress for the role, as much as you reasonably can.
9. Be up when you go in for your reading.
10. Look for the humor and the drama in the scene.

11. Indicate all important business; that is, business that propels the scene.

MONOLOGUES

A word about monologues: Agents and casting directors seem to have a fascination with monologues, which I find hard to understand. They will ask actors and actresses to "bring in a monologue," with the result that monologues take on a unwarranted importance as a necessity in an actor's repertoire. To me, a very important thing to learn about an actor is how that actor relates to another actor, how that actor "listens." Why, then, a monologue? Books of them are published and purchased hungrily. Classes are formed for the express purpose of teaching actors how to do monologues, usually at great cost to the actors. Why? In truth, actors doing so-called "monologues" are often encouraged do them like soliloquies, rather than conversations. "To Be or Not to Be" is a soliloquy; Hamlet is talking to himself, or better still he is speaking his thoughts. An actor doing a monologue in limbo usually winds up doing the same thing.

Actually, the only thing that can be called a monologue is something that is written in limbo, with no reference to anything that happened before or after it. It is a long series of sentences, usually calling for an emotional attitude of some sort, which the actor has to try to figure out. If it is related to something, and is a long speech that is part of a play or screenplay, then it's no longer a monologue. It's simply part of a role, which must be played in relation to all that has happened in that script up to the moment the speech starts.

Jennie's speech near the end of Neil Simon's *Chapter Two* is an excellent example. She says what she says because her new husband has not been able to forget his deceased first wife, and the marriage is now at stake. She loves him and wants the marriage to work; that's what prompts this wonderful speech. And that's what the actress should be dealing with if she chooses to do it. *She's talking to another person and she must relate to what she is "hearing" from him as she speaks*, because that determines where her performance goes as she moves from the beginning of the speech to the end.

This should be true of all "monologues." Forget "monologue"; think "speech in context." Study it in relation to what your bottom line is, and then set out to fulfill that need, making sure you "hear" the obstacles and respond to them. It's a moment in the life of the character, so play it that way.

25

······································

Working with the Director

An actor will work with many directors in his lifetime. Doing television he will work with more directors than in any other medium.

In our Directors' Lab (a class of selected students who work with a different film director each week), the actors quickly learn that every director is different. Each has his own way of getting what he wants, even of interpreting the same scene. It is vital that you learn to work with any directorial approach; in order to do that, you must learn to *listen* to the director.

Actors have a tendency to want to prove to the director that they are way ahead of him at all times. When the director starts to give some piece of direction, many actors will nod and say, "Yes, yes," long before they truly understand what the director wants.

When a director talks to you, it is best to give him 100 percent of your attention. You must not only listen carefully so that you hear every word, but listen with your intelligence and your senses and your craft so that you can grasp the *total* meaning of what he is asking for and the results he is looking for. In other words, a director might say, "Speak a little more slowly," when what he means is that your responses are not honest or that they are rhythmically inaccurate or that you are making the character too perceptive and bright or that he wants you to be puzzled as you speak—there could be any number of things he is really after.

You might logically ask, "Why doesn't he say so?" Well, maybe he himself is not sure what's specifically wrong, only that for him it is wrong.

Not all directors are good directors for actors. You will frequently find yourself receiving no help at all from a director, or hearing such peculiar phrases as, "The scene isn't magenta enough"

(I didn't invent that; an actor told me about it). It doesn't help any-one for you to say that the jerk isn't articulate enough and doesn't know how to get what he wants or doesn't even know what he wants; I have to remind you that in the final analysis it is your mag-nificent face on the screen, and there will be no subtitles offering explanations and cop-outs as to why your performance is not as good as it should have been. I've said it before, but I have to say it again: you must develop your instrument and your craft to such a peak of excellence that your performance will be good no matter what the problems.

So when you listen to the director, give him all your attention and listen with your ears, your emotions, your mind, and your senses. Look for the *full* implication of what he is after; don't make him have to stop you and ask for it three or four or ten times—and perhaps ultimately give up in despair and mumble, "Don't ever hire that actor again." The director is not interested in how smart you are; he is only interested in your final performance.

When the director says "Action," don't wait for inspiration, don't worry about the techniques you've learned, and especially don't worry about the semantics of your approach; just do it.

It doesn't matter if you can't define every beat and every aspect of the scene. If you can't find an infinitive form for the need, don't stop now to hunt for it. The hell with it; play the results if you have to, but start working. You'll be surprised how often just doing it will unlock doors. We stifle ourselves by intel-lectualizing during the performance; don't. There comes a time when all the lessons, all the definitions, and all the intellectualiz-ing need to be thrown away, and that time is when the director calls "Action!"

The more you think, the less you feel. Thinking is for prepara-tion; listening and feeling are for performance. If your preparation has been right, if your training has been any good at all—and if you have some talent—most of what happens will be right. Trust it.

On "Action!" that's what the director expects—no rational-izations, no excuses. He just wants you to start playing the scene. So start.

The television director is the most rushed director of all. His time—both for preparation and for actual filming—is limited. He has the least amount of time to work with actors and very likely the least amount of patience. I must say to the credit of most of the directors I know in the industry, their ability to control their impatience is staggering.

The director wants his actors thoroughly prepared. He wants them to have studied the script and the role. He wants them to understand the role in relation to the other roles. He wants the actors to make contributions, but not to fight to the death for them to be accepted. Very often a director will say, "Let's see what you've got." He wants to be able to listen to your ideas and say yes or no. If he says no, that should be the end of it; if he says yes, he wants to feel that you can implement your own ideas and deliver what you have just offered.

Speaking of contributions: when you feel an honest impulse to do something, do it. If you feel like touching the other actor, do it. If you feel like moving, do it. If a piece of business occurs to you, do it. I said "an honest impulse," not just something you thought of at home or that you saw another actor do, or that you think might be good. An honest impulse is a rare thing, so let it happen. Don't censor it, or frustrate it. Do it. The worst that can happen is that the director will say, "Don't do that," or "That doesn't work." He won't fire you, because it's too costly in terms of time and money to start trying to replace you at this time. It's much quicker and cheaper to just say, "Don't do that." On the other hand, if it's really good—and if it came from an honest impulse it probably will be—he may kiss your feet, because you brought something fresh to his work. So make sure you wear clean socks every day!

The director would also like to know that he can give you a piece of direction once and that you will carry it out. He wants you to know your craft so that you won't start before he says "Action" and you won't stop before he says "Cut." He wants to know that you care about your work and that you have respect for your profession and your fellow performers.

The director would also like to feel that if he doesn't give you any direction at all, you will still deliver a good performance. If he

can count on that, he will hire you often. Remember, he may have
to count on that; his time is limited, whether for a major feature,
a documentary, or a commercial being made in a small city. When
he is doing a television series, the very nature of the beast frequently makes it mandatory that he give all of his time to the stars
and little or no time to the guest actors, particularly those not in
the guest star category.

Remember, too, that before the first day of shooting, the director has probably spent a hectic period of time picking locations,
helping to cast, and doing his own directorial preparation for each
scene to be filmed. He must concern himself with the time allotted each day for the work to be done and must decide which
sequences should be given the most time and care and which the
least. He is on the set early, and he is undoubtedly working late at
night to prepare himself for the next day's work. If he seems to
expect miracles from you, it is understandable. If he seems to have
little time for you, it is understandable, even if it is discomforting.
That's why he would like to have the very reassuring knowledge
that when he hires you, he is hiring an actor who will be prepared,
who knows his craft, who will behave professionally at all times,
and who will, with or without help, deliver a performance that is
good and inventive and will help make his picture look good.

How do you work with a director who yells and screams at
you? That question was asked of me by one of my former students
when she went to work in a major feature film. It was being directed by a top Hollywood director who had a reputation for yelling
and screaming at actors and embarrassing them in front of the
crew and other members of the cast.

My advice to her is my advice to everyone: no director has a
right to insult you and degrade you in front of the company, or
even when you're alone, for that matter. There are a number of
directors in the industry who do work that way, and there's no
doubt in my mind that in virtually all cases, their need is sadistic
and should not be tolerated.

What I told the actress was: Let him yell for the first day or two.
Once he has a couple of days of your work on film, he will have an
enormous investment in you. Then when he yells or insults you, go

to him quite calmly and say, "Sir, I cannot work when you're yelling and screaming at me. It upsets me, and I can't function. So I'm going to my dressing room and I will be there when you're ready to resume work on a mature, calm, creative basis." Then turn around and walk to your dressing room.

Let the director threaten you, let the studio threaten you, let them raise hell as much as they want to. The point is you are not in breach of your contract; they are. I'm sure your union will stand behind you, and I'm sure your director will realize that he has made a mistake in his approach to you.

I do suggest that you do not make a public scene out of this moment, but rather take him aside and do it quietly so that he can back down without losing face. I promise you that you will win your point, because it will be too expensive to replace you and reshoot the material.

26

•••••••••••••••••••••••••••••••••

Working from the
Outside In—Or Not

There has been a lot of discussion among acting teachers and actors about whether to work from the inside-out or from the outside-in.

First, let's define the terms. Working from the "outside-in" means starting your character preparation with his external appearances and behaviors. For example, it is my understanding that Laurence Olivier, perhaps the most famous exponent of the outside-in approach, looked first for the physical attributes when he played Othello. How would he walk? How would he talk to people? What would his posture be? What have I seen other actors do who were playing similar roles?

All good questions. Having determined what are probably the correct answers to those questions and changing himself accordingly, the actor is ready to begin rehearsals.

Using the physical attributes would presumably help generate the feelings called for in the performance. There's no doubt that they might. They would certainly affect the actor in some way. The question is, what is the correct result? If you walk stooped over for a little while, your psyche begins to be affected. You will develop certain attitudes that might be different from those you normally hold. If your choice of physical attitude is correct, you may even generate some proper feelings out of this.

But the process is this: you *thought* of something, applied it, and something else happened as a result. This whole thing is an *intellectual* approach to finding how to play the role. It may lead into the reasons for those physicalizations, and if it does, good. But then again, it may lead to an intellectual, nonempathetic performance. There is also the danger that this may lead you into *playing the job*, rather than *the person who happens to be holding that job*.

Not all doctors walk the same way, or even think the same way. Not all accountants are stoop-shouldered, and not all army majors stand straight and tall. So you have to play *the person* who happens to be in some particular job—*and every person in that kind of job is an individual.*

Now let's talk "inside out." By now I'm sure you know where my heart is.

The problem with the "outside-in" approach above is that the best physicalizations can only be the result of an inner impulse. The way we walk, the way we look at or don't look at other people, the way we handle objects, are all the result of how we *feel.* Therefore, it seems to me that the first and most important thing we must touch in the role is what the person we are playing *needs,* and how he *feels* about things. That's what our preparation must find for us. The clues are almost always clearly laid out in the material, in the ways the author has given us to respond to the stimuli which hit us throughout the script. Once we give ourselves over to the feelings, they will begin to generate the proper physicalizations, and those physicalizations will be true ones, because they came from an honest feeling, not from some cerebral idea of how the character might act or look.

Let's suppose you are playing the head of a major corporation. Big job, big pay, very big power. How would you walk? You would walk head up, with powerful strides. How would you deal with people? With authority. What would your rhythm be like? How quickly would you cross the normal bridges you would be dealing with? Answer: quickly. Good.

Now you look closely at the script. There are scenes about how long it takes you to make a decision. You're in scenes in which you hesitate, in which you don't seem to know the subject as well as others. You discover that you inherited the business from your father; you didn't build it. Maybe you didn't even want it. But you control most of the stock, so you are "The Boss."

Well, that's different. You'd better start feeling your insecurities rather than your position in the company. Once you do that, you may begin to understand that you're not as smart as some of your underlings, so you begin to retreat into yourself—the head comes down as part of that. You don't have all the answers; your rhythm slows down, because you don't want to move too fast and make a mistake. Your stomach hurts, and you may hunch a little to ease that pain. By now you're totally different physically than when you started out with an intellectual concept of "The Boss."

This physical persona would be much more effective, because it would be the result of your inner activity, the result of your being the kind of person you are. The outer you and the inner you would be completely in synch, and therefore very real. Because that is true, the inner and outer would help each other get you to the fullest reaches of the role you are playing. The outer you would have been shaped almost without effort, almost automatically, because it was the inevitable result of what you are internally.

In a perfect world, I would opt for a combination of the two approaches, with the proviso that the outside-in work come only after a great deal of study and thought about the inner workings of the character. Then the inner and outer can work together, and be tried and experimented with on an inner path. If the things you tried externally don't seem to be right at this later stage, then dump them. Go with what happens naturally as a result of *feelings* and *need*.

27

•••••••••••••••••••••••••••••••••••••

In a Nutshell

OK. You want the preceding pages in a nutshell? You've done your preparation very thoroughly, and now you want to know what to do when the director calls, "Action"? This is it:

STOP ACTING, START LISTENING.

PLAY THE BOTTOM LINE FOR
EACH MOMENT OR SCENE.

PLAY ONE MOMENT AT A TIME,
AND KEEP IT SIMPLE, WITHOUT LOSS
OF PASSION. (LESS IS NOT MORE!)

COMMIT YOURSELF!

HAVE FUN! YOU DON'T HAVE
TO SUFFER TO BE GREAT!

IF YOU ARE HAVING A PROBLEM,
JUST ASK YOURSELF, "WHAT IS THE TRUTH
ABOUT HOW THE PERSON 'I HAVE BECOME'
WOULD SPEAK AND BEHAVE IN
THESE CIRCUMSTANCES?"
YOU'LL FIND ALL THE ANSWERS IN
THE SAME PLACE—IN THE TRUTH.

That's it. And you thought it was complicated!

The Machinery of Film and Tape

28

Day One on the Set

The director is ready. And there you are on a motion picture soundstage for the first time in your life, ready to start work on your first film role.

It's a very strange place to be. You're apprehensive. You're frightened. There are so many strange and unfamiliar things, unfamiliar sounds, and unfamiliar words.

You look up. Above the set there is a platform on which lights are mounted. Electricians are moving around on the platform, adjusting the lights at the command of the gaffer, who is responding to the wishes of the cinematographer.

Suddenly you are startled by an object snaking out over your head—the boom. You notice the camera mounted on an unfamiliar wagon of sorts. Someone is standing behind it, prepared to push it, along with the operator and the focus operator, who sit on it. Someone runs a tape measure from the camera to your face and makes a note somewhere.

You've been given your starting position, and the rehearsal has begun. You're told to move here, then there. Each time you stop where the director tells you to stop, someone sticks a piece of masking tape on the floor at your feet. The camera follows you around, slowly, because the people operating it aren't too sure yet where you and they are going. The cinematographer watches and calls for light adjustments, and the person on the boom talks quietly to someone you can't see.

"You're in her key light!" You. The statement is made to you. You realize you are casting a shadow on the face of the actress near you, and you jump back. You sneak a look; you notice there is a spotlight shining on her face.

The rehearsal continues. The operator wants you to make one move more slowly. The boom operator wants you to speak up a little. You get through the scene, and someone yells, "Second team!"

What? The other actors in the scene move away; you figure you'd better do the same. You watch another group of actors move to where you were standing.

In a little while the assistant director calls, "First team!" The other actors from your scene move toward the set; you do, too. You all move to your starting positions.

Now you rehearse again. You're beginning to tense up; you're close to actually doing the scene. You finish rehearsing the scene. The director says, "Let's go for a take." The assistant director calls for quiet. The other actors move to their first positions; you do the same.

"Roll it!" That was the assistant director. A pause. "Rolling," someone says. A buzz. "Speed," another voice says. You hear, "Fourteen, take one." A person holding a small blackboard-type object places it in front of your face, then slaps a hinged portion of it down on the larger section, which carries some names and symbols. "Action!" the director says.

This is it. The scene starts. Halfway through it, the director says, "Cut!" You turn to him. "Let's do it again," he says. Why did he stop you? He doesn't say. You go back to your first position, and the ritual repeats itself. This time you do the entire scene. The director calls, "Cut!" then says, "Print it."

He moves on to the set, with the cinematographer at his heels. He points out what he wants next, and you find you are in the way. You quietly move off the set a short distance. In a while, someone calls your name. It's your close-up. The makeup person checks your makeup. The ritual starts again and repeats until the director says, "Cut! Print it!"

This action goes on all day. Finally, the director says, "That's a wrap." Everyone relaxes. You're given your call for tomorrow by the assistant director, and the crew begins to put the equipment away for the night.

You've had your first day in film. You're excited, worried, happy, full of questions about what went on around you, and curious about many of the words you heard for the first time.

You wish you had heard them before.

What I described above is what happened to me on my first day on a movie set. Keep reading. It won't happen to you.

29

The Motion Picture Studio and the Soundstage

Although filmmakers are using actual locations more and more, the motion picture studio and the soundstage still remain the heart of the industry.

The typical motion picture studio is made up of a number of soundstages and numerous auxiliary buildings and departments involved in the making of a film. There are projection rooms, editing rooms, dubbing stages, music stages, scene shops, prop shops, makeup rooms and shops, costume shops, special effects shops, metal working shops, offices, publicity and accounting departments, executive offices, and, in most cases, a fire department right on the studio premises.

The soundstage, which is where you will undoubtedly do most of your acting, is usually nothing more than a very large and rather high room that seems more like a warehouse than a center of creative activity. It is soundproof—at least to a degree—and has almost nothing in it until someone is ready to use the stage for the making of a film. At that point, lights are brought in. The sets, which were constructed in the shops, are brought in, assembled, and given final touch-up. Props and set dressing are added. Usually makeup tables with lights and mirrors are brought in, and even small trailers that serve as dressing rooms for the leading actors.

It is unfortunately true that soundstages are frequently cold in the winter and hot in the summer, in spite of the best efforts to control the temperatures. They do not have the glamour of a theater, and there is almost a sense of clutter and even confusion surrounding the making of a motion picture. However, the magic is there; if the work is good, all the confusion and distractions seem to disappear when the real work begins.

The back lot (a studio area containing sets of exteriors such as Western streets, New York streets, and river ports) is rapidly becoming a thing of the past in Hollywood. The real estate on which the studios sit is so expensive that it is no longer economically practical to preserve the many exterior streets and sets that have been built over the years to accommodate various productions. Twentieth Century-Fox had a magnificent back lot that is now Century City, and MGM has sold everything but its main studio property. Universal has a substantial back lot, and The Burbank Studios (which used to be Warner Brothers) has some back lot available. Producers working out of The Burbank Studios will also use the nearby Ranch, which offers a number of exterior sets and locations as well as having several soundstages.

Security systems at all the studios are strong, and entry is difficult without a pass. If you are coming to Hollywood and have never been to a motion picture studio, I suggest that you take the tour at Universal. It is dressed up considerably for the public, but if you get a proper guide and take the tour on a good day, you will at least see what the soundstages and back lot look like, and you will get some idea of what is really involved in the making of a motion picture. You won't really understand it all until you begin to work as an actor, and, of course, we expect that that will be very soon.

30

Some Specifics of Film

I have mentioned that film demands simplicity and subtlety in performance. The physicalizations need not be as large as in the theater because the audience is usually only a few feet away, disguised as a camera and a microphone. The acting tools that we talked about will indeed apply to acting wherever it happens, and they will work in film if the actor remembers that the distance of communication must be taken into consideration. Film presents other elements, however, which are peculiar to itself and are not part of the theater.

Filmed performances are recorded on two separate media. The picture, or image, is recorded on film, in principle the same way as home movies or still pictures. The sound is recorded on magnetic tape in a totally separate process. The film is sent to the lab, the negative is developed, and a copy (or *print*) of all the material that was acceptable to the director—the good *takes*—is sent to the producing company. The sound, which was recorded on tape in conjunction with the film, is transferred to *magstripe*, which is nothing more than blank film with a strip of one-quarter-inch magnetic tape on it.

The film editor now takes the two separate components (the *work print*, which carries the picture, and the magstripe, which carries the sound), synchronizes them, and begins the process of selecting those pieces of film and sound that will ultimately make up the finished structure of the picture.

When the filmed sequences are assembled in a way that is satisfactory to the director and producer, sound effects and music are added. The various sound elements are put on different pieces of tape. Finally, all the sound tapes are united through a process called dubbing. All the audio portions of the final motion picture are joined and balanced, then transferred, with the picture and visual optical effects, to the final film.

171

On that film the sound is no longer represented magnetically; it is represented optically, by a thin strip of varying light patterns at one side of the picture. Those light patterns will be translated back into sound when the film goes through the projector. The final combination of picture and sound on one strip of film is called a *composite*.

Now let's define some terms. I assume you will be familiar with at least some of them.

Camera. A camera is the instrument that houses the film on which your glorious face is imprinted forever. There are many kinds of cameras, and each camera works with many kinds of lenses. Lenses of long focal length will photograph a smaller area—a close-up area—and lenses of a short focal length will photograph wider areas. To add to your confusion, I want to tell you that the higher the focal length number of the lens, the smaller the picture. In other words, the smaller the number, the larger the picture; the bigger the number, the smaller the picture. Got that?

Figure 30.1 illustrates different effects achieved by merely altering the focal length of the camera lens, while maintaining the same positions by actors and camera. A 50-millimeter lens was used for the wide shot. The second shot was taken with a 150-millimeter lens.

Camera dolly. A camera dolly is a wheeled platform that holds the camera and the camera operator, plus the focus operator. There are many kinds. The two best-known types are these:

1. *Crab dolly*. A unit designed to move like a crab. It can move forward, back, or at any side angle with a simple adjustment of the wheels.
2. *Chapman crane*. A very large unit mounted on a truck. The camera is mounted at the end of a long, counterweighted arm. There is provision for the operator, director, and focus operator to sit at the camera. The arm is raised or lowered or rotated sideways by hand, by a grip standing on the ground or on the bed of the truck. The carrier itself is battery-powered when filming, so that its movement is silent.

Figure 30.1   Effect of size of camera lens on the picture. Top, a wide shot on a 50-millimeter lens. Bottom, the same scene taken with a 150-millimeter lens.

The boom. The microphone is usually connected to the end of an arm on a moveable platform, the boom, on which sits a sound man who must make sure that the microphone is always pointed in the right direction and is as close to the actor as it can be without being in the picture. (Sometimes the microphone gets into the picture, and sometimes it's even more interesting to watch than the actor, but even then such accidents are not desirable.)

The microphones used are extremely sensitive, so it is not necessary for actors to use a great deal of volume when speaking. The simplest rule is to speak to the other person in relation to his distance from you, as if there were no microphone present. Speak softly if you are in an embrace, a little more forcefully if you are seated across from the other actor at a table, and with a good deal more volume if you and the other actor are shouting at each other from opposite ends of a football stadium. Speak as if the situation were real; the microphone will do the rest.

Lights. Lights are numerous in style, form, and function. All you need to know about the lights is that a *key light* is usually directed toward your face, and general lighting and fill-light illuminate the set. Be aware that the other actor in the scene also has a key light on him, and if you see a heavy shadow suddenly fall across his face, see if you are causing it. If you are, shift your position slightly before the leading man gives you a belt in the mouth or before you drive the cinematographer up the walls.

Movieola. The Movieola is a machine used by the film editor to do his preliminary editorial work. All the material that has been filmed, together with the corresponding sound tracks, is sent to the editor. It is coded so that every frame can be identified. The editor then begins the initial work of putting together the finished product. The director will frequently work with him, and together they will ultimately reach what is called the *director's cut*, the film assembled as the director visualizes it. Generally speaking, the producer will have the final word on the editing, unless the director is one of those rare birds who has the contractual right of final cut. Under the best circumstances, the final version is a cooperative effort between editor, director, and producer.

Since the first edition of this book was written, the film editing process has changed radically. Most of the preliminary editing is now done electronically, using videotape and electronic editing machines. The film is transferred to videotape after each day's work;

it is all coded carefully so any frame can be found quickly. The various tapes of the film shot are place in synchronized videotape machines, and the electronic editing equipment makes it possible to switch from one tape to another in seconds. The edits are done electronically, and can be changed quickly over and over again so that many editing ideas can be considered, and all versions can be saved for reference. All this work is done in seconds; no manual splicing is necessary until the final cut is achieved, and then the negative is cut and spliced to conform to what was determined electronically. If the director wants to see a version on a big theater-sized screen, the desired sequences are printed and edited manually based on what has been done electronically.

Master shot. The master shot is a wide shot that includes one or more actors. It tracks with the movement of the performers in the scene. A master shot may be uninterrupted from the beginning of a scene to the end of a scene, or it may be interrupted several times because the director knows that he will break it up in its finally edited form anyway.

Two-shot. A two-shot includes both people in the scene. (See Figure 30.2.)

Figure 30.2   A two-shot.

Figure 30.3   A pair of over-the-shoulder shots.

Over-the-shoulder. This is a shot in which we look across the back of one actor to the face of the other. Over-the-shoulder shots are almost always done in pairs so that the camera looks at both backs and both actors from similar, but opposite, vantage points. (See Figure 30.3.)

Close-up. A close-up is a shot that includes only the face, or the neck and face, or (in a looser version) the neck and face and shoulders, of one actor. For close-ups, the on-camera actor is lighted and placed carefully; the off-camera actor stands alongside the camera and plays his portion of the scene from there. Unfortunately, many times the off-camera actor, knowing he is not being filmed, will save his energy and not give much of a performance. That leaves the on-camera actor to do whatever needs to be done to make his performance responsive to what the off-camera actor will do on film, and not what he is now doing off camera. In some instances the other actor will not even be there; his lines may be read by a script supervisor or by the director. Some stars do not feel that it is necessary or worthwhile for them to spend their time and energy working when they are not on camera. That attitude is rude and unprofessional, but it does exist.

When I came to Hollywood and got my first film-acting job, I had no idea about the special nature of acting in films. When the director came to me after the first master and said, "Okay, now we do your close-up, don't move," I played the scene terrified that I might move and the world would come to an end. When I saw the film, I almost made the director's world come to an end; I was as stiff as a board.

You *can* move in a close-up; just remember that your face is all that is on the screen, and there are certain limits to how much you can move. Ask the director what those limits are, and then relax and behave normally within those limits.

Bust shot. This is a shot of a single actor, framed at the bust.
Waist shot. This is a shot framed at the waist.
Full shot. A full shot is framed at the feet, or beyond.

If you're not sure what the director is shooting and, therefore, how much of you will be visible to the camera, there is no harm in asking him what kind of shot it is and where it is framed. He will not resent you for asking, and you will avoid ruining the take by doing something inappropriate.

Figure 30.4   Setting the mark for actor's position.

Hitting the mark. When a scene is staged by a director, the actors' positions become critical, so marks are generally put on the floor to indicate the position of your feet at the end of each move. (See Figure 30.4.) You will be expected to move to those marks without looking at them so that the audience will be unaware that you are moving to a predetermined location. It may sound frightening at first, but the technique is really logical and simple. Count the paces from the mark to your starting point and then simply turn around and take that number of paces. After you have practiced this technique for a while, you will find that it is quite easy and demands very little of your attention. A better device is to use a piece of furniture as a reference point. The edge of a desk or the arm of a chair might easily become your mark. Of course, if you are moving to another actor who is standing still, that actor may supply all the information you need to reach the proper mark.

The need to hit a mark with reasonable accuracy is determined by the needs of the camera and the cinematographer. The entire set is not lighted, as a stage would be. Since the light values are critical to a good cinematographer, he will carefully light faces against backgrounds and fill-lights so that color and shading have cinematic value. It is necessary for the actor to be where the lights have been focused, since they cannot follow him around.

Another important element that necessitates hitting the mark is camera focus. When a position for the camera is determined, it is still necessary for a camera assistant to measure the distance from the camera to your face and then set the focus. If you or the camera then move, the focus must be measured and noted again at the new position.

When you do not hit your mark, you also adversely affect the composition of the shot. Most importantly, you may block another actor if you are off your mark.

Matching. A filmed scene is made up of many pieces. The usual procedure is to shoot a master shot, which includes the content of the scene in a wide shot covering as much of the scene as possible, and then to go in for *coverage*, which includes close-ups and over-the-shoulder shots. The various pieces are then put together in a series so that there is a continuous and connected and logical action on the screen. It is important, therefore, that what the actor does in the master shot is repeated almost exactly in the over-the-shoulders and close-ups; in other words, in all the coverage.

Let me give you an example. In a master shot, the actor says, "It's time to go to the store," picks up a cup of coffee, takes a sip, holds the coffee in front of his face, and says, "I wish I didn't have to." In the over-the-shoulder, the actor doesn't pick up the cup of coffee; he just says, "It's time to go to the store. I wish I didn't have to." If the director and the editor decide to go from the master shot to the over-the-shoulder at that point, they will have the actor saying, "It's time to go to the store," picking up a cup of coffee, and holding it in front of his face, and then they will cut to a close-up in which there is no coffee being held in front of the actor's face. Obviously, that sequence would be ridiculous, and the director and editor would be forced into choices they didn't want to make. When a problem is serious enough, the company must reshoot part of a sequence, and that's very expensive.

Here is another example. (This is a gross error, but I'm using it for the sake of illustration.) Suppose you're playing a two-page scene, and you start the master standing up, then you sit in the middle of the scene. The next day, when you shoot the close-up, you sit down after the first line. Now when the director tries to go from the master to the close-up, he will be intercutting from you standing, to you sitting, and back to you standing, without ever seeing you make the move. Obviously, that's an impossible situation.

The script supervisor has the primary responsibility for making sure that movements match, that clothes match, that hairdos match, and that tears match. However, it is also your responsibility to know what you're doing and to make sure that you are properly matching your sequences. There are instances where it may not matter whether a small piece of business is duplicated in master and close-up, since the director knows he may ultimately use only one or the other, but that is a decision for the director to consciously make, and not one that should be forced upon the production team because of a mistake made by you and the script supervisor.

Setup. Every new camera position or change in photographic composition is called a "setup."

Overlapping. In most circumstances one microphone is used to cover a scene. When you are doing your close-up, the microphone will be very close to you, and there will be no microphone near the off-camera actor working with you. As a result, your voice will be recorded with clarity and with presence, but the other actor's voice will sound distant and booming. It is important that your voice and his never overlap when you are doing a close-up, because if they do, the mixed sound of a clear voice and a booming voice will be unpleasant and unnatural. There must be at least a tiny pause so that your dialogue, clear and present, can be separated from the off-camera dialogue; then, later, the clear and present dialogue of the other actor, taken from his close-up, will be tied to yours.

There will be instances when more than one microphone will be used or when the mike and actors will be set in such a position that an overlap will not only be acceptable, but perhaps desirable. Whether or not to overlap will be for the director to decide. The general rule to remember is that when you are doing close-ups, do not overlap the other actor, whether you're on-camera or off-camera.

Even when you have an interrupted speech, you must not over-lap; you must interrupt it yourself, or if you are doing the interrupt-ing, you must not begin speaking until the other actor has stopped. The feeling will be strange in the beginning because you will seem to be left dangling, but the procedure is technically necessary.

Cheating. Frequently the film actor is asked to cheat. (This does not refer to hanky-panky with your costar.) Because of the needs of the camera, an actor sometimes has to assume a physical posi-tion that is not natural in real life, or he has to look at something other than the person or thing upon which he is supposed to be focused. You may have to cheat your physical position by tipping slightly from what would otherwise be natural and comfortable, because the camera needs you to be lower or higher or a shade to the left or right. In Figure 30.5 Joanne is looking down at someone seated. Because her eyes are not visible, she must "cheat" her looks upward.

A more common problem that demands cheating occurs when an actor leans out to make direct contact with a partner's eyes. In Figure 30.6, Joanne is leaning out, and as a result, is blocking her partner. She must cheat her look, playing the scene to Heaths's left eye, or even his ear. Of course, the audience must never be aware that you are cheating; everything that finally appears on the film must look natural, and comfortable.

Sometimes you will be asked to cheat the rhythm of a move-ment because the camera operator has difficulty following you, or because the shot is such that the rhythmic effect on film would give the illusion of being different from what you and the director want it to be at that moment.

One frequently encountered mechanical reason for cheating the speed of a movement is in the extreme close-up of the telephone. When the hand comes into the shot, lifts the receiver, and carries it to the ear, the hand must always move a little more slowly than is nat-ural; otherwise, it will appear to be moving at an extraordinarily fast clip, and the camera operator will very likely be unable to follow it.

There are innumerable cases in which you might be asked to cheat a look or a position. You must do it, and it is your obligation

Figure 30.5   Cheating a look. Top, the actress is looking down at someone seated. Her eyes are not visible. Bottom, the actress is looking higher, cheating her look to the top of the off-screen actor's head. Now we can see her eyes.

to make it look natural and to continue to deliver the same performance you would deliver if you were unencumbered by the cheat.

Spatial relationships to other actors. Film actors are placed inside a frame (the screen), where the space around them affects the

Figure 30.6   Cheating a look. Top, to make eye contact with actor, actress turns the back of her head to the camera and blocks the actor. Bottom, actress clears her partner by cheating her look, focusing on actor's left eye or ear.

viewers' perception of the space between them, causing an illusion of distance that is different from true distance. The true spatial relationship between actors is often seen as untrue from the point of view of the audience. Frequently, therefore, it becomes necessary for an actor to play so close to another actor as to feel uncomfortable at first, but such placement by the director is correct and even necessary because the audience will perceive the distance as correct. A space of only a few inches between faces will feel awkward to the actor, but it will seem perfectly natural to the viewer.

If the director wants a tight two-shot, he can't achieve it with the actors placed as they are at the top of Figure 30.7, where they are about two feet apart, a natural conversational distance. Instead, the actors must move closer—to within a foot of each other—and play the scene there. As you can see from the bottom of Figure 30.7, that spatial relationship seems perfectly natural, even though the actors may at first feel uncomfortable close.

Take. A take refers to a scene that is actually being filmed, as opposed to a rehearsal.

"Print it." This phrase is used by the director to indicate that the take just completed is good, and that a print of it should be made.

Pickup. The term "pickup" is used by the director to indicate that he wants to redo a small portion of a scene. When a scene is good until a certain point and then falters, the director will pick up the scene near that point and go on to the end. Or he may want to do another take of a section of a scene that has just been printed. In other words, the director may like all of a two- or three-minute scene except for one moment that doesn't work as well as he wants it to, or a moment when an actor fumbled with a line and then corrected it. Knowing how the film will be edited, the director knows that he can go back and just pick up a few lines without having to reshoot the entire scene.

Action. This is the word the director uses when he wants the actors to start performing. You *must* wait for him to say "action," because otherwise you might start the scene before the film is rolling or up to speed or before the technicians involved are ready.

Cut. This word is the director's instruction to stop the scene.

Figure 30.7   Spatial relationship necessary for film acting. Top, actors are about two feet apart, natural conversational distance for real life, but too far apart for acceptable film composition. Bottom, actors are within a foot of each other, uncomfortable spacing for real life but right for the camera.

Interruptions. During a take there might be some kind of distraction. It is generally best for the actor to ignore it.

For instance, if one of the stagehands kicks over a light, your first impulse might be to stop. However, it is best never to stop until the director says "Cut," just as you must never start until the director says "Action." If the scene is going well, the director may not want to stop it, even though he knows that he will have to pick up the particular moment where the light was dropped. It is even possible that the light was dropped at a point where for one reason or another, the sound track won't be used, or it may have been dropped during a pause, so the editor can easily eliminate the sound.

Sometimes, the director will talk to the actors in a scene without interrupting the take. He might ask you to repeat a line or two or to go back and pick up the scene from a given point. When this happens, don't break focus; don't break concentration. Try to give the director what he is asking for without making it necessary to stop rolling the film.

A director sometimes feels it necessary to talk an actor through a scene while the camera is rolling. That is his choice and his right, and it is important that you learn to be able to take such direction without breaking focus and without breaking concentration.

If, during the course of a scene, you bobble a line, there are several alternatives available to you. The least desirable is that you stop. Let the director be the one to say "Cut." You should go on, on the assumption that the director might like the way the scene is going and will come back and do a pickup to cover the bobble. He might even like the bobble if it has a natural sound to it. In many cases, the director will instruct you to go back a line and pick it up, without stopping the camera. Experience will help you decide how you want to go at it.

My advice is to continue the scene if the bobble is small, and then when it's over, and the director has said "Cut," make sure that he is aware that you bobbled. If there is a serious mistake, or if you have gone blank and forgotten your line, interrupt the scene by simply saying, "I'm sorry, I blew it," and the director will then decide whether he wants to call "Cut" or keep the cameras rolling and guide you to a new start.

The actor's call. You can expect to be called at least an hour before the first assistant director anticipates that you will be needed.

Usually the assistant will protect himself by calling you even earlier than that. As soon as you arrive, report to the assistant director so he knows you're there.

If you will be working in the first setups planned for the morning, you will probably be called to come in to makeup and wardrobe any time from an hour to three hours before the start of work, depending on how complicated your makeup will be. In most cases an hour is about the allotted time.

I suggest that you make a point of being on the stage at least a half hour before your call. First, that kind of planning allows for unforeseen delays on the way to the studio. More importantly, however, the extra time allows you to acquaint yourself with the set in which you are going to work. You should become familiar with the furniture and the props, the look of the set and the feel of it, particularly if the set is supposed to be your home or office—in other words, a place where you live.

All too frequently, actors walk into a set to play a scene and never do anything to give the impression that they really live there and are familiar with the furniture and the props. But it is important for the actor to appear to "belong" in his own home or office, for much of what we call truth is affected by how one relates to one's surroundings, and it is vital that you are familiar with, understand, use, and respond to, your environment. A familiarity with your physical surroundings will often trigger some interesting acting values, or even emotional values.

Unless you are on actual locations, your environment is unreal, but it must never appear so to you, because if it does, it will appear so to the audience. Even on real locations, you should get to the location in plenty of time to make a strange place a familiar one. You must learn to create your environment—to make the heat, or the cold, or the desolation, *real* to the point where it affects how you feel and what you do.

Another very important reason for being on time, and even early, is that the cost of a crew and actors who might be sitting around waiting for you is enormous. Professionalism includes courtesy to the producer, the studio, and the director, as well as to the actors and technicians with whom you will be working. It is unfair and unprofessional for you to cause the studio to spend large amounts of money just because your discipline is poor. Be on time, and be prepared.

The film crew. The film crew, whether it be for a TV episode or a feature film, is large. A feature, with its larger budget and often more complicated needs, might have a substantially larger crew than that of the TV episode, but the basic group is the same. It includes the following:

1. *The camera crew.*
   A. *The cinematographer.* The cinematographer is responsible for the photographic excellence of the film. He is responsible for the lighting, choice of proper film, the proper exposure, the correct use of lenses to fulfill the director's creative needs, and for supervising the entire crew. The actor is definitely affected by the cinematographer's needs. Your position might need to be altered, even made uncomfortable in special circumstances, to accommodate some special requirement of the camera. You will have to be accurate about when and how you move, or the work of the cinematographer and the camera operator will be for naught.
   B. *The camera operator.* The camera operator actually handles the camera during the shooting. He follows the actors, tilting or panning as required. He is responsible for achieving the final composition, as it was determined by the director and cinematographer.
   C. *The focus operator.* This crew member is responsible for making sure that the actors are always in focus. Before the take, the focus operator measures the actual distances from camera to performers, and he must make sure that the focus knob on the camera is turned to accurately accommodate the actor-to-lens distances throughout the take.
   D. *The dolly pusher.* A member of the Grip department, the dolly pusher is responsible for moving the camera dolly to

positions predetermined by the director, so that each moment in the scene will be filmed from the position the director wants. The position of the dolly also determines the position of the camera in relation to the actors, so the composition is also dependent on the accuracy and smoothness of the dolly pusher's moves.

E. *The film loader* or *camera assistant*. This crew member is the general all-around helper. He loads the film into the camera as needed and he may also hold the slate. The slate is a small blackboard-type device that carries information needed to identify each setup: name of company, name of production number (or both) of film being shot, director, cinematographer, day or night sequence, date, and whether the film is accompanied by sound or is silent. The assistant holds the slate where the camera can photograph it. When the camera and the sound recorder have reached speed, the assistant lets the arm of the slate fall against the slate itself, creating a sharp slap that the editor can then use to synchronize the sound track and the picture track.

   The slate brings to mind an amusing Hollywood legend, perhaps true, perhaps not. It seems that in the early days of talkies a scene was being shot without sound. Since the scene was silent, the slate person wanted to know how to mark the slate so that the editor would not go crazy looking for a nonexistent sound track. The director was one of the Hungarian directors who dominated the film industry at that time; without hesitation, he said, "Mark it 'Mitout sound.'" So the slate carried the abbreviation "M.O.S.," mitout sound, a designation that is still in use.

2. *The sound crew.*
   A. *The mixer.* The mixer is the crew chief. He is responsible for the overall quality of the sound. Wearing earphones, he sits at the tape recorder, starting and stopping the audiotape as needed. He adjusts the gain level of the tape

recorder when required, making sure that the actors' dialogue is in the clear and that no unwanted sounds are being recorded.

B. *The boom operator.* There is usually only one boom operator, but there may be more. The operator is responsible for making sure that the microphone is in the best position to pick up dialogue as the scene is played. He must move the microphone as the actors move, keeping it turned in the proper direction to favor the speaking actor at all times. He may actually be on a boom, or he may handle a fishpole, which is a long, lightweight pole holding the microphone. The fishpole is designed to allow microphone coverage in places a boom cannot reach.

C. *Cablemen.* They are general all-around helpers.

3. *The lighting crew.*
   A. *The gaffer.* As the crew chief, the gaffer is responsible for making sure the proper equipment is available and functioning. He is an important aide to the cinematographer. The gaffer often makes a significant creative contribution by setting lights so that the final picture will have the feeling the director and cinematographer are seeking.
   B. *The "best boy."* He is the assistant crew chief.
   C. *Operators.* They handle the lighting instruments.
   D. *Generator operator.* One or more generator operators are needed when the company is on location and generators are used.

4. *The Grips.*
   A. *The head grip.* He is the crew chief. His crew is responsible for all sets, carpentry, handling of sun reflectors, and movement of camera dollies.
   B. *Grips.* The number of grips varies, depending upon the needs of the filming unit on any given day.

5. *The prop department.* This department consists of property master and assistants. Their responsibility is to provide the

sets and actors with all necessary dressing and props. The prop men can sometimes be the actor's best friend, especially when the actor comes up with a wonderful idea that requires a new prop that the wonderfully efficient prop master happens to have on hand.

6. *The wardrobe department.* Members of this department are responsible for all wardrobe and wardrobe needs.

7. *The makeup department.* Members of this department are responsible for all makeup. Actors rarely put on their own makeup in films. The makeup artist is often exactly that—an artist. He may turn out to be your best friend.

8. *Drivers, still photographers, animal handlers, etc.*

9. *The first assistant director.* He is responsible for keeping order on the set and for making sure that production keeps moving. The production manager and producer depend on him to make sure that the director is not delayed, and also for making sure that the director himself does not delay production. The assistant's ability to keep the director moving depends on the power of the particular director in question, but in television episodes, the first assistant director seems to be there all the time, prodding the director and urging him to get the planned amount of shooting done each day.

10. *The second assistant director* (and third, etc.). They handle the many details involved in preparation. They will set up actors' calls, call actors, go hunt for them if they are not in place on the set when they are needed, and take care of many, many other details that make a day's shooting possible.

31

• •

Shooting a Scene

Here is a scene as you would find it in a screenplay. Following it are three more versions. The first two demonstrate what might happen to the scene as it is photographed and then edited. The third version will give you an idea of what would be shot in the various setups.

INT. TONI AND NICK'S APARTMENT—NIGHT

TONI *is sitting in front of the TV, sipping a glass of milk. She is absorbed in the drama on the tube, and doesn't look up when NICK enters. She is aware of him, though, and waves the hand holding the glass of milk in his direction.*

NICK *comes over to her, glancing at the set to see what she is watching as he approaches. He leans down and kisses her, then straightens up, wiping his hand across his mouth with feigned distaste.*

NICK

Yuchh! Milky kiss.

TONI

It's the only way I can get you to drink any.

NICK

Ha ha.

TONI

This'll be over in a minute.

NICK *nods, tossing his jacket on the couch. Without looking up from the TV,* TONI *points the milk-hand toward the closet.* NICK *sighs, picks up his jacket, and goes to the closet to hang it up.*

He goes to the kitchen, checks the pot on the stove. His reaction is noncommittal as he replaces the lid.

The drama on the TV is over; we hear the commercial start. TONI *gets up, switches off the set. She downs the last of her milk, wipes her mouth carefully with her napkin, sets the glass down, and goes to* NICK. *With no preamble, she puts her arms around him and gives him a sensational kiss. She really loves him.*

TONI
[After kiss]

Hi.

NICK

Hi, yourself.

TONI

Do you fool around?

NICK

Yeah, but I'm not very good at it.

TONI

Want lessons?

NICK

How much?

TONI

Just eat your dinner like a good little boy.

NICK

What's for dessert?

TONI

The lesson.

NICK

How come you always talk dirty?

TONI

How come you always listen dirty?

NICK

My religious upbringing.

TONI

Ha ha to you.

NICK *goes to a small table near the sofa and looks through the mail. As he is doing that,* TONI *moves over to the stove, checks the pot.*

NICK
[Referring to a letter]
What the hell is this?

TONI
[At stove]
What?

NICK

This letter from the May Co. About a new kitchen set you bought.

TONI

Oh, yeah. Didn't I tell you?

NICK

(*Crossing to her*)
You know damn well you didn't tell me.

TONI

Oh. Well, I bought a new kitchen set.

NICK

What the hell for?

TONI

Because we need it.

NICK

Why don't you ask me about something like this
before you spend all that money?

TONI

Hey. Remember me? I work. I have a right to
spend some of our money. Or my money.

NICK

What if we decide to get married some day? We'll
want to buy a house. And we need to save for
that. You spend money like my meter ticks all day
long. At double speed.

TONI

You're beautiful when you're macho. Take me!
Take me!

                    NICK

I'm serious!

                    TONI

That's your trouble.

                    NICK

Very funny.

                    TONI

What was our agreement when we decided to
move in together?

                    NICK

All right, all right. But we also said that after two
years we'd decide about getting married. And it's
two years.

                    TONI

Tuesday.

She gives NICK *silverware and napkins. He moves to the table, begins
to set it.* TONI *fills the bowls, brings them to the table. They both sit
and start to eat.*

                    NICK

OK. What happens Wednesday?

                    TONI

I don't know. It's only Thursday.

                    NICK

Go ahead. Tell me you haven't thought about it.

TONI *stops eating, sets her spoon down.*

                        TONI

I have thought about it. But Nick—I don't know
how I feel. Or I should say I do know how I feel,
and that's the trouble. I feel—afraid.

                        NICK

What the hell are you afraid of? You know I don't
beat you.

                        TONI
                      [Laughs]
That's not it. I guess I'm afraid something might
go wrong.
[NICK *starts to say something, but she stops him*]
I know—nothing's gone wrong yet. But—it's hard
to explain. I see marriages breaking up all around
us. Candy and Bill. Your sister. And I think
Ginger and Eddie are about to split.

                        NICK

Who told you that?

                        TONI

Nobody. But I talk to Ginger all the time. And
she ain't happy.

                        NICK

What's she so unhappy about?

                        TONI
                     [Shrugs]
She won't tell me. But she is. And we're good

together, Nick. Right now. The way we are. And maybe I don't want to rock the boat. Can you understand?

NICK

No.
[TONI sighs]
But I'd rather have you this way than twenty other women any other way. So I guess this is the way we stay.

TONI

Not forever, Nick. Just a little while longer, OK?

NICK

Do we have to eat this grass all the time?

TONI

[Laughs]
It's health food. Eat and shut up.

CUT

The scene you just read was photographed at the Workshop, as it might be done on film, single camera. Obviously there are many ways to stage and shoot a scene; what follows is only one possibility.

The photographs shown here portray only a few of the moments that would be part of the entire master, or group of master shots. Later, we will look at the way the scene might be edited with all the coverage included.

INT. TONI AND NICK'S APARTMENT—NIGHT

TONI *is sitting in front of the TV* (Figure 31.1), *sipping a glass of milk. She is absorbed in the drama on the tube, and doesn't look up when*

NICK *enters. She is aware of him, though, and waves the hand holding the glass of milk in his direction* (Figure 31.2).

NICK *comes to her, glancing at the set to see what she is watching as he approaches* (Figure 31.3).

He leans down and kisses her, then straightens up, wiping his hand across his mouth with feigned distaste (Figure 31.4).

> NICK

Yuchh! Milky kiss.

> TONI

It's the only way I can get you to drink any.

> NICK

Ha ha.

> TONI

This'll be over in a minute.

NICK *nods, tossing his jacket on the couch* (Figure 31.5).

Without looking up from the TV, TONI *points the milk-hand toward the closet* (Figure 31.6). NICK *sighs, picks up his jacket, and goes to the closet to hang it up.*

He goes to the kitchen, checks the pot on the stove. His reaction is noncommittal as he replaces the lid.

(The shot of NICK at the stove will be picked up after the entire master shot has been photographed. At this time, we will keep the camera on TONI as the scene continues, letting NICK walk out of the shot. We will not try to hold both people, since NICK will be too far away for the camera to hold both. After we have shot the entire master, we will come back to shoot this much of the scene in matching singles of NICK at the door and TONI on the couch. After those singles have been shot, we will not necessarily go in sequence and shoot NICK at the closet. That shot can wait; we will first shoot all the coverage we can with the camera pointing in the same general direction to minimize the amount of time necessary for lighting changes and changes in camera position.)

The drama on the TV is over; we hear the commercial start. TONI *gets up, switches off the set* (Figure 31.7). *She downs the last of her milk, wipes her mouth carefully with her napkin, sets the glass down, and*

goes to NICK (Figure 31.8, Setup 3).

(The camera has followed TONI to NICK, so that we are in a continuing master two-shot as the scene continues. Later, we will get a shot of NICK alone at the sink as he arrives and checks the pot. In the master, we will dolly [or zoom slowly, which often replaces the dolly] to a tight two-shot.)

With no preamble, she puts her arms around him (Figure 31.9) *and gives him a sensational kiss. She really loves him.*

                         TONI
                      [After kiss]
Hi.

                         NICK
Hi, yourself.

                         TONI
Do you fool around?

                         NICK
Yeah, but I'm not very good at it.

                         TONI
Want lessons?

                         NICK
How much?

                         TONI
Just eat your dinner like a good little boy.

                         NICK
What's for dessert?

                         TONI
The lesson.

                         NICK
How come you always talk dirty?

                         TONI
How come you always listen dirty?

NICK

My religious upbringing.

TONI

Ha ha to you.

(This whole sequence will be covered later in two tight over-the-shoulder shots that get the sense of intimacy. Now the camera will go with NICK, losing TONI, to continue the master. Later, NICK will bring us back to TONI at the stove, where the master again becomes a two-shot. When we have completed the master, we will get the necessary coverage, including a single of TONI at the stove, that will match what we have on NICK alone at the table.)

NICK *goes to a small table near the sofa and looks at the mail* (Figure 31.10). *As he is doing that,* TONI *moves to the stove, checks the pot.*

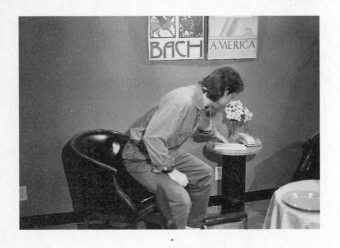

NICK
[Referring to a letter]
What the hell is this?

TONI
[At stove]
What?

NICK
This letter from the May Co. About a new kitchen set you bought.

TONI
Oh, yeah. Didn't I tell you?

NICK
[Crossing to her] [Figure 31.11]
You know damned well you didn't tell me.

(At this point, the camera will follow him, taking us into a two-shot.)

TONI

Oh. Well, I bought a new kitchen set.

NICK

What the hell for?

TONI

Because we needed it.

NICK

Why don't you ask me about something like this before you spend all that money?

TONI

Hey. Remember me? I work. I have a right to spend some of our money. Or my money.

NICK

What if we decide to get married some day? We'll want to buy a house. And we need to save for that. You spend money like my meter ticks all day long. And at double time.

TONI

You're beautiful when you're macho! Take me! Take me!

NICK

I'm serious.

TONI

That's your trouble.

NICK

Very funny.

TONI

What was our agreement when we decided to move in together?

NICK

All right. All right. But we also said that after two years we'd decide about getting married. And it's two years.

TONI

Tuesday.

She gives NICK *silverware and napkins* (Figure 31.12).

He moves to the table, begins to set it (Figure 31.13).

(The camera will follow Nick to the table and hold him, keeping the master continuous. Later, we will come back and get a matching shot of TONI at the stove, plus the necessary coverage: over-the-shoulders and close-ups. When TONI moves to the table in the following scene, we will let her move out of her shot and into the master. We will cover the following sequence with over-the-shoulder shots and close-ups.)

TONI *fills the bowls, brings them to the table. They both sit and start to eat.*

NICK

Okay. What happens Wednesday?

TONI

I don't know. This is only Thursday.

NICK

Go ahead. Tell me you haven't thought about it.

TONI

stops eating, sets her spoon down (Figure 31.14)
I have thought about it. But Nick—I don't know
how I feel. Or I should say I do know how I feel,
and that's the trouble. I feel—afraid.

NICK

What the hell are you afraid of? You know I don't
beat you.

TONI

[Laughs]
That's not it. I guess I'm afraid something might
go wrong.
[NICK starts to say something, but she stops him]
I know—nothing's gone wrong yet. But—it's hard
to explain. I see marriages breaking up all around
us. Candy and Bill. Your sister. And I think Ginger
and Eddie are about to split.

NICK

Who told you that?

TONI

Nobody. But I talk to Ginger all the time. And she ain't happy.

NICK

What's she so unhappy about?

TONI

[Shrugs]

She won't tell me. But she is. And we're good together, Nick. Right now. The way we are. And maybe I don't want to rock the boat. Can you understand?

NICK

No.

[TONI sighs]

But I'd rather have you this way than twenty other women any other way. So I guess this is the way we stay.

TONI

Not forever, Nick. Just a little while longer, OK?

NICK

Do we have to eat this green stuff all the time?

TONI

[Laughs]

It's health food. Eat and shut up.

CUT

Now we will go back and shoot all the coverage I spoke of previously. Since shooting the closet will necessitate turning the camera around 180 degrees, that will be the last setup.

To illustrate technique, I photographed the scene with only one master. In actual practice, it is not likely that there would be only one master in a scene of this length. It would take more time to set up and rehearse such a complicated master than to break it into sections. Since the editor will intercut to coverage from time to time, returning to a master as necessary, the use of several masters will not make the editing look jumpy.

In a feature film, long masters are more possible than in television episodes, since the TV director must work on a very tight schedule and must take all the shortcuts he can find. It is also unlikely that there would be so much movement for a TV episode, again because it takes too much time to stage, rehearse, light, and shoot a sequence with a lot of movement. The TV director would more likely be forced to simplify, and the scene would necessarily be more static.

There are more setups for this scene than might actually be necessary. However, if there is a great deal of time, it can be a distinct advantage to shoot all the setups, for that will give the director and editor greater flexibility in the final editing of the scene.

Each setup takes a certain amount of time. It may be only a couple of minutes, or it may be hours. It is best if the actor spends this period in preparation for the upcoming scene, as discussed earlier.

All the takes that were printed from all the setups will be screened at dailies. Then the editor will assemble the film, and he and the director will begin the work of re-editing again and again until they have a finished product. One version of their efforts might be cut together like this.

INT. TONI AND NICK'S APARTMENT—NIGHT

TONI *is sitting in front of the TV, sipping a glass of milk* (Figure 31.15, Master—Setup 1).

She is absorbed in the drama on the tube, and doesn't look up when NICK *enters* (Figure 31.16, Setup 10).

She is aware of him, though, and waves the hand holding the glass of milk in his direction (Figure 31.17, Setup 2).

NICK *comes over to her, glancing at the set to see what she is watching as he approaches. He leans down and kisses her, then straightens up, wiping his hand across his mouth with feigned distaste* (Figure 31.18, Setup 10).

                         NICK
Yuchh! Milky kiss.

                         TONI
                (Figure 31.19, Setup 2)
It's the only way I can get you to drink any.

                         NICK
Ha ha.

                         TONI
This'll be over in a minute.

NICK *nods, tossing his jacket on the couch* (Figure 31.20, Master—Setup 1). *Without looking up from the TV,* TONI *points the milk-hand toward the closet.* NICK *sighs, picks up his jacket, and*

goes to the closet to hang it up (Figure 31.21, Setup 11).

He goes to the kitchen, checks the pot on the stove (Figure 31.22, Setup 3). His reaction is noncommittal as he replaces the lid.

The drama on the TV is over; we hear the commercial start. TONI gets up, switches off the set (Figure 31.23, Master—Setup 1). She downs the last of her milk, wipes her mouth carefully with her napkin, sets the glass down, and goes to NICK. With no preamble

she puts her arms around him (Figure 31.24, Setup 17) *and gives him a sensational kiss. She really loves him.*

                    TONI
                 [After kiss]
Hi.

                    NICK
Hi, yourself.

                    TONI
Do you fool around?

                    NICK
              (Figure 31.25, Setup 4)

Yeah, but I'm not very good at it.

                    TONI
Want lessons?

                    NICK
How much?

                    TONI
              (Figure 31.26, Setup 17)

Just eat your dinner like a good little boy.

                    NICK
What's for dessert?

                    TONI
The lesson.

NICK
(Figure 31.27, Setup 4)

How come you always talk dirty?

TONI
(Figure 31.28, Setup 18)

How come you always listen dirty?

NICK
(Figure 31.29, Setup 5)

My religious upbringing.

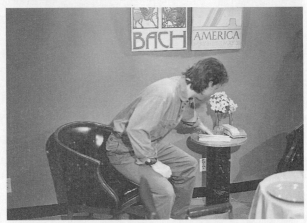

TONI
(Figure 31.30, Setup 18)

Ha ha to you.

NICK *moves to the table near the sofa and looks through the mail* (Figure 31.31, Master—Setup 1). *As he is doing that,*

TONI *moves over to the stove, checks the pot* (Figure 31.32, Setup 6).

NICK
(Figure 31.33, Setup 13)
[Referring to a letter]
What the hell is this?

TONI
(Figure 31.34, Setup 6)
[At stove]
What?

NICK
(Figure 31.35, Setup 12)
This letter from the May Co. About a new kitchen
set you bought.

TONI
Oh, yeah. Didn't I tell you?

NICK

(Figure 31.36, Master—Setup 1) [Crossing to her]
You know damned well you didn't tell me.

TONI

Oh. Well, I bought a new kitchen set.

NICK

What the hell for?

TONI

Because we needed it.

NICK

Why don't you ask me about something like this
before you spend all that money?

TONI

Hey. Remember me? I work. I have a right to
spend some of our money. Or my money.

NICK

What if we decide to get married some day? We'll
want to buy a house. And we need to save for
that. You spend money like my meter ticks all day
long. And at double time.

TONI

(Figure 31.37, Setup 6)
You're beautiful when you're macho! Take me!
Take me!

NICK

(Figure 31.38, Setup 13)
I'm serious.

                    TONI
That's your trouble.

                    NICK
Very funny.

                    TONI
            (Figure 31.39, Setup 6)
What was our agreement when we decided to
move in together?

                    NICK
            (Figure 31.40)
All right, all right. But we also said that after two
years we'd decide about getting married. And it's
two years.

                    TONI
Tuesday.

She gives NICK *silverware and napkins* (Figure 31.41, Master—
Setup 1). *He moves to the table, begins to set it.*

TONI *fills the bowls* (Figure 31.42, Setup 6), *brings them to the table. They both sit and start to eat.*

NICK
(Figure 31.43, Master—Setup 1)
OK. What happens Wednesday?

TONI
I don't know. This is only Thursday.

NICK
(Figure 31.44, Setup 14)
Go ahead. Tell me you haven't thought about it.

TONI *stops eating, sets her fork down* (Figure 31.45, Setup 7)

                          TONI
I have thought about it. But Nick—I don't know
how I feel. Or I should say I do know how I feel,
and that's the trouble. I feel—afraid.

                          NICK
               (Figure 31.46, Setup 14)
What the hell are you afraid of? You know I don't
beat you.

                          TONI
               (Figure 31.47, Setup 7)
                      [Laughs]
That's not it. I guess I'm afraid something might
go wrong.

[NICK *starts to say something, but she stops him* (Figure 31.48, Master—Setup 1)].

                              TONI
I know—nothing's gone wrong yet (Figure 31.49,
Setup 9). But—it's hard to explain. I see marriages
breaking up all around us. Candy and Bill. Your
sister. And I think Ginger and Eddie are about to
split.

                              NICK
                   (Figure 31.50, Setup 15)
Who told you that?

TONI

(Figure 31.51, Setup 9)

Nobody. But I talk to Ginger all the time. And she ain't happy.

NICK

(Figure 31.52, Setup 16)

What's she so unhappy about?

TONI

(Figure 31.53, Setup 10)

[Shrugs]

She won't tell me. But she is. And we're good together, Nick. Right now. The way we are. And maybe I don't want to rock the boat. Can you understand?

NICK

No.

TONI [*sighs*]
(Figure 31.54, Setup 16)
But I'd rather have you this way than twenty other women any other way. So I guess this is the way we stay.

TONI
(Figure 31.55, Setup 10)
Not forever, Nick. Just a little while longer, OK?

NICK
(Figure 31.56, Setup 16)
[No dialogue. Reaction shot]

Now we will look at how the scene was broken down for shooting. I used nineteen setups to shoot the scene, the last one being Nick at the closet.

In the following pages, the start of each setup is indicated by the initial of the character favored: T for Toni, N for Nick. A vertical line is drawn through whatever is included in that particular shot. The end of the setup is indicated by a horizontal line at the bottom of the vertical.

The numbers indicate the order of shooting. The various setups are shot out of sequence because, in most cases, all shots for which the camera is pointed in the same general direction are shot before those for which the camera has to be turned around. Thus, the shots over Toni's shoulder toward Nick as Toni goes to him after turning off the TV are followed by the single of Toni at the

NICK
(Figure 31.57, Master—Setup 1)
Do we have to eat this green stuff all the time?

TONI
[Laughs]
It's health food. Eat and shut up.

CUT

For the sake of illustration, I've used more cuts than might be needed. Simplicity and clear articulation of ideas are as important in filming and in editing as in acting.

• •

stove, the shot over Nick's shoulder to Toni after Nick discovers the letter from the May Company, and Nick's single as he checks the pot on the stove. Before the reverses are shot (over Nick's shoulder to Toni, etc.), the coverage at the table that favors the actor at our right is shot. Then the camera is turned around; the coverage at the sink is shot, then at the table, and so on.

The reason for shooting everything in the same direction first is that it takes time to change the lighting each time the camera is moved. When the camera has to make a 180 degree turn, the lighting change is extensive, so those moves are held to a minimum. The actor has the problem of shooting out of sequence, but that is part of the craft the film actor must develop: how to shoot out of sequence, but never lose the sense of continuity in the scene.

INT. TONI AND NICK'S
APARTMENT—NIGHT

MASTER 1   T 2

TONI *is sitting in front of the TV, sipping a glass of milk. She is absorbed in the drama on the tube, and doesn't look up when NICK enters. She is aware of him, though, and waves the hand holding the glass of milk in his direction.*

N 11

NICK *comes over to her, glancing at the set to see what she is watching as he approaches. He leans down and kisses her, then straightens up, wiping his hand across his mouth with feigned distaste.*

                         NICK

Yuchh! Milky kiss.

                         TONI

It's the only way I can get you to drink any.

                         NICK

Ha ha.

                         TONI

This'll be over in a minute.

MASTER 1   T 2   N 11

NICK nods, tossing his jacket on the couch. Without looking up from
the TV, TONI points the milk-hand toward the closet. NICK sighs,
picks up his jacket, and goes to the closet to hang it up.

        He goes to the kitchen, checks the pot on the stove. His reaction is
noncommittal as he replaces the lid.

        The drama on the TV is over; we hear the commercial start.
TONI gets up, switches off the set. She downs the last of her milk,
wipes her mouth carefully with her napkin, sets the glass down, and goes
to NICK. With no preamble, she puts her arms around him and gives
him a sensational kiss. She really loves him.

                                TONI

                            [After kiss]

        Hi.

                                NICK

        Hi, yourself.

                                TONI

        Do you fool around?

                                NICK

        Yeah, but I'm not very good at it.

MASTER 1   T 17   N 4   N 5   T 18

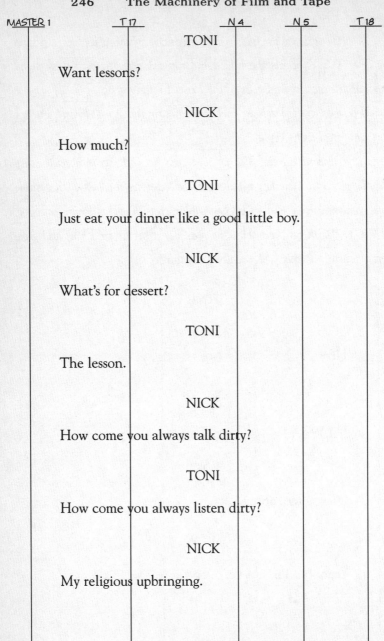

TONI

Want lessons?

NICK

How much?

TONI

Just eat your dinner like a good little boy.

NICK

What's for dessert?

TONI

The lesson.

NICK

How come you always talk dirty?

TONI

How come you always listen dirty?

NICK

My religious upbringing.

MASTER 1　　　　　　　T 17　　　　　　　N 4　　　　　N 5　　　T 18

TONI

Ha ha to you.

T 6　　　　　　　　　T 7　　　　　　　N 12　　　N 13

NICK goes to a small table in the hall and looks through the mail. As
he is doing that, TONI moves over to the stove, checks the pot.

NICK

[Referring to a letter]

What the hell is this?

TONI

[At stove]

What?

NICK

This letter from the May Co. About a new kitchen
set you bought.

TONI

Oh, yeah. Didn't I tell you?

NICK

[Crossing to her]

You know damn well you didn't tell me.

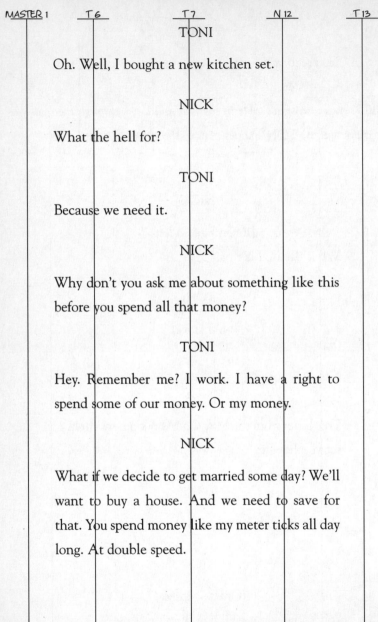

MASTER 1   T 6   T 7   N 12   T 13

TONI

Oh. Well, I bought a new kitchen set.

NICK

What the hell for?

TONI

Because we need it.

NICK

Why don't you ask me about something like this before you spend all that money?

TONI

Hey. Remember me? I work. I have a right to spend some of our money. Or my money.

NICK

What if we decide to get married some day? We'll want to buy a house. And we need to save for that. You spend money like my meter ticks all day long. At double speed.

MASTER 1   T 6   T 7   N 12   T 13

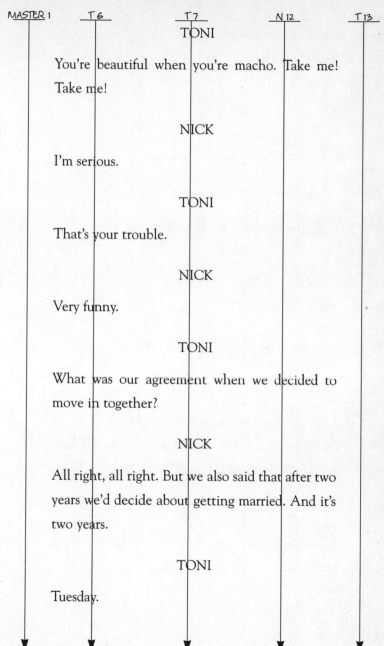

TONI

You're beautiful when you're macho. Take me!
Take me!

NICK

I'm serious.

TONI

That's your trouble.

NICK

Very funny.

TONI

What was our agreement when we decided to
move in together?

NICK

All right, all right. But we also said that after two
years we'd decide about getting married. And it's
two years.

TONI

Tuesday.

MASTER 1   T 8   T 9   T 10   N 14   N 15   N 16

*She gives NICK silverware and napkins. He moves to the table, begins
to set it. TONI fills the bowls, brings them to the table. They both sit
and start to eat.*

                         NICK

         OK. What happens Wednesday?

                         TONI

         I don't know. It's only Thursday.

                         NICK

         Go ahead. Tell me you haven't thought about it.

TONI stops eating, sets her fork down

                         TONI

         I have thought about it. But Nick—I don't know
         how I feel. Or I should say I do know how I feel,
         and that's the trouble. I feel—afraid.

                         NICK

         What the hell are you afraid of? You know I don't
         beat you.

MASTER 1   T 8   T 9   T 10   N 14   N 15   N 16

TONI

[Laughs]

That's not it. I guess I'm afraid something might
go wrong.

[NICK *starts to say something, but she stops him*]

I know—nothing's gone wrong yet. But—it's hard
to explain. I see marriages breaking up all around
us. Candy and Bill. Your sister. And I think
Ginger and Eddie are about to split.

NICK

Who told you that?

TONI

Nobody. But I talk to Ginger all the time. And
she ain't happy.

NICK

What's she so unhappy about?

TONI

[Shrugs]

She won't tell me. But she is. And we're good
together Nick. Right now. The way we are. And
maybe I don't want to rock the boat. Can you
understand?

MASTER 1   T 8   T 9   T 10   N 14   N 15   N 16

NICK

No.

[TONI *sighs*]

But I'd rather have you this way than twenty other women any other way. So I guess this is the way we stay.

TONI

Not forever, Nick. Just a little while longer, OK?

NICK

Do we have to eat this grass all the time?

TONI

[*Laughs*]

It's health food. Eat and shut up.

SEQUENTIAL LIST OF SETUPS

Setup 1: The Master. Starts with a medium shot (about knees) of Toni. Camera pulls back to include TV set and door, catching Nick as he enters. Hold two-shot until Nick leaves, when camera holds Toni. Hold Toni as she comes to TV, turns it off. Carry Toni and truck right (camera and dolly both move right) as she goes to Nick. Hold two-shot, moving in a little to make the shot tighter. Stay with Nick as he moves to the coffee table. Hold Nick as he moves back to Toni, letting him carry us to a two-shot. Hold two-shot until Nick moves to the table with the silverware, staying with him as he moves. Toni will come into the shot as they both sit. Hold both until the end of the scene.

Setup 2: On Toni, sitting at table with milk in hand. Framed at about her waist. Hold until she walks out of shot after turning off the TV set.

Setup 3: Waist shot of Nick at stove.

Setup 4: Bust shot of Nick, shooting from the left. Toni will walk into shot, giving us a shot across her to Nick. Hold until he walks out of shot to go to coffee table.

Setup 5: Start tight on Nick. Toni will come into shot, making it a tight over-the-shoulder two-shot. Hold till Nick leaves.

Setup 6: Waist shot of Toni at stove. Hold until she moves out of shot when she goes to the table. Will tighten to bust as needed for "macho" line.

Setup 7: Bust of Toni at stove. Hold until she moves out of shot.

Setup 8: Medium two-shot across Nick to Toni when both are seated at the table. Camera will be framed at start of scene before Nick sits into the shot. Then he and Toni sit into shot. Hold until end of scene.

NOTE: Very often the actor will not be in the shot at the start of the scene, or when the director says, "Action!" In that case, the actor need only be a step or so out of frame, even though he is supposed to be coming from someplace farther away. On "Action!" the actor moves only the distance necessary to indicate the last bit of movement, the settling-in. The director wants that movement because it sometimes make a more interesting cut.

Setup 9: Close-up of Toni seated at table. Hold throughout scene.

Setup 10: Extreme close-up of Toni seated at table. Hold throughout scene.

Setup 11: Waist-shot of Nick at door. Camera will be framed on the final composition before Nick enters, and he will walk into position. Hold him until he walks out of shot to go to the closet.

Setup 12: Three-quarter (knees) shot of Nick at coffee table. He will walk into shot. Hold him until Toni gives him the silverware, keeping him about the same size throughout.

Setup 13: Bust of Nick at coffee table. Hold him until Toni gives him silverware.

Setup 14: Medium (about waist) two-shot across Toni to Nick, both seated at table. They will sit into shot. Hold throughout scene. Composition should match that of Setup 8.

Setup 15: Close-up of Nick seated at table. He will sit into shot. Hold throughout scene. Composition should match that of Setup 9.

Setup 16: Extreme close-up of Nick. He will sit into the shot. Hold throughout scene. Composition should match that of Setup 10.

Setup 17: Bust shot of Nick at sink, shooting from the right. Toni will walk into shot, giving us a shot across him to her. Composition should match that of Setup 4.

Setup 18: Tight over-the-shoulder shot across Nick to Toni. Shot will start on Nick, and Toni will walk into position. Composition should match that of Setup 5.

Setup 19: Nick at closet, hanging up his jacket. He will walk into shot. Hold until he walks out of shot.

32

The Television Studio

Many of the Hollywood studios that are used to tape TV shows are converted film studios. Not all converted studios were designed the same way, of course, but the overall plans were similar. Wooden floors were overlaid with concrete or some other smooth, hard surface to allow vibration-free camera dollying. Control booths were built to house the console table (for the director, technical director, associate director, and program assistant) and the audio mixer. Sometimes the lighting director and the video control operators were assigned space and equipment in the booth as well.

There are still some converted stages that have no functioning control booth. Mobile units outside the studio proper house the necessary personnel and equipment, while the stage proper has only the sets, cast, cameras, booms, and lights.

The true television studios (such as at CBS-TV's Television City) are different from the converted studios in a number of ways. The control booth is permanent. Lights that are easily lowered and raised are hung from pipes, as opposed to being hung from fixed wooden scaffolding or on the walls of the sets. Dressing rooms, makeup rooms, rest rooms, and wardrobe rooms are more easily accessible. The entire complex is more confined, and more functional.

The control booth is an electronic marvel. A panel of buttons and levers on the console table allows the technical director to change the picture going out on the air by pushing a button that sends a picture from one of several cameras photographing the show, or from a film chain or slide chain being used in conjunction with the cameras. The control panel also has devices that allow for dissolves, fades, superimpositions, wipes (eliminating the picture from one side as another enters to take its place), and numerous special effects patterns to appear on the screen.

The console is designed to accommodate the technical director, the director, the associate director, and the program assistant.

The associate director's function varies, depending on where the studio is located and which union controls that studio. At CBS, where the International Brotherhood of Electrical Workers (I.B.E.W.) is the union, the A.D. (associate director) readies the shots for the director, alerting each cameraperson (there are usually four) to what his next shot will be. For example, he might say, "Camera two, close-up of Henry," or "Camera three, get a two-shot." The cameraperson immediately gets the correct shot, so that it is ready when the director wants to cut to it. The shots have all been rehearsed, of course, but many shows are so complex that having the A.D. ready each shot is a very necessary and valuable part of the shooting.

At ABC and NBC, where the National Association of Broadcast Engineers and Technicians (N.A.B.E.T.) is the union with jurisdiction, the A.D.'s function during broadcast or taping does not include readying the cameras. If it is necessary, the T.D. (technical director) will do it.

Whoever readies the shots, the camerapersons generally have cards listing their shots in sequence as well. As each shot is required, the director signals the T.D., usually by snapping his fingers; the T.D. presses the necessary button or special effects switch and causes the shot to be put on the air (or tape). In this way the entire sequence of shots is set up and effected.

Seated next to the A.D. in the control booth is the P.A. (program assistant), who must keep close track of the time at each moment in the shooting, check that the dialogue is correct, and so forth. During the editing process, the P.A.'s script is invaluable. The script must be accurate, since it is the only record of what each shot was, and when it happened.

In front of the console are monitors for each camera in use, plus the line monitor. During a live broadcast (very rare these days), the line monitor carries the picture that is going out on the air. During taped shows the monitor carries the "on-air" edited version of the scene being shot. For most series being taped, the shots taken by several or all of the cameras are recorded on separate tapes for later editing. The on-air version may work very well as edited during the performance, in which case editing time is significantly reduced. The other tapes are used later as desired, to change angles and to facilitate making cuts for time or for esthetic reasons. Sometimes these *slave* tapes are used sparingly; sometimes an entire episode may be edited from them, one shot at a time. The same general procedures apply to game shows and soaps, but in most instances, editing for them is minimal or nonexistent.

To one side of the control booth are the sound booth and the lighting booth. The CBS Television City sound booths allow individual control of sixty-four separate microphones, as well as giving the mixer control of the echo chamber and numerous other special effects. The lighting director's booth allows him to communicate to personnel on the studio floor and to the person at the light patch panel, where all the lighting instruments are connected to proper dimmers. The lighting director also has television monitors in front of him so that he can see what the pictures look like.

To further simplify the process of making a TV show at CBS, the scene dock, paint shop, wardrobe, makeup, and special effects departments are all in the same building as the four studios. It is, in effect, a true Television City.

Since the original edition of this book, CBS has added full animation departments and electronic special effects equipment, which makes possible those extraordinary images and combinations of images that have become so commonplace. CBS has also built two more large studios just a few yards from Television City, giving them six studios in all.

33

•••••••••••••••••••••••••••••••

The Multiple-Camera
Show

In the early days of television, all shows were shot with three or four video cameras and transmitted live, including the first dramatic shows, which were usually a half hour in length. As soon as people recognized that television was here to stay, dramatic shows began to shift to film, using only one camera at a time, while the comedies were still shot with three or four video cameras before a live audience. The "I Love Lucy" show was the first comedy to change from electronic cameras to a multiple film camera system, keeping the live audience. Today, most comedies are shot with three or four film or electronic cameras.

For the actor doing television comedies, his approach is really more related to the theater than to film. There are several reasons: first, entire scenes are played at one time and shot from three or four different angles simultaneously. Usually, individual pickups are shot afterward using only one camera. Second, because there is an audience, the actor's energy and voice levels are generally much higher than they would be if the same material were being shot with one camera and no audience. The audience gives the actor the feeling that he must communicate beyond the person to whom he is speaking, the distance of communication being determined, at least to a large extent, by the presence of an audience, rather than by the presence of a camera and a boom. Comedy generally demands higher energy than drama, and the presence of an audience increases that demand even more.

There is a further similarity between the theater and a multicamera show. Unlike a one-camera show, a multicamera show is rehearsed for several days before it is shot in front of the audience—as in the theater. Preparation, therefore, is substantially different than for the one-camera show, and generally much easier, since there is a rehearsal period during which the actor can work, think, discuss with the director, and listen and relate to the other actors as he searches for what his ultimate performance is going to be.

The dramatic soap opera is a multicamera show that is different from the usual comedy performed in front of the audience. Here the actor must perform in long sequences as he does on the stage, but there is no audience present. Since there is no audience and since the material is dramatic, the kind of energy, particularly vocal energy, used in the three-camera comedy shows would seem highly exaggerated and artificial. The distance of communication is the same as in single-camera drama; the actor only needs to reach the person or persons to whom he is speaking. The actor must never forget, however, that the level of inner energy must always be high so that the performance will have dynamics and excitement. In the main, there will be very few pickup shots, so that the actor will be performing an entire scene or sequence of scenes in a continuous flow, just as he would on the stage.

Just to recap and avoid confusion: the inner energy, the level of truth, must always remain the same, whatever the film or tape media in which the actor works. What may change from a one-camera drama or multicamera soap approach to a multicamera comedy approach are the physical energy and vocal energy. These are directed by two main factors: (1) the need for more vocal energy in comedy than in drama and (2) the presence of an audience, which affects the distance across which an actor must communicate.

In the theater, the actor must generally communicate to the distant audience through the other actor. In one-camera dramatic film or in the soap opera, the actor need only communicate directly to the other actor; the audience (as the camera) is so close that the distance of communication to them need not be considered.

34

•••••••••••••••••••••••••••••••••••••

Stunts

You may be asked to do stunts at some time or other. If a stunt is complicated and dangerous, I advise you not to do it unless you've been trained for it. A simple fall can be very dangerous if you don't know how to do it. And certainly falling off a horse, or falling out of a car, or spilling on a motorcycle, can be extremely dangerous. When such acts are called for in the script, the smart production company will provide a double to do that work for you; let him do it. Don't be brave, and don't feel that you are shirking your job, because if you do the stunt yourself you can wind up with a broken arm or leg, or a broken neck.

On the other hand, you should learn how to do some simple things you will probably be called upon to do. You should learn how to fall, because you will undoubtedly be asked to do that at some time in your acting career, either because you're shot, or because you stumble, or because you're hit on the head, or whatever. Learn how to take a blow and roll with it. Learn how to give a blow without touching or hurting the other person.

Heights will almost always be faked so that you will be safe from falling any distance, but make doubly sure that wherever you are, the footing is safe. For an episode of a television series called "Climax!" the sets were outlined with tape on the floor of the rehearsal hall where we worked. Edward G. Robinson came to me at one point (I was the associate director) and asked me about a balcony ledge that he was supposed to walk on as he went from one balcony to another. I said, "It will be about a foot and a half wide." He said, "I'm not worried about that, how high is it off the stage floor?" I said, "Well, according to the plans, it will only be about six inches, so there's nothing to worry about." His answer was, "There's plenty to worry about. One of the worst accidents I ever had was when I fell off a carpet."

It is almost inevitable that one day in your career you will have to hit someone or be hit by someone. Obviously, when you see two men on television delivering bone-crunching blows to each other's face and body, they're not actually hitting one another. They are very carefully timing each blow in such a way that the camera cannot detect that it misses; and most importantly, the person *receiving* the blow is taking it in a way that makes it look real. The part of his body that is supposedly being struck moves in the direction of the hand or object hitting him, as it would if he were really being hit. Obviously, it is also important that the actor make emotional and physical adjustments to the pain the blow would cause.

If you are being slapped, you must move your head in the same direction as the hand striking you, timing your move so that it happens as the hand gets to your face. If you move before the hand gets to you, that anticipation is obvious to the viewer, and the blow looks phony. If you move too late, you're liable to actually receive the blow or look nonresponsive to it—the first possibility is uncomfortable for you; the second is uncomfortable for the audience.

In the theater it is necessary that a slap actually be a slap, because one cannot fake the sound that accompanies it. On film, however, the sound can be added afterward, so unless the director or the actors actually want the slap to be real, it can be faked. Obviously a closed-fist punch cannot be real in either case.

Let me repeat that it is the *receiver* of the blow who makes it look real. If you are the receiver, it is up to you to rehearse with the person delivering the blow so that you very carefully choreograph the fight, whether it be one punch or ten. If the blow is to your midsection, it must cause you to double over and perhaps step back or fall back, depending on the demands of the fight. Emitting a grunt as you are hit will help. Don't concern yourself with how good the grunt is or whether or not it will be used later, because it doesn't matter; if it is not good, a better-sounding grunt will be added. The fact that you grunt will help make the moment look real. And that's what does matter.

Don't be afraid to take a good healthy swing at the person you're fighting, but practice with that person first so that you become aware of one another's sense of timing and of the distance necessary to make the sequence work. When you're delivering a slap or a blow to the face, the blow should be a roundhouse, that is, a full, round swing and not a short, choppy one. From the point of view of the camera, your hand should actually disappear behind the face of the person you are hitting (Figure 34.1) and then come across to its completion—with the person being hit turning his head at the proper moment to make that swing possible. If the camera is placed in such a position that the face and hand are blocked (Figure 34.2), then you can just swing across the front of the face and miss it by several inches without the audience's being aware that you have missed.

Do not deliver an uppercut blow, because there is a limit to where the receiving head can go, and the blow can cause serious injury. For the same reason, do not deliver a straight punch into the face. The blow should come across the face, and it should be taken with a head movement or a head and body movement, including perhaps a fall, depending on who's fighting and how hard the blow delivered is supposed to be. When hitting, make sure you swing as though you mean it, and make sure you miss the other person.

The really good fights that you see on film are almost invariably staged between stunt people, a carefully trained, highly specialized group that is among the most professional in Hollywood. A fight scene will be shot in masters, using the stunt people; then it will be repeated in close sequences, using the actors to make the audience believe that the actors are indeed fighting. Obviously, the stunt people must resemble the actors as much as possible, and they must be dressed the same, so that the audience never for a moment doubts that it is in truth the actors who are fighting.

I can't stress enough the importance of learning how to take and deliver blows. When I had a small role in a film starring Dana Andrews, I reported to the set and was informed that Andrews would not be available to shoot for several days because he had a black eye. In a fight scene, the man who delivered the blow was careless and actually hit Andrews in the face. That carelessness cost the company thousands of dollars and Andrews a great deal of

Figure 34.1   Delivering a slap, front camera view. It's clear that she's not hitting him.

Figure 34.2   Delivering a slap with the face and hand blocked from the camera. Now the audience would believe she slapped him.

discomfort. I know I wouldn't want to get popped in the nose, and I don't think you would either—nor would you want to be responsible for giving the star of a feature (or anyone else) a black eye.

FIVE

The
Film/Tape
Career

35

· ·
Beginning Your Career

Let's take the process an actor goes through from the time he first arrives in Hollywood until the magic moment when he first hears the director say "Cut" at the end of a glorious first performance.

I genuinely believe that if you have the stamina and the determination to become an actor, and if you can take the disappointments that will probably be your lot, you will eventually make your living as an actor, even though you may not become a star. You must, however, have the determination, and you must work, work, work, and continue to work to perfect your craft—to free and develop your instrument so that when an opportunity comes, you will be ready for it.

The first step is to become involved with other actors. It is a good idea to get into a class or workshop that is professional in its attitude, so that your instrument keeps getting trained and keeps building on its own experience. If you're lucky enough to have a teacher you can trust, wait until that teacher feels you are ready to start. Then you will need an agent.

Getting an agent is tough. Most agents are reluctant to take beginners unless there is some immediate and magic charisma about them. It takes a lot of hard work and persuasion to convince the studios to take a chance on a newcomer, and when all is said and done, the agent may have earned you one day's work at about $500, of which he will get the magnificent sum of $50—less than he spent at lunch that day.

So what do you do? First, get a list of franchised Screen Actors Guild Agents from the Screen Actors Guild at 5757 Wilshire Boulevard in Hollywood. Don't sign with any agent who is not franchised by the Guild—nonfranchised agents have little or no access to casting directors of SAG films, or AFTRA shows. The chances are he will be unable to do anything constructive for you, and he may exploit you.

A legitimate, franchised agent charges you nothing to represent you. He does not earn or see one penny of your money until after you receive your paycheck, from which he deducts 10 percent—no more, no less. If anybody propositions you with anything else in the way of representation, run the other way.

Managers are something else, but their contracts are also controlled by state law, and you should check the laws very carefully if you are ever approached by a manager.

As an actor, you will have little need for both an agent and a manager unless you become a major star. If that happens, you should examine your needs and make your decision accordingly. Meanwhile, to get an agent, send letters and composite photographs—good composites made by professional photographers—to twenty or thirty agents, asking them for an interview. Pray that three or four will answer, and that you can then persuade at least one of them that he will become a millionaire if he handles you.

If the letters get no results, the next best thing is to get into a group where you can perform and be seen by agents and industry people, but be careful not to work with poorly trained amateurs. Work with a professional group, either in a theater or in a classroom. In the latter case, make sure that the teacher is fully conversant with the needs of the profession and with film and videotape media.

You will need photographs, and you should choose them carefully. First of all, don't rush to a photographer. You won't need pictures until you are ready to look for an agent. If you take them too soon, you may find that your look has changed, or that the image you want to project is different. Also, if an agent becomes interested in you, you will want his advice about the kind of pictures to take or where to take them.

You should get two types of photographs. First, you need some head or bust shots that are an accurate reflection of what you are really like. They should look unposed, so that you will not look totally different from the pictures when you walk into someone's office for an interview. These shots are for acting work.

You will also need pictures for commercial work if you are interested in commercials. In that case, you will want a composite—a group of pictures that will show you in different poses and wardrobe—on one sheet or on two folded sheets. These photos should be posed to give prospective employers some idea of how different you can look. Remember, the people hiring for commercials will not be as interested in how well you can act as in what kind of quality or character you can project for a short period of time. Can you be funny? Can you look strong? Are you feminine? Are you sexy? Can you make them believe you could be a service station attendant selling oil or a sailor who loves Old Spice? Could you be convincing as a woman who plays a lot of tennis and eats a particular kind of cereal?

A word of caution: Before you settle on a photographer, check him out as much as possible. There are many good photographers and many bad ones.

If you go to a teacher or to a manager or agent who insists you go to a specific photographer, be careful. It's very possible that the person recommending the photographer is getting a kickback, and that the work will be second-rate.

Many places passing themselves off as talent placement centers charge a fee, send you to their photographer, then send your picture, along with dozens of others, to a few casting directors; they call that a service. It isn't. Make sure you have a choice of photographers, and that the choice is yours. After all, you are the one who has to be pleased and proud of the pictures you send out.

Having secured an agent, you will very likely be sent on a number of interviews. There you will have a chance to meet some casting directors, and then, we hope, you'll be given a chance to read for a part.

Cold reading, as I said earlier, is seldom required, because only a fool of a director or producer will ask you to read a script without giving you a chance to look at it first. After all, his best wish is that you are perfect for the role. If he doesn't give you a chance to look at the material before you read it, he is not giving you a proper chance to prove that you are the right person to play the part.

Generally you will be given a script, or the pages that constitute the scene you are being considered for, and you'll be given anywhere from ten minutes to twenty-four hours to study the role before the reading. You will then be faced (in all probability) with a terrifying group of people consisting of a casting director, director, associate producer, producer, executive producer, and studio executive, plus, perhaps, a secretary who will make notes or read with you. On the other hand, it might be the casting director who will read with you, or the director, or anyone else in the room; you can never be sure whether you're going to have a chance to work with an actor or whether you're going to be reading against a monotone delivered by whoever is handy.

You probably will not get any kind of decision or evaluation of your reading at the time you read. Casting people are generally noncommittal until they have seen all the actors scheduled. Your agent will have to carry the ball for you and find out if you are their choice for the role, or work like hell to convince them that you are the only possible choice for the role. If your fortunes follow the usual pattern, you won't get the first ten or twenty roles you try out for; but if you're good, if you keep working, if you are persistent, and if you stay "up," sooner or later you'll get that first part, and the ice will be broken.

A word of encouragement about reading. The people for whom you are reading are your friends, not your enemies. They are on your side, not against you. They would love nothing better than for you to be the perfect choice for the role in question. If you are, not only is their job easier, it is over, and they welcome such news. They are probably bored with the whole process of casting and would like to get on with other things. They are rooting for you to be great so they can pack it in and call it a day. Remember that when you walk into an office full of people with impressive titles. They want you to be good.

Your problems will not be solved because you've landed your first role. However, the first role is a toughy, and after that you can at least say, "Yes, I have worked in film! And I have my SAG card!"

About that elusive SAG card: the need for it presents somewhat of a vicious circle. You can't get your first job until you have a SAG card; you can't get your SAG card until you get your first job.

At the time of writing, Screen Actors Guild is fining producers who hire non-SAG members for less than three days' work, so producers are reluctant to start new people in small roles, where most new actors must start. However, a clause in the Guild contract permits a producer to hire you with no penalty if you have studied for a reasonable length of time at a recognized school and clearly intend to make acting your career. So take heart.

Now let's assume that you've gotten the role. What happens? First of all you go out of your mind with joy and have to crush an overpowering desire to kiss your agent. Then you may experience a sense of deep, deep despair because you "know" you're just not good enough. In addition, you will receive a script (if you're lucky) or the page or pages that involve your role. Study the pages carefully. At that point, it would be a very good idea to look over the material in this book on preparation and learning a role, because however small or large the part, the approach to learning it is the same.

Your preparation for film is done mostly by yourself, and as a consequence, it is far more difficult than preparation in the theater. There you have the advantage of hours upon hours of rehearsal with the other actors, so that the work you do at home alone is coupled with work with the other actors and the director. In film, you must do virtually all your preparation at home.

You must know the role so thoroughly that you are able to perform well even if you get no help from the director or the other actors. You must be so thoroughly prepared that nothing that happens on the set can throw you, whether it be mechanical failures, pressure and personality blowups, or last-minute rewriting of your scene. Above all, you must be so thoroughly prepared that you come to work with a clear idea of how you will perform your role; yet you must be flexible. If the director is in disagreement with your approach and wants to change it, you will be able to do that and deliver a performance that is satisfactory to both you and him without undue strain and tension.

Usually, you'll have a chance to rehearse your scene a couple of times on the set. If you're very lucky, you will have a chance to run over it with the other actor or actors before rehearsal with the director. On some sets, there is a dialogue coach, and he may have the time and inclination to go over the role with you.

A couple of rehearsals is about all you can expect before you are dismissed temporarily to allow the cinematographer to light the scene for filming. The lighting and other technical matters may take a few minutes, or they may take several hours. The director may call you to rehearse with the other actors until the scene is ready to be shot. If he doesn't, go to your fellow performers and suggest that you rehearse on your own. Look for every opportunity to rehearse as much as possible before you go for a take.

You have an obligation to stay nearby and to maintain contact with your role and with what you've just rehearsed. You will be called upon soon to do it again. That will probably be your last rehearsal before the director says, "Let's go for a take."

Because film is shot out of sequence, it is an excellent idea to look at the script while you are waiting for the lighting setup, studying the scenes *immediately preceding* the one you are about to shoot. It is very important to do this, because the upcoming scene is obviously part of a continuity; it is connected to what has happened before. Therefore, in order for you to know exactly where you should be emotionally, intellectually, physically, and sensorially at the beginning of this scene, you must know where you were when you were last on the screen and what happened to you in between. When the director says "Action!" you must be able to start the scene at the required emotional and physical levels.

The director is responsible for making sure there is an emotional continuity, and an energy and general performance continuity. However, there is no guarantee that he will fulfill that responsibility, or that he will be aware that the way you are playing this scene will not ultimately connect with a scene you are going to play at some time in the future. The only protection you have is to know your craft so well that if you get no help from a director—which is unfortunately sometimes the case—your performance will still be a first-rate, professional, rich performance. If you do get help from the director, that's gravy, and you can consider yourself fortunate to work with a person who understands and cares about actors and has found the time to work with them.

I cannot stress enough the importance of good preparation. You must find those techniques that work for you and that bring you to performance level at a moment's notice. Sometimes a moment's notice is all you have, because of somebody else's failure or because the script was rewritten at the last minute. The audience doesn't know or care that you didn't have enough preparation time; all they care about is what they see on the screen. The only way you can protect yourself and make sure you will always look good to them is to prepare yourself completely as an actor, so that your body, your mind, your senses, and your emotions will do all the things you want them to do at the right time. Then, meticulously prepare every scene each night before you go to work. Thorough preparation separates the professionals from the amateurs.

An exceedingly painful subject to most actors is *turning down a role*. However, part of an actor's ability to succeed lies in his being seen in a favorable light at all times. To be seen in a favorable light, you must accept roles that you know you can handle and that are right for you. (I'm talking about your work in the professional world, not in the classroom or in some distant summer stock experiment, where you are allowed to stretch.)

It is important that you have an honest image of yourself that will help you know what you look like, what quality you project, what characters you can easily make credible, and what characters it will be difficult or impossible for you to make credible. It's hard to say no to a job offer, but sometimes in the long run that's the way to make the most money and to have the longest and most successful career. Recognize your limitations. At the same time, however, *face your strengths* as well.

The chances are that it will take a while for you to get started in your career. The worst mistake that any young actor can make is to be idle during the waiting period. It's not sufficient to make a halfhearted effort to get into nonunion films or plays. The smartest course you can take while you are waiting is to involve yourself in any aspect of the entertainment industry. It is far better to sweep a soundstage than to wash dishes in some restaurant, because at least with the former you will be somewhere in the ballpark. It's better to be a secretary for a producer or a writer than to be the best shoe salesman at the Broadway.

Work for nothing in a nonunion film, or work backstage in little theaters if you can't get onstage. In that way you will become a member of a working company; you will be spending your time in the entertainment industry, and as long as you're doing that, you're going to be learning something and growing a little. Also, you will be more aware of what's going on, and you are more likely to be in the right place at the right time. That is frequently the most important step of all: to be in the right place at the right time.

There's something else you can be doing while you are waiting to become a star. Are you aware that most people in the industry think actors are bores? They do. Mostly because actors talk primarily about themselves. It's understandable; the actor is the only professional who is always out of a job or about to be out of a job— the only professional who is always looking for his next assignment. With that kind of insecurity, is it any wonder that he thinks and talks about himself? It may be understandable, but, nevertheless, it's boring. So use your free waiting time to delve into new interests. Find things outside the entertainment world that excite you, and give them some time. Meet people outside the industry. Talk to them; it will be helpful in your acting.

By taking some interest in the world outside the narrow sphere of film or television, you may turn out to be such an interesting person that producers and directors will enjoy having you around. And we both know the price they'll have to pay for that.

A question I am always asked when I teach my seminars in cities outside of Los Angeles is, "What do you think about going to New York or Hollywood?" My answer is always the same: If you want to work in the theater, go to New York. If you want to work in film or television, go to Hollywood. If you can live without it, don't go to either one. If you *can't* live without it, don't let anybody stop you.

36

Film and Television Unions for Actors

Two unions have jurisdiction over actors in the camera media. Screen Actors Guild (SAG) covers all work done on film. The American Federation of Television and Radio Artists (AFTRA) covers the actors who work on videotape shows. The jurisdictional lines are pretty clearly drawn, and most actors find that it is necessary to belong to both unions. At the time of this writing, there is talk of a merger, but that is probably some time away.

SCREEN ACTORS GUILD (SAG)

Screen Actors Guild is located at 5757 Wilshire Boulevard, Hollywood, California 90036. The phone number is (213) 549-6778.

You can join SAG only if you have a commitment for a film job or have had a film job with a production company that is a signatory to the SAG producers contract. At the time of application, if you have not worked on a film, you have to present a letter from a motion picture producer or his representative stating that you are wanted for a principal role or speaking part in a specific film. That application cannot be presented more than two weeks before actual filming. (My assumption is that this regulation is designed to prevent people from joining SAG on the basis of a promise of work in a film that never gets made. Two weeks prior to shooting implies that the film is already funded and is actually in preparation.)

If you have already worked in a film, you can join SAG by presenting proof of employment—a contract, a payroll check or stub, or a letter from the production company—that contains the following information: your name, your social security number, the name of the production company (which must be a signatory to SAG), the name of the specific production or commercial in which you worked, the salary paid, and the dates worked.

The membership fee is $1,080.00. In addition to that, you will have to pay the first semiannual basic dues of $42.50. The amount of dues you will subsequently pay will be determined by your earnings, with the amount being increased as your earnings increase, to a maximum of $1^1/2$ percent of earnings over $5,000 per year, up to a maximum of $150,000 in earnings.

SAG will not accept personal checks for membership. The money must be in cash, cashier's check, or money order.

If, at the time of application, you have been a paid-up member of one of the affiliated Guilds for a year or more, and if you have worked as a principal performer in that Guild's jurisdiction at least once, you may be able to join SAG without a commitment for a job in a film or filmed television show. In that case, the initiation fee is reduced, based on a formula derived from consideration of the amount you paid to join the original affiliated Guild.

The affiliated Guilds are AFTRA; American Guild of Musical Artists (AGMA); American Guild of Variety Artists (AGVA); Screen Extras Guild (in the process of merging with SAG at the time of this writing)(SEG); and Actors Equity Association(AEA).

Following is a list of SAG offices throughout the country as of 1997:

NATIONAL OFFICE
5757 Wilshire Blvd.
Los Angeles, CA 90036
(213) 954-1600

ARIZONA
1616 E. Indian School Road #330
Phoenix, AZ 85016
(602) 265-2712

ATLANTA
455 East Paces Ferry Rd. NE #334
Atlanta, GA 30305
(404) 239-0131

BOSTON
11 Beacon Street, Room 512
Boston, MA 02108
(617) 742-2688

CHICAGO
75 E. Wacker Drive, 14th Floor
Chicago, IL 60601
(213) 372-8081

COLORADO, NEVADA, NEW MEXICO, UTAH
950 S. Cherry Street Suite 502
Denver, CO 80222
(303) 757-6226

DALLAS–FORT WORTH
6060 N. Central Expressway
Suite 302, LB 604
Dallas, TX 75706
(214) 363-8300

DETROIT
28690 Southfield Rd. #290 A&B
Lathrup Village, MI 48076
(313) 559-9540

FLORIDA
7300 N. Kendall Dr. #620
Miami, FL 33156
(305) 670-7677

Central Florida
Sun Bank Plaza
3393 West Vine St. #302
Kissimee, FL 34741
(407) 847-4445

GEORGIA
455 E. Paces Ferry Rd. NE #334
Atlanta, GA 30305
(404) 239-0131

HAWAII
949 Kapiolani Blvd. Suite #105
Honolulu, HI 96814
(808) 538-6122

HOUSTON
2650 Fountainview Drive #326
Houston, TX 77057
(713) 972-1806

NASHVILLE
1108 Seventeenth Ave. South
Nashville, TN 37212
(615) 327-2958

NEW YORK
1515 Broadway, 44th Floor
New York, NY 10036
(212) 944-1030

PHILADELPHIA
230 S. Broad Street, 10th Floor
Philadelphia, PA 19102
(215) 545-3150

SAN DIEGO
7827 Convoy Court Suite #400
San Diego, CA 92111
(619) 278-7695

SAN FRANCISCO
235 Pine Street, 11th Floor
San Francisco, CA 94104
(415) 391-7510

WASHINGTON/BALTIMORE
5480 Wisconsin Ave., Suite 210
Chevy Chase, MD 20815
(301) 657-2560

AMERICAN FEDERATION OF TELEVISION AND RADIO ARTISTS (AFTRA) (LOS ANGELES LOCAL RULES)

AFTRA'S jurisdiction covers taped television shows, radio, transcriptions, some phonograph records, and some nonbroadcast material.

You can join AFTRA without a job commitment. You will need to pay the initiation fee of $800 and the first year's dues of $42.50. After that the dues schedule is determined by your earnings, as in SAG. If you do join without a job, you will have to sign a rider acknowledging that you are aware that AFTRA offers no work guarantees and that membership in AFTRA does not guarantee membership or access to any of the other performer unions (AEA, AGVA, AGMA, SAG, SEG).

If you are a member of one of the other performer unions at the time you join, your membership fee and dues will be less than the standard fee.

Under the Taft-Hartley law, if you get a job under AFTRA jurisdiction, you are not obligated to join the union immediately. You will have thirty calendar days during which you can work without joining; then, if you continue to work, you will have to pay the membership fee and dues.

The Los Angeles office of AFTRA is located at 6922 Hollywood Blvd., 8th Floor, Hollywood, CA 90028-6128. The phone number is (213) 461-8111.

Membership and fees in locals outside of Los Angeles may vary. If you are interested, contact an office near you and get the specifics from them.

AFTRA LOCALS AND CHAPTERS

ATLANTA
Ms. Melissa Goodman,
Executive Director
455 East Paces Ferry Rd. NE, Suite 334
Atlanta, GA 30305
(404) 230-0131
(404) 239-0137 fax

BOSTON
Ms. Dona Sommers, Executive Director
11 Beacon Street, #512
Boston, MA 02108
(617) 742-2688
(617) 742-4904 fax

BUFFALO
Mr. Rick Pfeiffer, President
c/o WIVB-TV
2077 Elmwood Avenue
Buffalo, NY 14207
(716) 874-4410

CHICAGO
Ms. Grace Fair
Acting Executive Director
75 East Wacker Drive, 14th Floor
Chicago, IL 60601
(312) 372-8081
(312) 372-5025 fax

MILWAUKEE
Mr. Todd Ganser, Business Manager
5004 West Burleigh Street
Milwaukee, WI 53210
(414) 442-7000

CLEVELAND
Ms. Joan L. Kalhorn, Executive Director
1030 Euclid Avenue, Suite 429
Cleveland, OH 44115-1504
(216) 781-2255
(216) 781-2257 fax

DALLAS–FORT WORTH
Mr. William McCright
Executive Director
6060 N. Central Expressway, #302
L.B. 604
Dallas, TX 75206
(214) 303-8300
(214) 363-5386 fax

DENVER
Mr. Jerre Hookey, Executive Director
950 South Cherry Street, #502
Denver, CO 80222
(303) 757-6226
(303) 757-1769

DETROIT
Ms. Barbara Honner, Executive Director
28690 Southfield Road
Lathrup Village, MI 48076
(810) 559-9540
(810) 559-7163 fax

DETROIT, BROADCAST DIVISION
Mr. Dave Gebard, Broadcast Rep.
3172 Cedar Key Drive
Lake Orion, MI 48360
(313)391-1999
(313)383-3045 fax

FRESNO
Mr. Chris Ward, President
P.O. Box 11961
Fresno, CA 93776
(209) 764-7187
(209) 222-2342 fax

HAWAII
Ms. Brenda Ching, Executive Director
949 Kapiolani Blvd., Ste. #105
Honolulu, Hl 96814
(808) 596-0388
(808) 593-2636 fax

HOUSTON
Mr. Jack Dunlop, Executive Director
2650 Fountainview, #326
Houston, TX 77057
(713) 972-1806
(713) 780-0261 fax

KANSAS CITY
Ms. Linda King, Executive Director
P.O. Box 32167
4000 Baltimore, 2nd Floor
Kansas City, MO 64111
(816) 753-4557
(816) 753-1234 fax

LOS ANGELES
Mr. Mark Farber, Executive Director
6922 Hollywood Blvd., 8th Floor
Hollywood, CA 90028-6128
(213) 461-8111
(213) 463-9041 fax

MIAMI
Ms. Diane Hogan, Executive Director
20401 N.W. 2nd Ave., #102
Miami, FL 33169
(305) 652-4824
(305) 652-4846
(305) 652-2885 fax
1-800-330-AFTR (Miami)

MILWAUKEE
(see Chicago)

NASHVILLE
Mr. Randall Himes, Executive Director
P.O. Box 121087
1108 17th Avenue South
Nashville, TN 37212
(615) 327-2944
(615) 327-2947 nite line
(615) 329-2803 fax

NEW ORLEANS
Ken Hanson, Executive Director
2475 Canal Street, Suite #108
New Orleans, LA 70119
(504) 822-6568
(504) 837-4990 fax

NEW YORK
Stephen Burrow, Executive Director
250 Madison Avenue, 7th Floor
New York, NY 10016
(212) 532-0800
(212) 545-1238 fax

OMAHA
Bob Horder
3000 Farnham St., Suite 3 East
Omaha, NE 68131
(402) 346-8384

ORLANDO
Major Building
5728 Major Blvd., Suite 264
Orlando, FL 32819
(407) 354-2219 fax

Ms. Lorraine Lawless
Central Florida Rep.
(407) 354-2230

PEORIA
Mr. Garry Moore, Treasurer
c/o Station Week
2907 Springfield Road
East Peoria, IL 61611
(309) 698-3737

PHILADELPHIA
Mr. John Kailin, Executive Director
230 South Broad Srreet, 10th Floor
Philadelphia, PA 19010-1229
(212) 732-0507
(215) 732-0086 fax

PHOENIX
Mr. Donald Livesay, Executive Director
1616 East Indian School Road, #330
Phoenix, AZ 85016
(602) 265-2712
(602) 264-7571 fax

PITTSBURGH
Mark Wirick, Executive Director
625 Stanwix Street, The Penthouse
Pittsburgh, PA 15222
(412) 281-6767
(412) 281-2444 fax

PORTLAND
Mr. Stuart Pemble-Belkin
Executive Director
516 S.E. Morrison, #M-3
Portland, OR 97214
(503) 238-6914
(503) 238-0039 fax

ROCHESTER
June Baller, President
87 Fairlea Drive
Rochester, NY 14622
(716) 232-3730

SACRAMENTO/STOCKTON
Mr. Michael McLaughlin, President
836 Garnet Street
West Sacramento, CA 95691
(916) 372-1966
(916) 925-0443 fax

SAN DIEGO
Thomas W. Doyle, Executive Director
7827 Convoy Court, #400
San Diego, CA 92111
(619) 278-7695
(619) 278-2505 fax

SAN FRANCISCO
Ms. Rebecca Rhine, Executive Director
235 Pine Street, 11th Floor
San Francisco, CA 94104
(415) 391-7510
(415) 391-1108 fax

SCHENECTADY/ALBANY
Jim Leonard, President
170 Ray Avenue
Schenectady, NY 12304
(518) 381-4836

Mr. Peter Rief
Shop Coordinator
c/o WGY-AM/WRVE-FM
1 Washington Square
Albany, NY 12205
(518) 452-4800

Mr. Jack Aernecke & Peter Brancato
Shop Coordinators, c/o WRGB-TV
1400 Balltown Road
Schenectady, NY 12309
(518) 346-6666

SEATTLE
John Sandifer, Acting Executive Director
P.O. Box 9688
601 Valley Street, #200
Seattle, WA 98109
(206) 282-2506
(206) 282-7073 fax

SAINT LOUIS
Jache Dietrich, Executive Director
906 Olive Street, #1006
St. Louis, MO 63101
(314) 231-8410
(314) 231-8412 fax

STAMFORD
Mr. Len Gambino, Shop Coordinator
c/o Station WSTC
100 Prospect Street
Stamford, CT 06901
(203) 348-1308

TRI-STATE
(includes Cincinnati, Columbus, & Dayton, OH;
Indianapolis, Indiana, & Louisville, KY)
Ms. Herta Suarez, Executive Director
128 East 6th Street, #802
Cincinnati, OH 45202
(513) 579-8668
(513) 579-1617 fax

TWIN CITIES
Ms. Colleen Aho, Executive Director
708 North First Street
Suite 343A Itasca Bldg.
Minneapolis, MN 55401
(612) 371-9120
(612) 371-9119 fax (call before faxing)

WASHINGTON/BALTIMORE
Ms. Pat O'Donnell, Executive Director
4340 East West Highway, #204
Bethesda, MD 20814
(301) 657-2560
(301) 656-3615 fax

37

The Star

What makes a film star? That's a terrific question, and I wish I had a terrific answer. I have a few theories, and I'll be happy to share them with you.

Before we continue the discussion of what makes a star, let's ask a related question: What makes a good actor? There are many opinions. I believe a good actor is (1) one who can articulate for the audience what the material is about; (2) one who can interest the audience sufficiently to make them want to stay and watch the performance; and (3) perhaps most important, one who is able to move the audience. It doesn't matter if a line reading is bad or if an emotion seems unfulfilled. What ultimately matters, and the only thing that ultimately matters, is that the audience was swept up in the material, believed and empathized with what it was seeing, and was moved. Surely, John Wayne, Gary Cooper, Gregory Peck, Joan Crawford, Barbara Stanwyck, Joanne Woodward, Anne Bancroft, and Glenda Jackson all accomplish those ends. Does it matter, really, whether or not each one fits into some subjective opinion about what constitutes good acting?

What does it matter if a film star could never succeed on the stage? Nobody's asking him to. He doesn't have to; he might not even want to. His medium is the film. What does it matter if a great stage star does not succeed in the accepted sense on film? Stars rarely are able to do equally well in both media, for the media are different, make different demands, and unquestionably have different audiences. Television and film audiences are, to a large extent, composed of people who have never seen, and never will see, a play, or people who will see only a few in their entire lifetimes. Most of the people in these audiences judge acting by different standards than theater audiences do. An average motion picture will reach far more people than any play could hope to reach, and the average television episode will reach even more people than most feature films can. If we go back to the definition of acting that stresses the actor's need to communicate ideas and emotions to the audience, isn't it sufficient if a film actor does exactly that and the audience enjoys being there and experiences something they afterward are pleased to have experienced?

Maybe we should change the phrase "good" actor to "effective" actor. If actors are effective, they are doing what needs to be done, and if I were a writer or the director or the producer of a movie, that's the kind of actors I would want, even if they could never play Hamlet or Lady Macbeth.

For many years I wondered, probably along with everyone else in the industry, why some actors became stars and *remained* stars. The first and most important factor is charisma, but there's no point in discussing it in depth because I don't know its component parts. I know that it is a quality that stars have and that great leaders have, but I don't know where it comes from. Let's just say that a great star has charisma, whatever that is, and go on to other things. They are the people I'm talking about, not stars who appear suddenly and disappear almost as suddenly. I looked for some quality or performance approach that they all had in common and was very hard put to find one. (Remember now, I'm talking about the screen and television star, not the star of the theater, who is a different breed in a great many respects.) Finally, I realized what one of the major factors was.

The leading man in the pilot for a new ABC series was an actor whose work I liked a great deal, but who never became a major star. I watched the pilot, and a lightbulb lit over my head during a scene in which the actor was faced with a group of men who he knew wanted to destroy him. They had trapped him in a corridor; helplessly, and with great terror, he cried, "Help me, help me." I would have felt exactly the same way; I would have been just as terrified, if not more so, and I probably would have screamed "Help me" a lot louder than he did. But I became aware that his responses were not strong responses, nor were they heroic responses, although he was, in the accepted usage of the term, the hero of the series. I began to think back to the work of such stars as Gary Cooper, Humphrey Bogart, Clark Gable, and Spencer

Tracy—some of the really big ones—and came to the conclusion that the difference between their work and that of the actor in the pilot lay in a very simple selection: they did choose strong, heroic responses.

The star plays a hero who is *never* terrified by danger; he is aware that it exists, and he is determined to survive, but instead of allowing the emotion of fear to overpower him, he plays a very dynamic intention: *to solve the problem and survive*. Gary Cooper might walk down a western street, holding a gun that has only two bullets in it, knowing that there are six men on top of various roofs waiting to gun him down. The Cooper-type actor is aware that death is at hand, but he is concerned not with the terror inherent in the situation, but with the need to survive—*to find a way to solve the problem*.

The last phrase is the most significant. Instead of being over-powered by the problem, the actor does what is necessary to *solve* the problem. Isn't it true that the person we respect and love and want to follow, as we must indeed want to follow heroes, is the one who faces a problem squarely and then proceeds to find a way to beat it?

Is that an oversimplification? It may be, but it also seems to be a truth. Right now it seems to be a very significant truth and one that bears a good deal of examination. Watch a surviving television or film star and you will find that that rule applies.

Maybe the problem is that most of the actors I'm talking about never had the talent and emotional capacity to experience or play fear. I rather doubt that that's true, although some of the most successful film actors of our time, like Gary Cooper and John Wayne, have been accused of being rotten actors. My guess is that we need to reexamine the usual definition of good acting before we condemn actors whom people have spent hundreds of millions of dollars to see.

I discovered another quality of a star as I watched a TV situation comedy. I was bothered by the leading lady, but didn't know why. The actress is a perfectly good actress (who has not become a major star), and the series was a very successful one (although I expect the major reason for its success was that it was sandwiched between two excellent and even more successful series). As I wondered, my wife said, "You know, there's nothing emotionally vulnerable about her."

In her casual way, my wife had put a finger on one of the most important characteristics of the star. People are vulnerable. Actors portray people, and if they expect their audiences to identify with them, to feel with them, and to like them, then they, too, must be vulnerable.

Perhaps a classic lady of strength is Lady Macbeth. One's first impulse in interpreting and attacking the role might be to give her more power than Macbeth himself possesses, since she is the one with the greater ambition and she is the catalyst that sets the tragedy of the numerous slaughters into motion. Yet those very tragedies drive her insane and, ultimately, send her to her death. She must, therefore, be vulnerable in spite of the apparent power—or she would have been the only one to survive the play. Without the vulnerability, it's difficult to conceive of the tragedy, and Shakespeare, who was a pretty clever fellow all round, had the good sense to draw the character that way. Unfortunately, not every actress has the sensitivity and awareness to play her that way; many actresses playing the role never achieve this most important value.

The vulnerability of successful male stars is also apparent—not on a level of weakness, but on an emotional level. One of the best examples I can think of is Humphrey Bogart. Look at the classic *Casablanca*. Bogart is tough, solid as a rock, self-sufficient—yet very vulnerable. Under it all, he is a pussycat.

Vulnerability—the chink in the armor that lets the audience know that you are human, that you can be hurt, that you are susceptible to failure, that you have an Achilles' heel—that's what gives the real strength to the character. It is the decision to forge ahead, even though you might prefer not to—to tackle and overcome obstacles in spite of the fact that you are not made of impenetrable steel—that most affects an audience.

Is vulnerability a quality an acting teacher can help you acquire? Possibly, but only if you are willing to lay your emotions bare and expose your true feelings. The absence of vulnerability is frequently the result of an actor's holding up strong defenses and refusing to show weakness, believing it to be demeaning or fearing to be hurt. Unless you show that you *can* be hurt, and that you do care about things on a very personal level, even though your feelings might be considered weak or corny, you will not project a sense of vulnerability. You will play your moment-to-moment life in such a way that the audience will feel no real empathy.

Another quality that we will find in any star—one we can, fortunately, develop, is *authority*. It is important that everything you do in your performance is done with certainty, with decision, and with clarity and economy of motion. It is those qualities that constitute a sense of authority, and it is the actor who works with authority who will get the audience's attention. Check in real life and see if you don't watch the authoritative person.

Whatever you do, it is important to believe that your choice is the right one, the only one, the inevitable one; then go at it with everything you've got. Even if you have made a wrong choice, if you do it with authority, the chances are that at least half the audience won't know that you're wrong, because you will have done or said it with such conviction.

In one of our sessions with Dr. Branden, we were astonished to discover that some people, in fact many people, were unable to stand up in front of the group and say to each person in the group, "I have a right to be alive," or "I have a right to stand here." It was equally difficult to say, "I take full responsibility for everything I say," or "I take full responsibility for everything I do." An astonishing number of us lack the very essential authority we need not only to be successful as actors, but to be successful and happy as human beings.

See if you can say those things with an easy sense of conviction. If you can't, stand in a comfortable position and keep saying them until you begin to believe them—and then keep saying them after that, or join a group of friends or actors and do it there, because it is necessary that you find the strength and security to say it to a number of other people. Don't kid yourself, though, and believe that saying the words is sufficient. It's not until you can say them and really *believe* them at a deep gut level that you've achieved what is necessary.

Uncertainty is one of the deadliest of acting sins. If you're going somewhere, go there. If you're going to move to a chair, move to it; if you're going to move to someone, move to that person; if you're going out of the room, go as if you have a purpose and a destination. Not only is a hesitant, sidling performer uncomfortable to watch, he is abrasive to an audience. Whatever you do or say, do or say it as if it is the only possible correct and inevitable thing that could be said or done in the life of the character, and believe it. The corollary, of course, is to believe that you are a good and effective actor—that you know what you are doing, and that you belong on the stage or in front of the camera and have a right to be there.

The other side to this coin is being able to evaluate yourself in a completely honest way and then to accept that evaluation with affection. Not many people can look in the mirror and see both the things that they like about themselves and the things that they don't like. All too often we are preoccupied with what we don't like about ourselves and are dragged down by it. We are determined that we are unworthy and incompetent; when we perform, we present that sense of incompetence and unworthiness with great authority because it's what we believe in.

Examine all the good things about yourself; examine the things that you do well as an actor, accept them as things you do well, and then look honestly at things you do not do well. We all have limitations; there is no actor alive who doesn't. That doesn't mean that you are an incomplete actor; it only means that you are a human being—that you have an instrument that is individual and could never conceivably be all things to all people.

Know where your strengths are, develop them and make them even stronger. Know where your weaknesses are, and work on them to turn them into strengths wherever you can. Face your limitations with courage and acceptance and put them aside for the time being. Face the fact that you are not a great tragedian or that you are not a great comedian, just as you would face the fact that you will never be able to sing opera if you can't carry a tune.

The inability to sing opera is no problem for most people; they accept it and don't try to have careers as opera singers. It's also no

294 The Film/Tape Career

problem for most very successful popular singers. Why, then, should you have difficulty saying to yourself, "I'm a terrific dramatic actor, I just can't play farce"?

Don't despair; sometimes the inability to achieve certain performance values is only temporary and is overcome as one matures as a person and as an actor. Meanwhile, don't destroy yourself and your career by insisting on doing those things.

Film, because of its intimacy, is a typecasting medium. The best thing you can do for your career is to find out what type you honestly are and develop and grow from there. Don't kid yourself about what type you think you are or would like to be.

Two of the questions I ask most new students who come into the Workshop are, "What kind of roles do you see yourself playing?" and "What actor or actress is doing the things you want to do?" In an astonishing number of cases, they will see themselves as leading men and women when they are unquestionably character people. There are others who see themselves in stereotyped categories such as gangsters or heavies.

My advice to them is to put aside all preconceptions about what kind of actors and actresses they are and to simply begin to work—to let us help them find the thing or things they do best, then to develop those things to a professional level. Then they should take an occasional experimental sortie into a good stretch role in order to broaden their acting parameters. My advice to you is the same. Go to some friends you can trust, who will be honest with you, and find out what you are. Then make the most of that, while you continue experimentally, not professionally, to stretch yourself so that as time goes by, your own instrument will become more versatile and capable of doing things it couldn't do years ago.

Ultimately, the audience, and only the audience, can determine who is a star. No matter how talented you or your peers in the industry may think you are, if the audience doesn't take to you, stardom is not your fate. Everyone in the entertainment industry would like to be able to spot a star, but no one has been able to do so every time out.

Audiences are fickle and frequently surprising. When we tested the first episodes of "The Man and The City," starring Anthony

Quinn, Quinn scored a 94 percent "excellent and favorable" rating, the highest any actor had ever received in those tests. Our elation was dampened, however, by the fact that in a series titled "Hondo," there was a dog named Sam—and he scored 95 percent. We never mentioned that to Quinn, incidentally.

38

· ·

Exercises for
Acting for the Camera

The following pages include a number of very effective exercises designed for the classroom, or for use with any small group of actors working together.

The exercises that follow were designed for our classes and for the book by Eric Stephan Kline.

Eric received his B.A. in Literature and Psychology from the University of California at Berkeley, and his M.A. in TV Production from San Francisco State University. He has been an instructor at the Film Actors Workshop since 1980, and he was a Visiting Lecturer in Dramatic Arts at the University of California at Irvine from 1982 to 1996. He has coached actors for hundreds of auditions, and for appearances in dozens of feature films, including City Slickers, Mr. Saturday Night, Crimson Tide, *and* The American President. *He is currently the principal instructor at the Film Actors Workshop.*

Again, a word of caution: When you built the house we talked about earlier, you didn't continue to carry your tools with you when you went into it to live, right? You put them away. The same applies to any acting exercises; don't take them into the work!

Remember, an exercise is only that. It is designed to help you to better understand a concept, or to help you reach an emotion that is eluding you. FORGET THE EXERCISES WHEN YOU PERFORM.

LONG SHOT AND CLOSE-UP
• •
(See Chapter 2)

When you are new to the camera you are going to have trouble trusting that the audience will get what you are feeling without your enlarging the performance physically or vocally, as you might on stage. To build up that trust, try this exercise:

Take a short scene from a film, and shoot it:

1. In a long shot, much as a theatrical audience might see it from the back row of a theater.
2. In a series of tight close-ups, much as a film audience might see it on-screen.

Now play back the tape and notice the differences.

In Take 1 the audience listens to the words. In Take 2 the audience watches what goes on in the silences.

In Take 1 the audience is moved when you physicalize what you're feeling. In Take 2 the audience is more likely to be moved by something they see in your eyes.

In Take 1 you are always in a two-shot. You must move to earn the audience's attention. In Take 2 the editing focuses the audience's attention on you, without your having to work for it. Once the camera cuts to you, there is nowhere else for the audience to look.

In Take 1 louder often seems to mean more dramatic. In Take 2 the most intense moments can just as easily be the quietest ones.

To sum up: in Take 1 you may have to work quite hard to reach your audience. In Take 2 the camera and the microphone are working with you to help you reach them.

VOCAL LEVELS

• •

(See Chapter 2)

Because you have not yet worked with a microphone, you may automatically believe that louder is better. But because the microphone has a "close-up" on your voice at all times, it gives you the freedom to use volume levels which would be impossible on the stage, levels which are *real*.

To begin to explore these possibilities, try this exercise. Take a short scene and videotape it. Arbitrarily change your vocal levels—not your interpretation, or attack—just your volume. Do the scene:

1. as rehearsed
2. with both actors shouting
3. with one actor speaking loudly, the other softly
4. with one actor speaking softly, the other loudly
5. both actors talking across "real distance"

To get a concept of what "real distance" means, put the script down and have a normal conversation with a partner, talking as yourselves. Then take note of your volume level.

Now watch how the power balances within the scene change with each volume adjustment. The effects will depend in part on your original interpretation of the scene. Generally though, the person who talks more softly will appear stronger. This effect will be surprising to most stage-trained actors, who are often conditioned to believe that the more you scream, the stronger you are.

EXPLORING YOUR QUALITY

• •

(See Chapter 3)

What you have to sell on-screen is your own uniqueness, rather than your ability to play a wide range of characters. If you have trouble believing that you have any distinctive qualities on-screen, try this exercise:

Get a partner. Go to a bar or restaurant and tape-record your conversation. Transcribe a three-minute section of the tape and memorize it as you would a scene. Videotape the scene and, if possible, show it to a small group of people. Ask them what your essential quality is. After they arrive at a consensus, ask them how they would cast you.

You may be surprised at the results. Even though you are playing yourself, your audience will see you as an interesting "character" with very specific qualities. When you realize that you have this much energy and impact just being yourself, you will be much less tempted to play "characters."

As Richard Dreyfuss once said in an interview, "British actors, because they come from a theatrical tradition, get to be stars by putting on a lot of make-up and playing a wide range of characters, like Olivier. American actors, because they come from a film tradition, get to be stars by being the best at being who they are. Cary Grant was the ultimate Cary Grant. Spencer Tracy was the ultimate Spencer Tracy."

Try being the best at who you are and see if your screen work doesn't gain more power and immediacy.

CHARACTER AND QUALITY
• •
(See Chapter 3)

On-screen you're always working from yourself. If you're new to the camera, especially if you're from a traditional theatrical background, this idea might make you a little uncomfortable. Your objection might be, "But I'm nowhere near as interesting as my character."

To get over these objections, try this exercise:

1. Take a short scene and tape it playing your needs as the "character."

2. Tape yourselves talking about the same subject as the scene—
    not using the dialogue from the scene and without any partic-
    ular needs, just as yourselves.

Play the tapes back and see which is more interesting. More
often than not it will be Take 2, when you are just being
yourselves. Surprising? Not really. As one director has said, "It's
impossible for an actor to try to be interesting on-screen. Either
he is interesting, or he looks like he's trying and then he's
dead."

Now look at Take 2 again and find the specific adjustments
that made it better: lower volume, more relaxed diction, slower or
faster rhythm, or less indicated emotion. Take these adjustments
and:

3. Try the written scene again, and compare it to the others.

LISTENING/SENSING: PRESENCE
(See Chapter 5)

One of the biggest differences between the stage and the
screen is that onstage you tend to play scenes at greater than normal distances in order to fill up the stage and to provide a justifi-
cation for talking louder.

On-screen, you tend to play scenes at normal, or less than normal, distances. Like everything else on camera, this spatial adjustment has an upside and a downside.

The upside is that you don't have to work as hard, vocally and
physically, because the other actor and the audience are so much
closer. In addition there is more stimulus available when the other
actor is six inches away than there is when he is standing sixteen
feet away. The downside is that this increased intimacy can be a
problem if you are not used to it.

To begin to understand what real sensing is, try this exercise. Take a very intimate scene and do it:

1. As you've rehearsed it, but standing very far apart—at least six to ten feet.
2. Just for yourselves, standing as close as you can to one another without touching and as slowly as you possibly can, so that the other person's physical presence begins to dominate your attention. These adjustments should make your sensing of each other much easier.

Now play back the tapes and watch what happens. The meaning of Take 1 usually derives from the words that you hear.

The meaning of Take 2 usually derives more from your hearing what is not being said: a pause, a blink, a look, a breath, a sigh. This additional level of stimulus often results in a big increase in the level of intimacy and moment-to-moment involvement in the scene.

THE TALK-BACK EXERCISE: LISTENING
• •
(See Chapter 5)

Once you understand the importance of listening on-screen you will find you won't have much trouble staying connected to the other actor as long as you are trading lines.

The trouble starts when the other actor has a "speech" of three or more lines. In this situation you will usually panic and succumb to what I call the "check-in–check-out" syndrome. You check into the scene to say your lines, check out again while the other person does his speech, then check back in again to say your next line.

Meanwhile, your face goes blank and your eyes glaze over. In your reaction shot you look like the "lights are on but there's nobody home." Onstage no one might notice the disconnection, but on-screen you're very much an actor caught in the act of "acting."

To begin to understand how to avoid this kind of disconnection, try this exercise. Take a so-called "monologue" from a scene in which both characters have strong needs.

1. Do the scene once your way, with your partner talking and you listening silently.
2. Do the scene again, this time turning the monologue into a dialogue by improvising your responses to the other actor's lines. Don't intellectualize, don't edit, don't make up character-based lines, just go on impulse, from your gut responses. Don't be grammatical. You don't have to wait for a pause, or the end of a sentence to speak, just jump in whenever you feel the urge.

    Have the other actor stop when you interrupt him, let your responses affect him, and then go on with his lines. Under no circumstances should he begin to improvise. It is very important that he stay with his lines.
3. Do the scene again, with your partner talking and you listening silently. Just let your responses happen, don't attempt to act them out for the audience.

Now play the takes back. You should notice a big increase in your involvement as you move from the first silent take to the second take, in which you "talk back" to your partner, because now you have converted the monologue into a dialogue. You are now actively processing the stimuli instead of passively receiving them. It's important to understand that there are very few monologues on-screen; almost everything is a dialogue, regardless of whether or not you have lines to support your responses.

You should still be able to retain most of this increased involvement when you go silent again in the third take. The result is a much more dynamic, and therefore much more usable, reaction shot.

THE TALK-BACK EXERCISE: THE SPEAKER

● ●

(See Chapter 5)

As I mentioned above, with a little practice you won't have much trouble staying connected to your partner as long as you're both trading lines. It's when you hit a long speech that panic sets in. Suddenly you will be tempted to abandon your need to get through to the other actor and settle for just getting through all those words. Ideas for arbitrary line readings will begin to buzz around in your head. "I could say them faster." Or "I could say them slower." "I could say them loud here, and then slow here."

To overcome these temptations, try the talk-back exercise from the speaker's point of view. Take a monologue from a scene in which both characters have strong needs and do it three ways:

1. Your way, with your partner listening silently.
2. With your partner talking back his responses. Make sure you don't override him, because that is a choice not to listen. Stop each time he interrupts, listen, let it affect you, then go on.
3. Your way again, with your partner listening silently.

Now play back the tapes. Take 1 will look more like a monologue, with a limited connection between you and your partner. You may find yourself speeding through the words just for the sake of getting the speech over with.

Take 2 should be much hotter emotionally because you are now hearing the resistance implicit in your partner's silences. Again, you're always in a dialogue, even though this time you have all the lines. You're never getting "nothing" from your partner. Even his silence can be a stimulus; you can "hear" it as resistance, or you can "hear" it as agreement.

Take 3 will often be less charged than Take 2, because the resistance is no longer as loud. Still it should be much more connected than Take 1 because you are working off of your partner now instead of just making a speech.

COMPLEX AND SIMPLE BRIDGES
• •
(See Chapter 5)

Most bridges are simple, like this one:
JOHN
Where did you go last night?
MARY
I went to the movies.
Assuming Mary is telling the truth, then the bridge is simple:
"Where did I go last night?" followed by the response "I went to
the movies." The bridge and the response follow logically from the
stimulus, "Where did you go last night?"

The problem gets stickier when the written stimulus and the
written response do not follow logically. Take this example:
JOHN
I got a job.
MARY
I'll never get married.
No matter how committed you are to listening, if you're play-
ing Mary, you're going to be tempted to just say the line. But that
would be wrong: you have no real stimulus, because "I got a job"
isn't the stimulus for "I'll never get married." It makes no sense.

Here's where a yellow flag should go up in your mind with the
words BRIDGE OUT printed on it in big red letters. It's a sign that
there's a connective missing in the text that you have to supply
yourself. You can think of it as a complex bridge or as unwritten
dialogue.

Let's try building this bridge. Start with the repetition of the
stimulus from Mary's point of view:

1. You got a job.

Now explore the implications:

2. Now you'll be working all the time.
3. You won't have time for me.

4. So we'll gradually drift apart . . .
5. and eventually we'll break up . . .
6. and so we'll never get married . . .
7. and so I guess
8. I'll never get married.

You could build this bridge in a hundred different ways, but in this example, Mary's response is eight thoughts away from the written stimulus.

Onstage all eight of these thoughts might be written into the dialogue in order to reach the back rows of the theater. On camera they are subtracted from the dialogue, so that the camera can see you think and feel your way through them in the silences.

To get a feel for these complex bridges, find a scene with a lot of discontinuities and changes of subject in the dialogue. Tape it:

1. Your way.
2. After working out the complex bridges as unwritten dialogue.

Now play the tape back and see whether your listening, your dynamics, and your overall level of involvement don't improve when you stop saying lines, and start crossing bridges.

LISTENING/SENSING: PHONE ACTING
• •
(See Chapter 5)

You're always responding to stimuli, but sometimes those stimuli are wholly or partly imaginary. Nowhere is this more true than when shooting a phone conversation. It's likely that the person you are talking to will be shot in a separate scene, in another location, on a different day. This means that, more often than not, you'll be talking to thin air.

Because there's no one on the other end of the line, you won't listen. You won't pause for the other person to get a word in. You won't react to what they're supposed to be saying. You just talk—

then, realizing that you're losing energy because the whole scene has been reduced to "talk," you will "act" to make up the difference. Later you may spend a good deal of time wondering why the scene seemed forced.

To begin to understand how to deal with this problem, try the following exercise. Take a short scene involving a phone conversation and do it three different ways:

1. As you've rehearsed it.
2. With another person on the other end of the line, who will turn it into a dialogue by improvising responses to all your lines.

Tape each of these in a tight close-up and analyze the results.

Notice how shallow the level of involvement is during Take 1, when you are only pretending to listen to the voice on the other end of the phone.

Notice how active the listening process becomes during Take 2, when the scene is converted into a real dialogue, instead of an imaginary one.

3. Now try this scene again, alone this time, but retaining the reactions developed during the improvisation.

See if you can sustain this level of involvement during Take 3, when the conversation becomes wholly imaginary again.

LISTENING: THE REACTION SHOT
• •
(See Chapter 5)

An actor once asked me, "What do you do when the camera is on you and you don't have any lines?"

"You listen," I told him.

"OK, but what else do I do?"

You may have similar feelings about being in a reaction shot with nothing to do or say. To begin to understand how uncomfortable this can be, try this exercise.

1. Take a short monologue and, after discussing the facts and circumstances, have someone read it to you. Videotape your reactions in a tight close-up.

Now play the tape back and analyze the results. You will probably be a little flat in this take, with very little energy or dynamics, because you are listening passively. In reality, listening is the most active thing you can do. In real life you do not simply receive information, you are constantly sorting, evaluating, judging, trying to decide whether what you are hearing is true or false, good or bad, worthless or worthwhile.

Take 1 also tends to be flat because you are listening too objectively. In real life you have opinions on everything and everyone, but once a scene begins you often become a model of restraint. This objectivity limits your involvement because it keeps you from reacting strongly, either positively or negatively, to the incoming stimuli.

It can also look flat because you are not working from yourself. You are not bringing your own responses to the listening processes. Your listening is at all times circumscribed by your concept of what the "character" should be thinking and feeling. In effect, you are playing your concept of what should be happening, rather than your own moment-to-moment responses to the stimuli.

To understand how much more powerful real listening is, try this exercise:

2. Keep the camera on you in a tight close-up while you watch another actor play the sentence completion exercise described in Chapter 5 with a partner.

Now play Take 2 back and compare it to Take 1. You should look more lively, more involved, because you are actively judging the validity of the other person's responses. You will probably try to anticipate the other person's answers. Sometimes you will succeed and be pleased with yourself. Sometimes you will fail and be surprised by the actual reply. Either way, your involvement with the event, on a moment-to-moment basis, will be much higher because the listening is active, subjective, and tied directly to your own unique responses.

BOTTOM-LINING: INVOLVING THE OTHER PERSON
(See Chapter 5)

In classical theater you do a lot of soliloquies. On-screen almost everything you do is a dialogue. You don't communicate to the audience directly, you communicate by interacting with the other character. In most scenes he's all that you've got to play with. But you may lose sight of this fact if you fail to include the other person in the bottom line. Then you may find yourself disconnecting from him when you do the scene, because you haven't given yourself a reason to listen to him.

To fix this problem, try this exercise. Take a scene in which you have a strong need to discover some information and do it two ways:

1. Bottom-lining with the need to figure out the truth. The obstacle is that you're confused about what the truth is.
2. Bottom-lining with the need to find out the truth. The obstacle is that the other person won't tell you.

Now play the tape back and analyze the results.

Take 1 should look a little disconnected, and for good reason: you've given yourself no reason to listen to the other person, so you don't. You're probably listening very well to yourself, but unfortunately, that's not what the scene is about.

Take 2 should look much more connected because you've given yourself good reasons to listen to the other person, both when you're pursuing the need, and when you're responding to the obstacles he puts in the way of that need.

Try putting both the need and the obstacle on the other person by asking "What do I need to do with this person?" and "In what way does he make the achievement of that need difficult?"

See if including the other person in your bottom line—both on the level of need and obstacle—doesn't increase your level of involvement.

COLD READING: BY THE NUMBERS
(See Chapter 5)

No matter how well you learn to listen, you're going to be tempted to go into "speech mode" when you hit a block of print in a cold reading.

To see what this approach looks like on screen, try taping this speech:

"Listen, you know I love you. I've loved you for a long, long time. This thing that's come between us, we can't afford to let that destroy what we had. It's your decision. I know that now. What do you think?"

Now play the tape back and see how it looks. Your natural tendency will be to plow through the print, disconnecting from the other actor. To overcome this temptation, you have to realize that most speeches consist of a number of attempts to achieve your need. The easy way to remember this is to number the attempts.

1. "Listen, you know I love you."
2. "I loved you for a long, long time."
3. "This thing that's come between us, we can't afford to let that destroy what we had."
4. "It's your decision."
5. "I know that now. What do you think?"

It looks like one speech, but actually it's five separate attempts to get your girlfriend to agree to stay, followed by five separate rejections. Therefore there's going to be five times more frustration generated than when dealing with it as a single speech.

Now tape the speech by the numbers. Be sure to see if you're getting through each time you try. Sometimes you can see the other person's reaction while you are talking. Sometimes you will need to pause a moment to see if they respond.

Now play the both tapes back and look at the results. You should see a big increase in involvement in Take #2. That's what happens when you have the numbers on your side.

VISUAL FOCUS
• •
(See Chapter 7)

Deciding where to look is often a problem for the actor. The simple remedy is to remember that the visual focus is usually where the emotional focus is.

Take this scene:

Agnes is an attorney, interrogating Christine.

AGNES

Now this is very important. When was the last time you saw the defendant?

CHRISTINE

On the night of the crime.

AGNES

But you said previously that the last time you saw him was two months ago.

CHRISTINE

I was mixing that up with another time I saw him at the same place.

Now try it this way:

1. Christine is telling the truth, and her bottom line is to convince the attorney that she is.

Now play back the tape and look at the results. If Christine is really connected to her need, her visual focus would be on the attorney, and it would appear that she is telling the truth.

Now try the moment again, but this time:

2. Christine is lying, but still trying to convince the attorney that she is telling the truth.

Her emotional focus is more on herself now, because she has to struggle against revealing that she is lying, so she will find it more difficult to look at the attorney. As a result, it's almost certain that she will appear to be lying, or at least hiding something.

3. Now play the scene again, this time with Christine fighting the need to turn away, struggling to look at the attorney in her effort to make the attorney believe she is telling the truth.

Look at this third take. This should be the most dynamic and interesting one, because Christine's inner conflict has been intensified. Commit to the bottom line; the visual focus will take care of itself.

ENERGY AND CARING: RAISING THE STAKES
(See Chapter 8)

"Where does an actor's energy come from?" Tony asked in one of his seminars.

"Food," someone shouted out.

Tony couldn't argue with that. "Besides food. An actor's energy comes from how much he cares about what is happening to him."

To begin to understand what that means, try this exercise.

Take a potentially volatile scene, such as the scene from *Kramer vs. Kramer* where Joanna tells Ted she is leaving him. Do the scene in the following way:

1. Minimizing the obstacles. Have Ted choose that she has left before and not followed through; consequently he is indifferent to her threats this time. Have Joanna choose that "the marriage is over," that she feels nothing for Ted, and is simply doing him the courtesy of telling him she is going before she leaves.

    Now play the tape back and watch what these adjustments do to the scene. You should notice an almost complete absence of energy and dynamics.
    Try the scene again, this time:

2. Maximizing the obstacles. Have Ted choose that he will die if Joanna leaves him. Have Joanna choose that she must convince Ted that leaving him is the right thing to do, that she cannot live with herself if she does not; that Ted will think she is a witch, and that he will teach her son to hate her.

    Watch the way these adjustments affect the energy level of the scene: the greater the stakes, the more you care; the more you care, the greater the level of emotional involvement, and the more explosive the resulting scene. Notice that changing how much you care about the obstacles you face changes the entire scene—without altering the written text.

THE EMOTIONS: THE COMBAT EXERCISE
(See Chapter 9)

If your anger is blocked you're going to find yourself acting "from the neck up" in confrontation scenes. You may scream, and your face may contort, but your body will remain strangely calm and relaxed.

In contrast, a really great actor experiences anger as an acceleration of all the body's inner rhythms. The heart rate, pulse, breathing, even the skin tension, all increase. As a result the body's external rhythms—the pace at which you move, walk, and talk, and think—often accelerate. In good acting, the body is never separate from the emotions and the mind: there can be no acting "from the neck up."

To overcome any blocks you may have with anger, try this exercise. Take a very volatile scene and tape it:

1. The way you've rehearsed it.
2. With the combat exercise.

This time hit the other actor on the shoulders with both hands each time you have a line, and let him hit you each time he has one. Test each other's limits beforehand so that you will not hurt each other.

Turn the scene into a dialogue of blows and let the spoken dialogue ride on top of the physicalization. The idea here is to physicalize the anger that drives the scene.

This physicalization will eliminate another common problem with highly volatile scenes: your tendency to become less, rather than more, angry while the other actor is speaking. In this exercise, the continual combat will keep your attention from wandering too far.

While you are still "hot" from this exertion:

3. Do another take, this time without the physicalization.

Play back the tapes and see what happens. Take 2 is usually better than Take 1 because the physicalization brings you into better contact with one another. But Take 2 will always seem slightly exaggerated because the physicalization causes you to react very strongly—much more strongly than the words alone.

Take 3 will be somewhat less volatile because the stimulus has changed; it is now much less physical, much more verbal. Consequently it should be the most true to life.

PLAYING AGAINST AN EMOTION
● ●
(See Chapter 9)

The camera allows you to play against emotions to a much greater degree than you normally do onstage. The suppressed emotion will usually result in some subtle form of physicalization, which the camera will pick up and deliver to the audience. But playing against the emotion presents you with yet another trap. You may tend to play against an emotion that is not really there. It is just a cerebralized idea of emotion, rather than an emotional reality.

For instance, you may be playing a husband who is angry with his wife. Because you fear that an emotional outburst may endanger your already shaky marriage, you suppress your anger. But if you are not experiencing real anger, your audience will see only the exterior calm, the cover, the mask. You are playing the result.

To see what this looks like on-screen, try this exercise. Take a short scene in which you are called upon to play against your anger. Do the scene in the following ways:

1.   Playing only the calm, or result.

Now play Take 1 back and analyze the results. Notice that the core emotion, the anger, is too weak to show through. The scene does not play because no one, including the actress playing your wife, or even you yourself, can really feel your anger.

Now try the scene again, this time:

2.   Fully playing only the underlying emotion—your anger.

Notice the difference between the takes. Take 1 usually lacks dynamics and interest because the core emotions are weak. Take 2, on the other hand, will probably be too "hot," too much expressed emotion.

Now try the scene again, this time:

3. Now with the emotions rolling, try masking those emotions—
    making it part of your need to cover them as much as possible.

Take #3 usually creates the impression of a bubbling volcano.
The suppressed emotions create physical tensions, and result in an
accelerating inner rhythm. What makes the scene more exciting
is your depth of involvement with your own emotions. Occasionally
they may become too strong for you to suppress entirely, erupting
momentarily, and in the process creating additional dynamics.

MULTIPLE TAKES: LADDERING UP
(See Chapter 9)

When you're new to the camera, you may "chase the emotion"
as director Barry Levinson calls it. You may tend to set a level for
the scene, then push yourself up to that level, even though you
don't really have the stimulus. The result is your performance
looks forced, and your face looks distorted by tensions in the eyes,
mouth, or forehead. Not a pretty picture. This performance tension is one reason why you have to stay honest and truthful to
what you're feeling on a moment-to-moment basis.

To get an idea of how important this is, try this exercise. Take
a fairly emotional scene and do it:

1. Once on the level you feel it should be played, regardless of
    whether or not that level is real for you at the moment.
2. As a series of five to ten takes, during which you play the
    scene at whatever level is real for you at the moment. When
    you are done with one take, do not laugh or talk away the
    emotion you've generated. Hold on to that emotion and use it
    as the preparation for the next take.

Now play back the tape and look at the results. Take 1 will usually look forced and unrealistic.

Most of Takes 2 to 10 will be usable—some better than others—because you are working honestly from yourself on a moment-to-moment basis. You may also notice that the level of emotion increases from take to take; that you are "laddering" your way up to the level that you're trying to reach by working honestly within each individual take.

Remember, you are not in a live performance, so not every take you do has to be perfect. As Sydney Pollack says, "I tell my actors, 'You only have to do the scene right once, then I can cut it into the film.'"

ANTICIPATION: DELAYING THE FLASH POINT
• •
(See Chapter 9)

One of the most common traps you face as an actor involves playing the end of the scene at the beginning. For instance, knowing that a scene will end in a fight, you might play that conflict right from the beginning of the scene, when your best interests might be better served by trying to avoid the conflict altogether.

This tendency can be so strong that it actually becomes unrealistic. One of the differences between most actors and real people is that real people tend to avoid conflicts, while most actors seem to seek them out.

To get an idea of what this looks like on-screen, try this exercise. Take a very confrontational scene and tape it:

1. Taking advantage of the earliest possible flash point to generate an explosion of emotion.

Play the tape back and watch how this choice affects the meaning of the scene. Take 1 will usually be very emotional, but it may be difficult to understand what you are fighting about. Consequently, you may not seem very sympathetic.

Now try the scene again, this time:

2. Playing against the conflict—delaying the flash point as long as possible.

This take may be less obviously emotional, but should make the relationships much clearer and more sympathetic. Because the conflict builds so gradually, and because you are relieved of the necessity of acting out highly charged emotions from the word "go," you may find that you are in better contact with the other actor.

Onstage this decision to delay the flash point is often a difficult one to execute. In the theater you are often looking for explosions of emotion to support the explosions of volume and physicalization necessary to communicate to an audience that is relatively far away. Play too much against an emotion for too long and the audience may lose touch with what's going on inside you.

On the other hand, the camera supports this approach. No matter how hard you play against the emotion, or how long you delay the conflict, the camera will see what is happening in your eyes and convey it to the audience.

So you could say that in addition to exploding, the camera gives you another alternative: imploding. You push down the emotion as long as is humanly possible, but eventually it will build to an unsustainable level and result in some physicalization—no matter how slight—that will be meaningful to the audience.

IMPROVISING A PRELIFE: MAKING THE BACKGROUND REAL
(See Chapter 11)

Too often actors will wait for the first lines of dialogue to begin the scene. Onstage, where the scenes are relatively long, and the action is continuous, you can often get away with this approach. On camera, where the scenes are very short, and often shot after long hours spent waiting for lighting, this habit can spell disaster. By the time you've worked your way into the scene emotionally, it's over.

To understand what this feels like, take a short, emotionally volatile scene and do it:

1. As you've rehearsed it, with no emotional or physical preparation.

Play the tape and notice how flat the scene is. The solution to this problem is to get your motor running before the first line of dialogue is spoken. One simple way to do this is to:

2. Improvise your prelife, the "moment before" the scene starts.

The two characters may have been together, or with someone else; in the same location, or another place entirely. Continue the improvisation until your "motor" is running. Then:

3. Do the scene again.

Now play back the tapes. Notice how much more energy the scene has after the improvisation.

BOTTOM-LINING: PREPARATION
(See Chapter 11)

Your emotional preparation is the third part of the bottom line. If you're like most actors, you'll be afraid to get deeply involved in this emotional preparation, concerned that it will make you "too big" for the screen.

To begin to understand what this approach looks like on-screen, try this exercise. Take a scene that requires you to be angry from the beginning and do it:

1.   Preparing with the idea that you are merely perturbed.

Now play Take 1 back. As you can see, the preparation can be more important when you are working on-screen than when you are onstage. Onstage you are often in continuous action for long periods of time, so it's easy to keep your energy up. Working on-screen you may sit around for hours while the cinematographer lights the scene, then be required to "nail it" in a few takes. Your emotional preparation is one way to bridge the distance between the part of you that's sitting around the set and the part of you that belongs in the scene.

Try the scene again, this time:

2.   Preparing with real anger.

Make sure that in this take you do not cerebralize the anger. Realize that most strong emotions will lodge themselves somewhere in the body. In addition to speeding up your rhythm, the anger may cause a tightness in your chest, or a churning in your stomach, or some other physical affect. Try to move your awareness out of your head and into this area, then pace in the rhythm of that anger as you think about, or talk out, what's causing it.

Now play both takes back and analyze the results.

Take 1 will likely look even more superficial. It may even tilt towards comedy because the emotional base of the scene is so cerebralized.

Take 2 should be much more dramatic and more powerful, because the emotional base of the scene is so much stronger. If you can still manage to play your needs and not allow this preparation to overcome them, then this take will most closely resemble a finished version of the scene.

To get more impact on-screen, give yourself a fuller preparation. Remember, whether you're onstage at the Taper, or on-screen with De Niro, the passion remains the same.

CUES VS. STIMULI
● ●
(See Chapter 14)

Real listening involves picking up the stimuli, not just picking up the cues. This ability to really listen is especially important on camera because the audience is so close to you. They can see when you're really thinking, and even worse, when you're not.

To understand the difference real listening can make, try this exercise. Take a scene with a number of long speeches and do it:

1. Responding only to your "cues" at the end of the other person's speeches. Simply wait for the end of the other person's speech and then begin your own.

Now play the tape back. You will probably find that the scene drags and lacks dynamics.

To remedy these problems, try another take, this time working from stimuli. To do this you must find the other person's word, gesture, or intonation that triggers your response. Finding this stimulus is tricky because it can occur at the beginning, middle, or end of his speech. Once you have isolated these stimuli, try the scene again:

2. Responding to the stimuli as they occur.

You may have to spend a good deal of time on Take 2 in order to find out what is really triggering you, but it will be time well spent. You should notice a large increase in the pace, energy, and dynamics of the scene, once you begin playing the scene from stimulus to response, rather than from speech to speech.

WORKING WITH A YELLOW HIGHLIGHTER

• •

(See Chapter 14)

If you're like most actors you memorize by rote: you say your lines over and over again until you get them right. This technique is deadly because you are programming yourself to work off your lines rather than listening to the other person. While he is talking, you're going to be thinking, "What's my next line?" and meanwhile, you won't have heard a thing.

How do you deal with the problem of memorization? You "study the other person's lines as much as you do your own, and find in them that thing that triggers you to say what you have to say at that moment." Then instead of memorizing by rote, you will be memorizing organically: from stimulus, *across the bridge*, to the response. Having memorized in this way, when you are in the scene you will no longer be thinking of your next line, you will be listening to the other person. You will be listening for the stimulus that triggers your next line.

The best way to do this is to work with a yellow highlighter on the other person's lines. You should highlight only those words or phrases that provide the stimulus for your next speech. How do you find this stimulus? Work backwards. Start with your response— your line—then work backwards to find the stimulus in the other person's speech that triggers it.

Here's an example:

JONES

That's crazy. You think I'd do that? That's insane. You think I'd kill my own wife? You think I'd pull out a knife and stab her seventeen times?

HENDERSON

I think you'd kill your wife, your first born, and your own mother if it would get you that insurance money.

Assume you're playing Henderson. Work backwards from your line, "I think you'd kill your wife. . . ." Find the stimulus for it in Jones's speech, and highlight it.

You should have highlighted "You think I'd kill my wife?" It's the logical stimulus for Henderson's line "I think you'd kill your wife. . . ." Read them in sequence and see how logically one flows from the other:

JONES

You think I'd kill my own wife?

HENDERSON

I think you'd kill your wife, your first born, and your own mother if it would get you that insurance money.

Notice that your response is almost always an echo, a repetition, or a logical extension of the stimulus. That's how you can identify it.

To get a feel for working this way, take a scene with fairly long speeches and cold read it:

1.   After studying it in your usual way.
2.   After working with the yellow highlighter.

Now play the tapes back. Notice how much better you are listening in Take 2. Notice how many more speeches you seem to have "memorized." Once you understand why you're saying what you're saying, at the moment you're saying it, most of the lines will take care of themselves.

BOTTOM-LINING: ACTIVE CHOICES
(See Chapter 14)

The temptation to make everything smaller for the screen can sometimes affect the way you bottom-line your scenes. Afraid to be too big for the screen, you settle for a passive choice. The result is that you feel like nothing's happening when you're doing the scene, and you look completely de-energized in the playback.

To remedy this problem, try this exercise. Take a scene in which your character asks a lot of questions, and do it:

1. Bottom-lining it with the need to be told some information.
2. Bottom-lining it with the need to find out the truth.

Now play the two takes back and analyze the results.

Take 1 will often look less dynamic because you have bottom-lined your need passively; you've programmed yourself to sit back and wait until you're told the information.

Take 2 should look more dynamic because you've bottom-lined your need actively. Very often this change will be most evident in your eyes. It's as though the lights have been turned on, as moment by moment you search the other person for the truth.

Try bottom-lining your needs in the most active way possible and see if it doesn't increase your energy on-screen.

RHYTHM

• •

(See Chapter 15)

To begin to understand how valuable rhythm can be in your work, try this exercise. Take a very volatile scene and tape it two ways:

1. After walking slowly around the room, letting the rhythm of the movement affect the way you feel, and speaking out your role-related thoughts.
2. After walking around very fast for some time, letting the rhythm of the movement affect you and speaking out your role-related thoughts.

Now play the tapes back and look at the results. You will probably see that Take 1 lacks drive and dynamics. The scene never "catches fire." As a result of the rhythmic disconnection between your emotions and your body, your anger will tend to disappear. Your body remains relatively relaxed and you move relatively slowly during the scene itself.

Take 2 should be very different. Now you are moving and thinking in the rhythm dictated by what you are feeling. Your involvement is total: mind and body. You should have little trouble finding the drive and dynamics that will lead you to the explosive climax that the scene requires.

PHYSICALIZATION: ADVANCE-RETREAT

●●

(See Chapter 17)

The first couple of times you're on camera you will probably freeze up. You'll try as hard as you can not to move, fearing that you'll fall off the screen if you do.

Giving in to this fear will leave you acting from the neck up, and your performance will suffer as a result. To fight this tendency, Tony encourages you to "feel the impulses down to your toes." These feelings will often result in some form of physicalization, which is just as important on screen as it is in the theater, though it can be a good deal more subtle.

To get an idea of how important proper physicalization can be, try this exercise. Take a scene in which a man is trying to get closer to a woman who is doing her best to avoid him. Do the scene three ways:

1. Your way.
2. Physicalize your needs. If you're playing the man, take a step toward the woman every moment you're pursuing your needs. Every moment that you're responding to her resistance, stop or take a step backwards.

   If you're playing the woman, take a step away from the man every moment that you're pursuing your need to avoid him. Stop or take a step toward him every moment that you're giving in to his persistence.

3. Your way again, using as much or as little of the physicalization as feels right for you.

Now play the takes back and analyze the results.

Take #1 suffers because no one advances, no one retreats. You both agree, out of politeness, to leave a demilitarized zone between you, which no one crosses. It's a safe performance, but not an exciting one.

Take #2 should be more lively for several reasons. The demilitarized zone has disappeared, and as a result, you are both more vulnerable to one another. Also, by physicalizing your needs, you are no longer acting from the neck up, so you have more energy. Finally, by committing yourself physically to the pursuit or frustration of the need, you are forcing yourself to listen more critically, which adds to the dynamics of the scene.

Take #3 should be the most comfortable because you are doing the *scene* again, rather than an exercise. Notice that many of the physicalizations you discovered in Take #2 have worked their way into the scene, though they may not all be fully physicalized.

Once you "feel the impulses down to your toes," you can physicalize them completely, partially, or try to suppress them, depending on your needs. Sometimes a movement of a few inches is all that's required.

BOTTOM-LINING: POSITIVE NEEDS
• •
(See Chapter 18)

You may often find yourself choosing dramatic needs with which you cannot personally identify, but which seem absolutely right for the "character." You rehearse the scene, but you feel "out of it." You tape the scene and it looks forced or unrealistic.

You've got a problem with the way you bottom-line your scenes. To begin to understand this problem, try this exercise.

Take a scene involving a great deal of anger and tape it:

1. Bottom-lining it with the need to punish the other person.
2. Bottom-lining it with a need with which you can personally identify. If possible, make it a positive need. In this scene, for instance, you could try to make the other person understand what you are saying, instead of punishing them. Make sure to establish for yourself why this need is important.

Now play the tape back and analyze the results.

Take 1 will be emotionally explosive, but it will tend to be one level. The reason is that every moment the other person resists your need to punish him, it's likely to frustrate and anger you. Every moment you are pursuing the need to punish him, you will likely want to show him how angry you are with him. So the dynamics of the scene go from anger and frustration to pure anger. A very small range.

Take 2 should be no less emotional, but should display better dynamics. Each moment you are responding to the other person's resistance (his unwillingness to listen or understand) your response is probably going to involve some kind of anger or frustration. But each moment you are pursuing your need to make him understand, you are going to try to suppress that anger. So the dynamics go from fully expressed anger one moment to your trying to be calm the next.

Take 1 may look forced because your needs cause you to play into the anger every moment of the scene. You feel as though you have to pull these violent emotions out of yourself. The result is a performance that often looks "indicated." Look for mouth, forehead, eye, or vocal tension as a sign of this tendency to push.

Take 2 will often look more realistic because your needs dictate that you play against the anger. Your job is to remain as calm as possible; it's the other person who's creating all the anger and frustration by resisting you.

Your face and voice should be much less subject to performance tension in this take.

In Take 1 your overall level of involvement may look limited.

It's usually hard for actors to get involved in negative choices like punishing someone. The basic rule of thumb is, don't play needs you can't personally identify with.

In Take 2 your level of involvement should be higher, because you're pursuing a positive need that you can really care about: making someone understand something that's vitally important for you and for him.

Try keeping your needs positive and see if it doesn't help bring more of yourself to the work.

THE BLACK HAT: PLAYING THE BAD GUY
• •
(See Chapter 19)

You will have more difficulty playing villains on-screen if you have trouble believing in the negative things you are doing. The audience is so close to you that this lack of commitment shows up much more readily on-screen than it does onstage. In essence you are saying to the audience, "It's not really me doing these terrible things, it's just my character." You are playing the bad guy. The result is often a performance that is unconvincing or unbelievable.

To get a feel for this problem, try this exercise. Take a short scene with one character who is clearly evil. Play the scene in the following ways:

1. Playing the villain as evil.

The solution is to give up playing the "bad guy" entirely. Define your needs in a positive way. Justify your "negative" actions by seeing them as part of some greater good (for example, a soldier often kills in order to save lives). Then play these needs as strongly as you can.

2. Playing the villain's positive needs very strongly.

PLAYING THE BAD GUY II
• •
(See Chapter 19)

When you're playing villains you may have a tendency to make judgments on the character. This tendency will separate you from the role, decrease your involvement in the moment, and thus reduce your impact on-screen.

To begin to understand this problem, try this exercise. Take a short scene with your role written as a villain and do it:

1. Playing the role with a value judgment on your role.

Now play Take 1 back and analyze the results. You may notice that you are not wholly involved in the role, or that you are playing the villainy in the role in an overly obvious way.

One solution to these problems is to take the negative judgment off yourself and put it on the other person. An example of this process is Michael Douglas's portrayal of Gordon Gekko in the film *Wall Street*. He does not play a greedy businessman, he plays a realist who's out to save America. His "greed is good" speech is chillingly effective, not because it's obviously evil, but because it's being delivered by a man who acts as though he's running for president of the United States. Gekko's judgment of the executives of Teldar Paper, of his young protégé Bud, and of almost everyone he meets, is that they really don't "know the score." This judgment becomes a part of almost every bridge Michael Douglas crosses. The resulting intensification of his point of view adds energy and dynamics to the listening process, and the role.

To get a feel for this process, try another take. This time:

2. Playing the role with a value judgment on the other person.

Now play the tape back and analyze the results. You should find that your involvement is much greater in Take 2. In addition, you may find that you are a good deal more sympathetic, now that you have given up "playing the bad guy."

INTERRUPTED DIALOGUE
● ●
(See Chapter 19)

One of the traps inherent in learning to listen is feeling that you have to listen to everything with equal weight: in practice, it amounts to the habit of giving everything a three-second thought pause. As Tony points out, this is not real listening, this is the attitude of listening. It's especially destructive in comedy scenes and scenes involving high levels of conflict. Both of these kinds of scenes run at a faster than normal pace, and are often written to accelerate to some kind of climax.

To get a feeling for what this attitude of listening can do to a confrontation scene, try this exercise:

1. Take the following scene and tape it, taking thought pauses before each of your lines.

JANINE

I want out of this marriage.

ROBERT

You want out of the marriage?

JANINE

Don't act so surprised.

ROBERT

You want out of our marriage?

JANINE

You must have known this was coming.

ROBERT

This is incredible.

JANINE

You're being so dramatic.

ROBERT

I can't believe this.

JANINE

Look, we can work this out.

ROBERT

I hate you for doing this.

Now try it another way, using the concept of interrupted dialogue. Remember that when someone says something new or important to you, it will sometimes provide the stimulus for your next three or four speeches. It's one of the ways writers make it possible for a scene to accelerate organically to a climax.

Let's assume you're playing Robert. To test for interrupted dialogue, take two of your speeches, and take out what's said by Janine in between. If those two speeches make good logical sense, you're probably not listening to Janine at that moment, you're listening more to yourself. In the example above, all of your lines are a response to one stimulus: "I want out of this marriage." They form one continuous response. See for yourself:

ROBERT

You want out of the marriage? You want out of our marriage? This is incredible. I can't believe this. I hate you for doing this.

In effect, the author is writing out the bridge for you, which is the absorption of this huge new stimulus. It is not until you get to "I hate you for doing this," that you are even ready to respond to Janine's demand to end the marriage.

To get a feel for interrupted dialogue, bracket all these speeches in your script. The brackets will help you remember that they are all one speech, one impulse, one idea. Even better, if the other person's lines are short, as Janine's are here, white them out on your script, so that you will not be tempted to wait around for something that you're not going to hear anyway.

2.   Try the scene again, this time as interrupted dialogue.

Now play back the takes and analyze the results. Notice that Take 2 builds much more organically to a much bigger climax. This explosiveness is one of the benefits of real listening.

Look for runs of interrupted dialogue in your comedy scenes and in very confrontational dramatic scenes.

DEALING WITH THE PAST: AVOIDING REVERIE
• •
(See Chapter 19)

You may find yourself going off into a dream world or reverie whenever you deal with the past. That is, you disconnect emotionally from the reason you brought it up, and end up with a very de-energized performance.

To begin to understand the problem this disconnection creates, try this exercise.

Take one or more speeches dealing in depth with the past and do it:

1.   Playing the past events and associations as past unrelated to the present need that brought them up.

Play this take back and you will see that it offers little in the way of drive or dynamics. To fix these problems, you have to remember that the need that caused you to bring up the past is what initially energizes you. However, if you go on talking about the past long enough, some or all of the emotions present at the events you are describing may begin to surface. Once your focus shifts to these past events and the emotions that surround them, you are still responding to stimuli, but those stimuli are for the most part internal. They come from inside you, not from the other actor.

How do you begin to access these stimuli? Realize that a so-called "monologue" is like an iceberg. An iceberg displays ten per-cent of its mass above the waterline; ninety percent below. In such moments only ten per cent of the experience being communicated is in the words, the rest is below the level of the words.

You can connect to this deeper level by finding the specific person, place, and things you are talking about. Say the word "person," and nothing happens. The imagination and the emotions do not respond to generalities or abstractions, they respond to specifics. Think of your mother, and all kinds of emotions begin to stir.

To begin exploring the iceberg, try another take, but first explore the speech(es). Attach a face to every name, a picture to every place. Know the details of every reference, and how you feel about each of these details. Then:

2. Do the speech(es) again.

Notice also how much more energy you seem to have. This energy comes from being connected emotionally to what you are talking about. You are no longer just saying words, you are responding to stimuli. The past is no longer past, it has started to become part of the present. The feelings that arise may become so strong that they draw you into yourself, making this take seem a little self-indulgent, even weepy.

Now go back to your original need, the one that made you bring up the past in the first place, and do another take:

3. This time playing the need, and fighting against the tendency to give in to the feelings. Try to stay connected to the other actor in order to achieve your needs.

This take should work the best, combining a sense of the emotional implications of the experience you are describing with the drive that comes from your commitment to achieve your need.

THE SUBCONSCIOUS
• •
(See Chapter 19)

As mentioned earlier in the book, you cannot play the sub-conscious drives and needs of the character because by definition they are not available to you.

Try the following:

Without telling the class what you are doing, pick a scene, or use one of the scenes in the book, and bottom-line it. In other words, reduce it to its simplest form: "I need to . . ." etc. Then play and, if possible, tape the scene. If you prefer, you can use this:

FATHER OF MINE

INT. KITCHEN—DAY

DEBBIE's mother, MATTY, is sitting at the kitchen table, head in hands, unmoving. After a moment, DEBBIE enters. She looks at her mother for a beat, shakes her head, then moves to the table.

MOTHER
Your breakfast is on the table.

DEBBIE
Thank you.

MOTHER
French toast.

DEBBIE
I can see.

She sits at the table, eyes on her mother, picks up her fork but doesn't eat.

DEBBIE
All right—what's wrong this time?

MOTHER

Nothing's wrong.

DEBBIE

I've lived with your moods all my life. I know one when I see one. What did I do this time?

MOTHER

It's not you.

DEBBIE

That's refreshing. So what is it?

MOTHER

I went to Walter Everson's funeral yesterday.

DEBBIE

God—why?

MOTHER

What do you mean, "why"? Because he died, that's why.

DEBBIE

I mean, why bother.

MOTHER

He was a very nice man.

DEBBIE

He was a sleazeball.

MOTHER

What?

DEBBIE

He was a sleazeball.

MOTHER

Don't say that!

DEBBIE

What's with you? You were never close to him. Not that I ever noticed, anyway. So why the broken heart?

MOTHER

Why did you call him a sleazeball? That's a terrible thing to call someone who just died.

DEBBIE

Because he was.

MOTHER

You don't know anything about him.

DEBBIE

He was a pig. A first-rate scum who should have been put out of his misery a long time ago.

MOTHER

Stop it!

DEBBIE

OK. I didn't want to say anything in the first place.

She stares at her mother, who sits silently, eyes fixed on the table.
DEBBIE *gets up and leaves.*

Now Debbie should invent and add some subconscious elements, but not tell the other members of the class what they are.

For example, her father locked her in a closet for three hours when she was three years old. Her mother whipped her brother and made him bleed when she was only two years old. And since childhood she has had a strong attraction to men (or women) who resemble a forgotten uncle (or aunt), no longer alive, who fondled her when she was very little.

Now play the scene, and tape it.

Look at the two scenes. See if the subconscious elements enhanced or cluttered the work. Think about the performance: was it easier or harder? My bet is that it was much harder.

Was it more interesting for you to play? If so, you're probably suffering from the "If I'm not doing a lot of stuff, I'm not acting" syndrome.

Now, most importantly, check the reaction of the class to the two scenes. Which was clearer, and most effective? Was there really any difference in the performance that they could detect? Could they figure out what the subconscious elements were? If not, was there any point in playing them?

If you had to make a choice of the two ways to play the scene again, which would you choose?

THE CONTACT EXERCISE
(See Chapter 19)

Actors who are new to the screen usually do not have much trust in the camera. They often give in to the temptation to "open the scene up," making gestures and movements directed towards an audience that is not there.

This tendency has the effect of de-energizing the scene, taking energy that is bouncing back and forth between two actors, and throwing it out into empty space where it will affect no one. You have to remember that in a close-up, the audience sees everything you see, feels everything you feel. Reach the other actor and you will reach the audience. Try to reach the audience directly and you will lose them: they will see you "acting."

To get a feel for what this kind of theatricalization can do to a scene, try this exercise. Take an intimate scene and tape it:

1. Taking every opportunity to refer to anything other than the other actor: people, places, or things.

Play this take back and notice that the repeated choice to "open the scene up" destroys any sense of intimacy. To remedy this problem, try another take, this time:

2. Touching the other actor at least once on every speech. Try to vary the contact, so that you do not repeat the same gesture over and over.

Now play back the tape and notice how this "reaching out" helps increase your involvement with each other, and how much warmer the scene is as a result.

If you are like most actors you are usually so obsessed with your lines that you ignore the other person in the scene; but it is almost impossible to ignore someone who is hitting you, or hugging you, or kissing you. You may shy away from this kind of contact at first because it is so intimate, but it is especially important for good screen acting.

Now try the scene again, this time:

3. Using as much or as little of the contact as feels right for you.

DEALING WITH PROPS
● ●
(See Chapter 19)

You may often find yourself beginning scenes by crossing to the center of the set, finding a chair, and sitting there until you run out of dialogue. It's a safe approach, but it doesn't usually lead to thrilling performances. To understand how it translates to the screen, try this exercise. Take a scene in which one or more of the characters are very "revved up." Do the scene:

1. Sitting at a table the entire time.

Play the tape back and analyze the results. It's likely to look pretty static. Adding props can sometimes overcome this problem by creating activities that will draw you into the reality of the scene.

In shooting most films, however, there's a limited amount of rehearsal time, so you can't rely on the director to give you these props or activities. You have to get used to developing them yourself.

To help develop an awareness of the value of using props, do another take of this scene:

2. With props strewn around the room. Feel free to explore these props during the scene and to develop bits of business with them, even if they seem unrelated to the lines of the scene.
3. With props again, this time incorporating one or two of the most appropriate bits of business into the scene. Be sure to make the appropriate adjustments so that the business does not violate your bottom line in the scene.

Notice how the scene changes with the addition of props. You should see an increase in energy, a better articulation of your needs, and an overall increase in the reality of the scene.

UNORTHODOXY EXERCISE
(See Chapter 19)

At times you may get so fixated on your lines that you will only play what is written on the page. As a result, your scene work will lack spontaneity: the impulses that generate movement, gestures, or business with props are stifled.

In a theatrical production, the director can fix what is lacking in your performance during the usual six weeks of rehearsals. In film and television, however, there is often very little rehearsal time, so you can't rely on the director. You have to do your own homework, and do it in such a way that you still are free to go with your impulses on the set.

If you're too locked in a scene and can't seem to generate any impulses, try this exercise. Do the scene:

1. The way you've rehearsed it.
2. As crazy as you can—doing whatever comes to mind, however inappropriate or illogical in terms of the meaning of the scene. Be as bizarre as possible: stand on your head when asked to sit down; shout when you should whisper, and vice versa.
3. Do the scene again, this time retaining the one or two bits developed during the crazy rehearsal that will work within the context of the scene.

This exercise is great fun and very useful in working with comedy.

THINKING FUNNY I

(See Chapter 23)

To get a handle on the differences between comedy and drama, try this exercise. Take a short comedy scene that has some physical business (a fight, a fall, etc.), and do it two different ways:

1. Playing the real gut emotions provoked by the physicalization: anger, hatred, pain, etc.

Play this take back and notice that the depth of emotion tilts the scene towards drama. To play the same scene as comedy you have to remember that the consequences of any action are not as great as in drama (i.e., death can be an annoyance in comedy rather than a tragic event), and that responses are oblique, childish, or illogical. It is the immaturity of these responses that often makes the scene funny.

Laurel and Hardy provide a perfect example of many of these adjustments. While they are walking down the street carrying a ladder, Laurel drops a banana peel, and Hardy slips and falls. The consequences of that fall are not real, in physical terms. Hardy never breaks his neck; he doesn't bleed; the film never cuts to a close-up of his face as he grimaces with unbearable pain. That would be a dramatic treatment of the situation, provoking deep emotions of anger and pain in the actor.

But these emotions must not exist in the world of comedy, so Hardy's fall is reduced to a mere annoyance. The consequences are social, not physical. That is, Hardy is made to look foolish, so he becomes frustrated or irritated with Laurel for making him look bad.

2.   As a comedy, taking the kind of adjustments suggested above to provoke lighter emotions: nervousness, anxiety, irritation, etc.

Play back the tapes and review the results. Notice that the lines have remained unchanged, but the different ways you have "heard" the physicalization have created two entirely different scenes in two completely different universes: the dramatic and the comic.

THINKING FUNNY II: DECEPTION
(See Chapter 23)

Another common comedy setup is deception. You can see it in many comedies, from Shakespeare's "As You Like It," in which Rosalind pretends to be a man; to *Beverly Hills Cop*, in which Eddie Murphy pretends to be any number of government agents, homosexuals, and art patrons; to *Tootsie* and *Mrs. Doubtfire*, in which Dustin Hoffman and Robin Williams, respectively, pretend to be women.

To get a feel for the comedic values of deception, try this exercise. Take a scene in which you are trying to convince somebody you are dying and do it in two ways: .

1.   Straight—you are dying.

Now play back the tape. You should see that Take 1 is tilted towards drama. When you tell the truth, what's at stake are the real implications of what's being communicated, and those implications often provoke very deep, and very dramatic, emotions.

Now try another take of the same scene, this time:

2.   Deceiving—as though you are not really dying, but you're trying to convince the other person you are.

Play the tape back and notice that Take 2 has shifted toward comedy. The adjustment involving deception has caused you to hear the incoming stimuli in a different way, producing lighter, but still real (on a moment-to-moment basis) emotional responses.

The reason? When you deceive, you do not deal with the real implications of what is being communicated and the deep emotions surrounding those implications. You only deal with whether or not the other person is buying your story or not. If he does, you're happy or excited. If he doesn't, you will become nervous, tense, or anxious. All of these emotions are perfect for comedy: they are relatively superficial, and they create a fast inner rhythm.

THINKING FUNNY: SEX AND LOVE
• •
(See Chapter 23)

The consequences of events are never as final in comedy as they are in drama. Nowhere is this more evident than in the treatment of sex and love. The consequences of love are very great, so emotions surrounding the loss of love tend to be very deep. Love can break your heart, and people have been known to die of broken hearts.

To understand how easily the idea of love translates into drama, try this exercise.

Take a scene about a girl rejecting a boy's affections and:

1. Play the scene as though you are deeply in love with the girl, want to marry her, and spend the rest of your lives together. Hear each of her rejections on as deep and as personal a level as possible.

Now play the tape back and see what happens. Ordinarily, you'll wind up with a drama of some depth. Real hurt and real sadness, appropriately applied, are emotions that are too painful to be funny.

Now try another take of the same scene, but this time:

2. Play the scene as though you just want to go to bed with her. Hear her rejections only as the simple frustration of your need for sex.

Play this take back and notice the difference. By dealing with sex instead of love, you have heard the stimuli in a more superficial way, provoked lighter emotions, and tilted the scene away from drama and into comedy.

Why? Sex is a strong drive with almost no serious consequences. No one has ever died from lack of sex, though some people do go a little crazy. Because of this, sex makes a perfect setup for comedy, because the feelings it provokes (anxiety, nervousness, irritation, frustration) are all superficial emotions with very fast rhythms—perfect for the speed and acceleration that comedy often requires.

THINKING FUNNY III:
MISCOMMUNICATION

● ●

(See Chapter 23)

Often when people communicate, it's drama. When people miscommunicate, it's comedy.

Another way to avoid playing really deep emotions in comedy is to look for miscommunication. Miscommunication is a common element in comedy. Why? When two people communicate, what's at stake are the real implications of what's being communicated. These implications are likely to provoke very deep, very dramatic emotions. When two people miscommunicate there are no implications because nothing is getting through. If you're talking and not being heard, you're going to respond with irritation, or frustration. If you're listening and not hearing anything, you're probably going to become confused.

Again, these light, fast emotions are perfect for comedy. To get a feel for miscommunication as a comedy setup, try this improvisation.

Take a situation in which a woman is attempting to leave her husband and he's trying to stop her:

1. Do it straight, as though this were a serious matter for both of you.
2. With a communication problem: put the husband in the shower. Assume that he can't hear her, and that she can't get through to him, and he keeps giving her inane answers.

Now play the takes back and watch how they change. Take 1 should tilt toward drama because you are both dealing with the real pain of divorce and the deep emotion connected with that breakup.

Take 2 should tilt (sometimes heavily) towards comedy because nothing is being communicated. The wife is only responding to her inability to get through, with superficial emotions like irritation or frustration. The husband, if he's listening at all, is probably only "hearing" his shower, and as a result is becoming progressively happier and more relaxed. The better he feels the more likely he is to drive his wife nuts. Result: comedy.

COLD READING
• •
(See Chapter 24)

When I asked one casting director what she looked for in an audition, she said, "Well, it's really nice when an actor makes a choice."

I didn't quite understand. "You mean a rich, dynamic choice?"

"No," she said, "just any choice. Ninety percent of the actors who audition for me just read the lines."

Why does this happen? In an audition, actors tend to tense up at the prospect of getting work, and as a result, their technique goes out the window.

To counteract this tendency, try this exercise. Take a scene you are unfamiliar with and bottom-line it: make a short statement of your needs and obstacles. Tape the scene immediately and play it back.

Notice how directly your choices translate to the screen. If your need is weak, the scene will lack drive. For example, in a scene about the breakup of a relationship you might choose "to let your girlfriend know that it's over." David Mamet says that letting someone know something is not a goal, it's an errand: you do it once and it's done. It will carry you through a moment, but it will not drive you through an entire scene. It would be better to choose a need like convincing her or making her understand the relationship's over. These needs will keep you continuously connected to your girlfriend as you monitor, on a moment-to-moment basis, whether or not you are getting through.

If your emotional preparation is weak, the scene will lack passion. For instance, you may have a tendency to cerebralize the emotional preparation. Many actors do. I once asked an actor how he felt about his girlfriend sleeping with his brother. "Perturbed," he replied. These literary ideas are unlikely to get you connected on a very deep level.

If you have not put the obstacle on the other person in a way that makes you care about their resistance, then your listening will suffer. Your need may be to make your girlfriend understand that your relationship's over, and your obstacle is that you're nervous. That obstacle puts your attention on yourself. You need to put it on her by asking "In what way does she make the achievement of my need difficult?" She may not want to listen, or she may be confused, or she may be hurt, or angry. Any one of these will get your attention off yourself and on to her.

Repeat this exercise until you instinctively make the strongest choices possible in terms of the need, the obstacle, and the preparation. You should begin to notice that between seventy and ninety percent of what ends up on the screen is the result of this kind of selection. The camera is so close that how you think about the work has a direct effect on the results.

COLD READING I: EYE CONTACT
(See Chapter 24)

When you cold read you have two very bad choices. You can look at your script while the other person is reading. This approach will give you pace but no involvement. Or you can look at the other person while he is speaking. This approach will give you involvement, but no pace.

To get a feeling for how awkward these alternatives can be, try this exercise. Tape a cold reading:

1. Looking at your lines while the other person is talking.
2. Looking at the other person the entire time he is talking.

Now play these takes back and analyze the results. Take 1 will usually have tremendous pace and drive, but no real involvement or listening. Take 2 will usually have real involvement and listening, but lack pace and drive.

One way to deal with these deficiencies is to realize that, at its most basic level, listening is about keeping track of whether or not you are getting what you want. Most scenes consist of a series of attempts to achieve your needs. In most cases, you are only obligated to listen long enough to determine whether your attempt is successful or not. Once you hear this rejection you have the stimulus to go to your next line, which usually consists of another attempt to achieve your need.

Try another take, this time:

3. Looking at the other person only for as long as it takes you to determine the success or failure of your attempt to achieve the need. You may have to listen to only a few words to make this decision, or you may have to listen to his entire speech. As soon as you decide, drop down and get your next line.

Now play the tape back and look at the results. Working this way in a cold reading will give you involvement, which can only come from really listening to the other person. It will also give you pace, because you are listening selectively, taking only what you need to determine how next to pursue your need.

In real life we don't listen to everything with equal weight. You can apply this principle to your cold readings and greatly increase your chances of success.

COLD READING II: MECHANICS
● ●
(See Chapter 24)

In a cold reading what you don't know is of paramount importance. You don't know the scene (either its shape or its place in the piece). You often don't know the story in any detail. You don't know the character, and to top it all off, you don't know the other actor (assuming there is one: often it's just the casting director reading with you).

So when it comes time to cold read, it's no wonder that you feel insecure, and more often than not you simply bury your head in your script—the one thing you have to hang on to—and proceed to deliver the most elaborate line reading you can manufacture at the time.

In addition to these problems, your unfamiliarity with the lines causes you to keep your eyes glued to the page, so you completely lose track of the other actor. You feel "out of it" during the reading, and after the audition you'll probably spend a lot of time wondering why you lacked "energy."

The answer is you tricked yourself into believing that the scene exists on the page. If that were true, plays would be read silently rather than performed. The truth is that the scene only exists between you and the other actor. If there is no contact between you, there is no scene; only two people reading from separate pieces of paper.

To overcome this tendency to work off the page, instead of the other person, try this exercise:

1. Videotape a scene while you cold read.

Now play the tape back and look for mechanical problems with the reading. You may notice yourself burying your head in your script, or leaving it on the table and looking down at it, in the process pulling your look away from the other actor. Try holding the script up so you can look over the top of the page and maintain eye contact with your partner.

You may wave your script around, trying to disguise the fact that you are working from sides. Notice that this excess movement draws attention to the script, and away from you. Try holding the sides still next time.

You may hold your script to one side, introducing head movement into the reading each time you look at the script, and encouraging you to look away from the other actor. Try holding the script directly in front of you, so that you minimize both your head movement and the tendency to break focus with the other actor.

You will probably notice that you're rushing through the reading. Next time, slow down until you can begin to make contact with your partner.

You will often notice yourself pushing the volume up to theatrical levels. Next time, remember you are only doing the scene for the other person, not for the audience.

When you have taken all these adjustments:

2. Try the reading again.

You should notice several differences. The reading should have less movement, more feeling; a little less pace, but more involvement; less volume, but more listening and dynamics.

The demand for moment-to-moment contact is at its highest during cold readings, even higher than during scene work. It's especially important in a film or television audition because, in general, the scripts are written much more sparsely than material written for the stage. There are many more reactions called for than are indicated by the dialogue, and you will miss a lot of them unless you fix the mechanical problems that encourage you to disconnect from the other actor.

WORKING WITH EXTRAS
• •
(See Chapter 28)

Like everything else in film, working with extras has an upside and a downside. The upside is that the added dimension of reality provided by the extras' presence will draw you deeper into the scene. The downside is that their presence might distract you, throwing you completely out of it.

To get an idea of the possibilities and pitfalls of working with extras, try the following exercise. Take a short scene set in a crowded public place and stage it in the following ways:

1. With only the two principals on a bare set.
2. With the two principals plus a number of extras as it would be staged on a film set. Be sure to choreograph the background action so that it articulates (and incidentally, intrudes upon) what the principals are doing.

Play back these two tapes and watch what effect the addition of background action has on your performance. Sometimes it will energize you, breathing life into the scene. Sometimes it will simply confuse you and destroy the scene, especially if you are not sufficiently focused on your bottom line in the scene.

Once you have adjusted to working with extras, try this exercise again with more elaborate background action.

Epilogue

● ●

I expect that as time passes, this book will be revised frequently, because I like to believe that we are always in a learning process. I do believe, however, that these pages offer a good starting point and hope that you have found them not only informative but also enjoyable to read—as enjoyable as I have found the work with my students, which helped me formulate what I have written.

Shortly after we organized the Film Actors' Workshop, I had a student who was undoubtedly the most corn-fed young man I had ever encountered. Pure back-hills, he was also extremely shy with girls, and he found it very hard to make contact of any kind in the exercises and scenes he did.

One day I set up an improvisation in which he was a used car salesman, and one of the very attractive girls in the class was a buyer. His intention was to get her to go to dinner with him, and he was reminded that he was permitted to do or say anything he wanted in order to fulfill his intention. He had always had that liberty, of course, but for some reason it registered this time. Before the improv was through, he had his arm around her, and both were laughing and enjoying each other's company enormously. When I finally called a halt to the improv, he turned to me with a huge grin on his face and said, "This here actin's a piece a cake."

And so it should be for every actor. Acting should be pleasurable and satisfying. If it is always hard work and a strain, chances are you aren't doing it very well, or maybe you shouldn't be an actor. So, have "a piece of cake."

Index

A

acting: approach to, 12–14; authority in, 292–293; craft and technique of, 17; defined, 15–18; film versus stage, 3–6; good, 288; as problem solving, 290; vulnerability in, 291–292

acting style: developing an, 8–11, for comedy and drama, 144–146

acting tools: 93, 97–163; for cold reading, 150–153; comedy, how to play, 144–149, 259; director, working with the, 155–159; dynamics, 110–112; inside-out character development, 160–162; listening, 11–12, 19–26, 20–21, 23, 32, 300–302; movement, 113–115; 160–162; object images, 138–141; personalization, 136–137; rhythm, 60–61, 97–109; selectivity, 122–135; summarized, 163; unorthodoxy, 142–143

action, 168, 184

actor's call, 186–188

Actors Equity Association (AEA), 276, 279

ad-libbing, 22–23

Adventures in the Screen Trade, 25

agents, 267–268

Ages of Man, 6

Albee, Edward, 37, 130

American Broadcasting Company (ABC), 111, 256

About the Author

. . . .

After receiving his degree from Washington University in St. Louis, Tony Barr began his career as an actor and stage manager on Broadway. Moving to Hollywood, he appeared in sixteen features and numerous television episodes before joining CBS-TV, where he became associate producer on such famous series as "Climax!" and "Playhouse 90." He subsequently spent thirteen years with ABC-TV, then left his position as a programming vice-president to return to CBS Television, where he served until his retirement as vice-president, CBS Entertainment Productions. He has served on the Advisory Board of the Communications Department of Stephens College, Columbia, Missouri, and on the Board of Governors of the Academy of Television Arts and Sciences. He is a member (on leave) of Actors' Equity Association and the American Guild of Variety Artists. He is a member of the Screen Actors Guild, and has been an active member of the Directors' Guild of America since 1952. The Film Actors Workshop, which he founded in 1960, is located in the Los Angeles area; phone number (310) 442-9488.

Currently Mr. Barr is teaching in Los Angeles on a limited basis, and conducts a number of two-day intensive weekend seminars in cities throughout the United States and Canada.